LA SALLE

LA SALLE

Explorer of the North American Frontier

ANKA MUHLSTEIN

Translated from the French
by Willard Wood

ARCADE PUBLISHING • NEW YORK

To Robert, on his thirtieth birthday

FIRST ENGLISH-LANGUAGE EDITION

Library of Congress Cataloging-in-Publication Data

Muhlstein, Anka.
[Cavelier de La Salle. English]
La Salle : explorer of the North American frontier / by Anka Muhlstein :
translated from the French by Willard Wood.
p.   cm.
Translation of : Cavelier de La Salle, ou, L'homme qui offrit
l'Amérique à Louis XIV.
Includes bibliographical references and index.
ISBN 1-55970-219-2
1. La Salle, Robert Cavelier, sieur de, 1643–1687. 2. Explorers —
America — Biography. 3. Explorers — France — Biography. 4. Canada —
History — To 1763 (New France) 5. Mississipi River Valley —
Discovery and exploration — French. I. Title.
F1030.5.M8413   1994
977'.01'092 — dc20
[B]   93-47991

Published in the United States by Arcade Publishing, Inc., New York
Distributed by Little, Brown and Company

10   9   8   7   6   5   4   3   2   1

BP

Designed by API

PRINTED IN THE UNITED STATES OF AMERICA

Contents

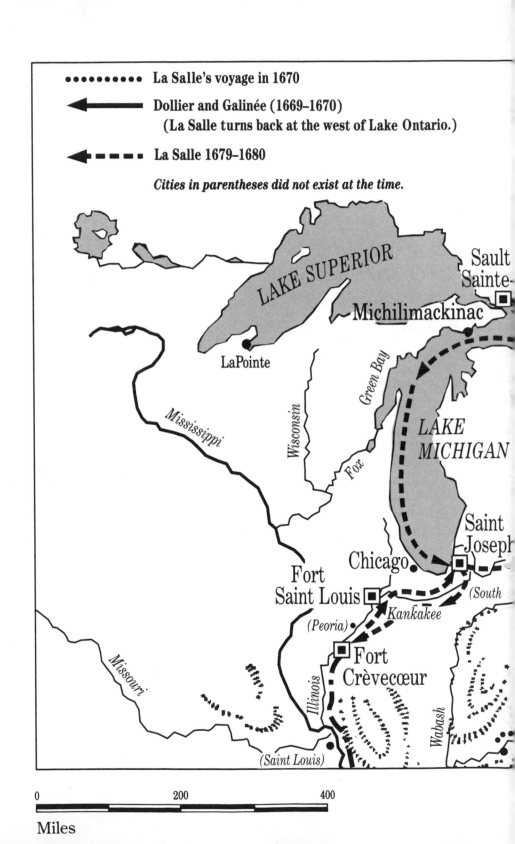

La Salle's voyage in 1670

Dollier and Galinée (1669–1670)
(La Salle turns back at the west of Lake Ontario.)

La Salle 1679–1680

Cities in parentheses did not exist at the time.

LAKE SUPERIOR

Sault Sainte-

Michilimackinac

LaPointe

Mississippi

Wisconsin

Green Bay

Fox

LAKE MICHIGAN

Saint Joseph

Chicago

Fort Saint Louis

(Peoria)

Kankakee

(South

Missouri

Illinois

Fort Crèvecœur

Wabash

(Saint Louis)

0   200   400

Miles

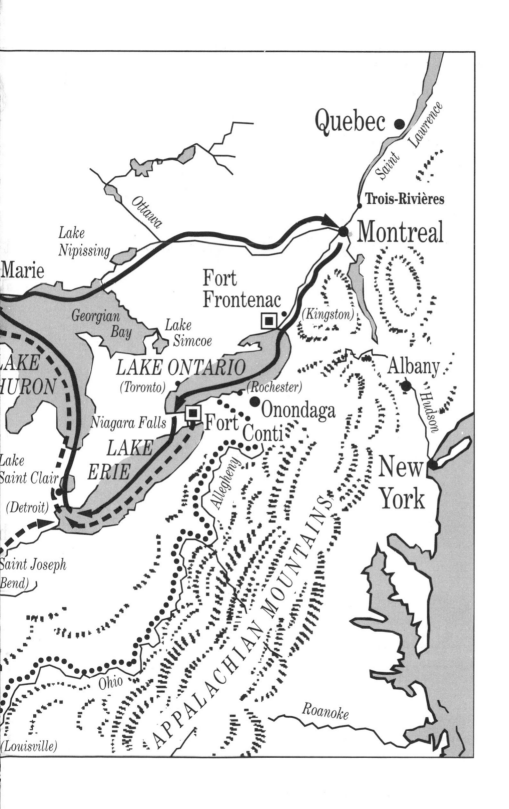

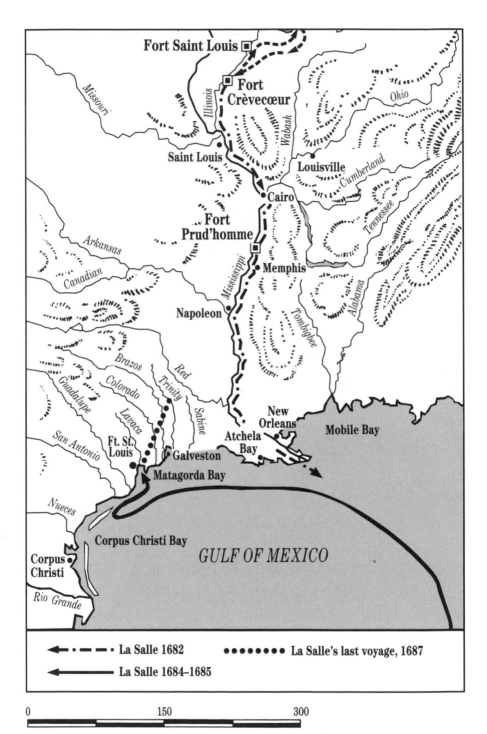

Fort Saint Louis

Fort
Crèvecœur

Missouri

Illinois

Ohio

Wabash

Saint Louis

Louisville

Cumberland

Cairo

Tennessee

Fort
Prud'homme

Arkansas

Canadian

Memphis

Mississippi

Alabama

Napoleon

Tombigbee

Brazos

Red

Colorado

Trinity

Lavaca

Sabine

Guadalupe

New
Orleans

Mobile Bay

Atchela
Bay

San Antonio

Ft. St.
Louis

Galveston

Matagorda Bay

Nueces

Corpus Christi Bay

GULF OF MEXICO

Corpus
Christi

Rio Grande

| ◄ — · — · — | La Salle 1682 | •••••••• | La Salle's last voyage, 1687 |
| ◄————— | La Salle 1684–1685 | | |

0   150   300

Miles

Author's Note

I became interested in the subject of this book under unexpected circumstances. I was flying from New York to Tokyo. It was winter, the weather was clear, the air transparent, and I was looking out the airplane window following the network of highways as they cut thin lines through the dark forest below me. Occasionally, a glistening ribbon showed where a river had frozen over; later, the giant cloverleaf of the Great Lakes blossomed across the landscape. The plane banked and angled northwest toward Alaska and for hours the ground was bare and featureless but for a desert whiteness, an unbounded blank on which lakes and contours in the terrain were indicated only by a different hue of white. From so high up, flying at such a rate, I could imagine the true immensity of this continent. But to cross it on foot?

I remembered later, without much surprise, that even after World War II unknown areas north of Hudson Bay were still being charted. Contemporary explorers traveled by airplane, like me, reducing distances and obstacles to insignificance. But how had their precursors, the voyageurs of the seventeenth century, accomplished their travels? What was this land like three hundred years ago, I wondered. And what kind of people were they, these early adventurers, who had the strength and the determination to set out in search of the new frontier, and not come back until they had found it? In answering this question I discovered one truly extraordinary man, a man whose journeys ranged from Canada to the Mississippi Delta, who learned the Iroquois language and native customs, who made mortal enemies and lifelong friends. His name was Robert Cavelier de La Salle.

LA SALLE

❖ 1 ❖

From Rouen to Quebec
1643–1667

By the start of the seventeenth century, North America had begun to reflect the character of Europe. The English were established in New England and Virginia; the Dutch at the mouth of the Hudson River, and the French, for their part, clung to the rugged, inhospitable lands to the north. A Frenchman, Jacques Cartier, had explored the Saint Lawrence as early as 1534 and to some extent opened the region to France, but the French were unable to convert their early start into territorial gain — the inordinate harshness of the winters and the bloody religious wars that ravaged the home country until 1598 prevented it. Not until 1603 and the arrival of Champlain was a true French colony founded. This time the French learned the arts of survival from the Indians and, with the backing of their king, eagerly set about exploring the New World.

Two main groups of explorers crisscrossed Canada during this period. There were the fur traders, who in their hunt for tribes rich in pelts continually sought new contacts; and there were the missionaries in quest of souls to save. A small group of madmen also existed, men fascinated by the unknown, by distant seas and undiscovered passages. New France, with a few thousand inhabitants, was too small a society for there not to be considerable overlap between the different groups. Missionaries needed to acquire trinkets to gain access to the Indians and attempt their conversion; they were no strangers to trade. Their knowledge of the country and their understanding of native behavior far exceeded the requirements of their missionary task. Traders (or voyageurs, as they were called, since the Europeans never hunted furs themselves and setting up in trade meant traveling in search of Indians) were often former pupils or servants of the Jesuits, and could not have managed without the counsel and support of the priests. Explorers, those who pursued exploration for its own sake rather than for furs or souls, engaged in trade to finance their expeditions and shared the schooling, science, and zeal of missionaries — they could never have endured their terrible hardships unless driven by the most intense curiosity. And so these men, whose aims were so profoundly different, were intimately linked.

No one straddled the various categories as boldly as Robert Cavelier de La Salle. He spent ten years or so as a member of the Jesuit order. Once in New France, he ran his successive seigneuries so competently that he could readily have amassed a considerable fortune, but he aspired only to the glory of discovering the lands along the great river the Indians called *Mississippi*, the Father of Waters. His exploration of the river was accomplished at a cost of inhuman toil, and he lost his life to it. But there was a time when, thanks to him, Canada and Louisiana were joined together by France in an enormous arc.

Robert Cavelier came from a family of wealthy merchants in the town of Rouen. It was a family whose thrift, solidity, and seriousness of purpose, aided by the high price of cloth, had provided such affluence over the generations that, in the reign of Louis XIV, the head of the family was able to dedicate two of his offspring to religious and intellectual careers. The elder was placed with the Sulpician order, while the younger and more gifted son, Robert, born in 1643, the same year that the five-year-old Louis XIV inherited the crown, was placed with the Jesuits. The father preferred this child over his five brothers and sisters, and gave him the property of La Salle. From then on, he was always referred to by that name. The family's confidence in this son's future is well demonstrated by the fact that they chose to send him to the Jesuit college. No better school existed. He was successful there, and his masters spoke highly of his gift for mathematics, while congratulating themselves on his moral qualities. The school's atmosphere was somewhat military and its schedule rigid: from wake-up at five o'clock until lights-out at nine, study halls followed prayer sessions and classroom recitations in close order, leaving little time for daydreaming or enjoyment.[1] But La Salle adapted so well to it that the fathers enjoined him to take his first vows in 1660. He was seventeen years old. Was it love of God or the attraction of that wonderful and mighty machine, the Society of Jesus, which moved him to enter holy orders? I tend to discard the first hypothesis. La Salle never showed any signs of mysticism, and he was faced with a simple choice: he could live the placid, narrow life of a Norman worthy, or choose the exalting and perilous calling of a missionary, as the Jesuits regularly sent their best candidates to China, India, and the Americas to convert, to learn, and to discover. He hardly hesitated.

At the hands of his schoolmasters, La Salle acquired knowledge of all there was to be learned in the seventeenth century — from astronomy to the exact sciences, from navigational theory to ancient and modern languages. His knowledge of Greek, Latin, Hebrew, Arabic, Spanish, and Italian gave him the confidence and ability to master the Native American dialects he would later encounter. The Jesuits also had a passionate interest in cartography and taught their students how to take sightings with an astrolabe. The sketches and information they had brought back from their voyages contributed to the burgeoning of this new science. For some time, the Portuguese and Italians had been producing atlases and navigational charts — in Venice, Messina, and Genoa. But it was near Dieppe, a port for ocean shipping often used as a departure point for America, that the parish priest of the village of Arques, Pierre Desceliers, endowed a chair for the study of cartography. He drew the first world map for Henry II and was a founder of the modern school of map-makers, whose work is more accurate than artistic. Interest in maps continued to grow during the seventeenth century, and the development of copperplate engraving made them relatively available. As for Canada, its coastline and the course of its major rivers were mapped as a result of the expeditions of Jacques Cartier in 1534 and those of Champlain after him. The native inhabitants, as it turned out, had a surprising talent for reconstructing the features of the land, and their sketches, on which the travelers based their own work, were wonderfully accurate. Nicolas Sanson, who was born in 1600 and received the title of professor of geography to Louis XIII, a post that he retained under Louis XIV, was the pride of French cartography. What set him apart was his great scientific rigor. Contrary to the practice of his Italian colleagues, he relegated decorative drawing to the borders and margins of the map, and stuck to pure and simple representation. Sanson was the first geographer to leave blank areas where he had no information, rather than to give free rein to his imagination. These were the very qualities that the Jesuits were trying to inculcate in their students.

They thought well enough of La Salle to send him to Paris to complete his studies, and from there to the college of La Flèche. But his independence of mind, his distaste for bowing to authority and submitting to rules, and a certain feverishness on his part, worried his superiors. "He is a restless boy," reads one of their reports.[2] Clearly, he had promise, but the priests attached too much importance to steadiness of character to send him on a mission prematurely. For La Salle, who spent his time dreaming of China and perfecting methods of surveying and measuring latitude and longitude, rather than in contemplation of his venial sins, the slowness of the Jesuit fathers began to rankle. Instead of crossing the seas, he was teaching grammar in a provincial town: first at Alençon, then Tours, then Blois. Proud, and with a driving ambition, he did not take well to being in a schoolroom with a group of boys, charged as much with disciplining them as with improving their minds, "for it was necessary to endow them with a sense of responsibility but also, perhaps, to reinforce their subjection."[3] In 1666 he appealed to his father superior to be sent to China, specifying that his father would pay his passage and provide him an income once there. His initiative was met with disapproval. In the Jesuit priesthood one does not ask for advancement, one waits for orders, and possibly one becomes a missionary in Japan, the Congo, Brazil, or Canada. La Salle's appeal was dismissed. He stubbornly petitioned for the position of professor of mathematics in Portugal. The Jesuit fathers refused just as stubbornly, posting him to study theology at La Flèche. Losing patience, La Salle sent in his resignation.

The father superior, aware that his student was too hot-tempered and inflexible ever to function as a member of the Society, allowed him to leave without a scandal, and La Salle's reputation remained intact. The desire for personal gain or pleasure played no part in La Salle's decision. Thirst for adventure and a hunger for risk and new experiences burned in him so strongly that he jauntily shook off his attachments. And yet his re-entry into the secular world was anything but easy. His father, who seems to have understood and supported him, had just died. Worse luck still, when La Salle had gone into holy orders and taken the obligatory vow of poverty, he had renounced his right to any share in the family inheritance. His brothers and sisters agreed, however, to provide him an annual income of 400 livres.[4] After a few weeks in Rouen La Salle knew enough to be convinced that he was not cut out for a life in the provinces. Not that Rouen was a sleepy town. On the contrary, its level of culture was very high — out of one hundred estate inventories of the time, forty mention libraries. Even more unusually, 85 percent of the storekeepers and 75 percent of the artisans were able to sign their marriage certificates in their own hand.[5] Easily accessible to Paris by two paved roads and by boat traffic on the Seine, Rouen opened readily to the larger world. Its merchants exported locally woven linen and hemp cloth to New France and to Spain, where they were further redistributed to South America. Colored cloth goods known as *rouenneries* were manufactured in the Rouen area, as were *siamoises,* whose thread was half cotton and half silk. Thomas Le Gendre, one of the richest merchants in town, a Protestant convert and "among those in the kingdom having the most extensive sea trade,"[6] had correspondents all over the world. He also had cousins in America, Holland, and England. His traders set the tone for the port of Rouen, where more than a thousand ships arrived annually.[7] A youth like La Salle was not drawn to the unknown by abstract longing; he had evidence of a world beyond the ocean right in front of his eyes. He decided to ship out for New France. His family paid him outright the capital set aside for his annuity, and he left France in the summer of 1667.

This decision, at once so reasonable and so visionary, accurately reflects La Salle's own nature. It was reasonable because Rouen traders had known for more than a century that the prospects of getting rich in Canada were very real. Some of them had brothers or relatives who had settled in Quebec, where they formed an aristocracy in the Company. Had not the Merchant Company of Rouen at one time held exclusive rights to the fur trade with New France? The cod fishery had enriched many Norman ship owners, and the hundreds of Normandy natives who had gone on this adventure reported back that in New France you ate meat every day and caught fish with a shovel, which was a great deal more fun than measuring out cloth in a dank and ill-lit shop. La Salle's decision was all the more natural as his elder brother belonged to the Sulpician order in Montreal, and his Le Ber cousins, who had settled in New France ten years before, had grown prosperous from the fur trade and the cod fishery. But La Salle's ambition transcended a desire to make a fortune, and his departure to the West answered a lifelong dream of freedom and exploration. Like many before him, he pursued a chimera and thought only of the glory attendant on discovering a passage to China and the riches of the Orient. Denied the grandeur of the missionary's calling, he was free to aspire to the explorer's prestige. As North America was still for the most part unknown territory, he would have his work cut out for him.

What knowledge did he have of Canada? A great deal more than most of his contemporaries. Rouen regularly outfitted two ships a year for Canada. A merchant's son, when not trailing the ships' crews around port, could post himself at the guardrail of the new bridge to watch for their arrival (the bridge, made of boats joined together and paved, rose and fell with the tides and was dismantled in winter so as not to be carried off by ice). The boy would pester the captains and officers with questions. During his apprenticeship with the Jesuits, he had listened to many travel accounts, had an opportunity to question the few missionaries who returned to France, and especially, had read the *Jesuit Relations* with fervor. The mission field of New France had been an outpost of the French Jesuits since 1634. Quebec, founded in 1608,[8] counted about fifty inhabitants in the 1630s, including five women and three nuclear families, under the governorship of Samuel de Champlain. A navigator-explorer commissioned by Henry IV to start new settlements in America, Champlain had been traveling the Saint Lawrence and the shores of the Great Lakes since the beginning of the century, and had also made incursions northward and explored Acadia. He had founded the trading post of Quebec to exploit more effectively the trade in hides and pelts with the tribes of the surrounding area. At the end of his life, grown sedentary and devout, he began to regret that his tiny capital was stagnant and that its lands were only slowly being put into production. Although explorers and the Frenchmen known as coureurs de bois, who disappeared into the forest to live like Indians, were making inroads into the unknown, and fur traders were expanding into new areas, the colony was still unable to supply its own needs. Ships from France brought over the basic necessities of life once a year, including everything from seeds to fabrics. But there was a risk that Richelieu, Louis XIII's minister, and his successor Mazarin might lose interest in the colony, since the returns it brought were relatively slight. Champlain therefore asked that priests and missionaries be sent over to convert the Indians and give leadership to the colonists. This was no small task, but it accorded with the religious climate in France, where the Counter-Reformation had inspired great zeal and fervor. At one time, the seventeenth century in France was called "the century of saints"[9] for the reason that France, although late to accept the directives of the Council of Trent (1545–1563) and Charles V's injunction to hold the line against Protestant reform, had within a century become the foremost nation of the Roman Catholic Church, its "eldest daughter." France produced such great preachers as Bossuet, who was renowned throughout Europe, and pious princesses who, following the example of Richelieu's niece, the Duchesse d'Aiguillon, financed convents, seminaries, and religious missions abroad. The Jesuits therefore took on Champlain's challenge as a welcome duty, meeting it with enthusiasm and intelligence.

They did not wait in the relative comfort of Quebec for Indians to arrive but set out instead along the waterways, dressed in their long black robes, a Bible and a crude dictionary in hand. Carrying their moccasins so as not to puncture the fragile bark of their canoes, these patient men pushed ahead into the dark forests, determined to live alongside the savages and win them over by the strength of their example. Every evening they were obliged to scribble down, often on a strip of birch bark, an account of their day's activities. Upon their return to Quebec, they delivered the report to the father superior. The father played the part of editor, cutting, pasting, and correcting the texts so that they could be sent to France at the end of the year as a coherent account, ready for publication. And every year since 1632 the *Jesuit Relations* were eagerly snatched up as soon as they were published and passed from hand to hand. The success of these accounts is perfectly understandable. Even today their mixture of description, commentary, and preposterous detail about the Indians' way of life — the food they ate, their customs, their hunting trips — makes lively reading. It is easy to imagine with what enthrallment the young La Salle would have read these narratives. There were also primitive atlases in circulation, based on the accounts of Cartier and Champlain. An illustrated edition of Cartier's voyages had been reprinted several times since 1545. Like all his contemporaries, La Salle thought that Canadian rivers flowed in from the west, a hypothesis he particularly planned to investigate.

He left, therefore, in the spring of 1667. For more than a century, ocean crossings had presented little risk.[10] The ships had become safer and the sea routes were well-known, but the voyage was still a long one — six to twelve weeks, depending on the wind — and very uncomfortable, even for men accustomed to hardship. The boats would seem quite small to us; the average vessel was eighty feet long, or about the size of a modern coastal trawler. Space was restricted further by the fact that women, and especially the nuns who went to Canada in large numbers, insisted that a special area be reserved for them. They were usually packed into the bottom of the boat. The crew were paired together in steerage with one hammock for every two men, since one would always be on watch while the other was resting. The captain, officers, and passengers of note occupied cabins in the highest section of the ship's stern. These were "in every way similar to a coffer in which a single man could barely lie down,"[11] partitioned with curtains and furnished with a hammock. Only the captain and one or two passengers had actual rooms with furniture and a straw pallet. Everyone else had a "cuddy" whose panels could be dismantled and stowed in the hold in case of battle or overcrowding. The lowest rank of passengers were assigned bedframes on one of the lower decks. Air and light filtered in through either slits in the bow or gratings on deck, which admitted quantities of water as well. Some sixty passengers lived belowdecks. The ship's upper deck was far too encumbered for passengers to take the air or stroll there, and was further reduced in size by the forecastle and the rear quarterdeck. One has to imagine the great piles of skiffs, coiled rope, and animal pens littering the deck. There were cows and calves on board as well as pigs — not to feed the passengers and crew but to build up live-stock in New France.

Who crossed the ocean from France at that time? Men from Normandy, Picardy, and Saintonge, most of them young and ready to try their fortune in the New World. Many were farmers' sons who had learned a trade — carpenters, masons, blacksmiths. It took money to pay one's way to New France and to settle once there. Surgeons and apothecaries also made the crossing, at least a few who were more adventurous than their colleagues, and poor youths might go if they had a contract of some sort, either with the Jesuits (who would feed the boys and possibly admit them to the order in return for three to five years' work — these lads were called *donnés*) or with settlers who needed colonists to clear their land. Nuns would sometimes chaperone groups of strong and healthy young girls, generally orphans in the Crown's care, being sent to marry colonists and produce as many babies as possible. The pitiful number of women — one marriageable girl for every hundred unmarried men — was a serious barrier to natural increase in the population. The young ladies were given a few weeks to recover from the voyage, then they were assembled in the town hall where the boys — stocky peasants suffering from embarrassment or more easy-mannered young city dwellers — would join them for mutual inspection. The numbers favored the girls, who could afford to look and compare before making their choice. But first they had to survive the long crossing!

La Salle seems to have embarked with Monsieur de Queylus, the father superior of the Sulpician order in Montreal (and therefore the superior of La Salle's brother), and a young Sulpician priest called Father Fénelon, half brother to François de Salignac de La Mothe Fénelon, the future archbishop of Cambrai. The Sulpicians had allowed the young priest to leave after only fifteen months in seminary school because the present moment was seen as highly propitious for arrival in Canada. In the previous period, 1640–1666, there had been a series of fierce wars between the Hurons, who were allies of the French, and the Iroquois. Constant attacks had ravaged the outlying areas of

Quebec and Montreal. Even a brief outing in the countryside might cost one's life. The Indians captured children, scalped women, and fractured the skulls of men with a single blow of their terrible war clubs. But Louis XIV and his minister, Colbert, were determined to regain control of the colony and had sent a regiment, the Carignan-Salières, which in two campaigns imposed a new respect for French arms among the natives. A number of the regiment's officers and soldiers had decided to remain in Canada, and these young and energetic men greatly strengthened the little outpost. Father Fénelon was planning to settle at Quinte, on the north shore of Lake Ontario, where the Sulpicians had established a mission. La Salle had no such specific destination, as he knew that to execute his plans he would first have to make money. As the coastline of America drew closer, his optimism can only have increased.

Birds now began to appear, as if to say that land was near. One morning, flocks of cormorants, skimming the surface of the water, seemed to accompany the boat. The passengers could make out in the distance, looking like large sails, the outspread wings of giant petrels, and on the bridge the men were trying to attract a solitary albatross. The horizon pulsed with the flight of thousands of snow geese, Canada geese, and eiders, crossing the sky with loud cries, heading toward the line of dark cliffs that now began to appear in the distance. A peal of thunder announced the rushing overflight of an army of passenger pigeons, large birds with dark wings, traveling in such numbers that their flocks darkened the sky during migration. The wind carried the delicious odor of pine trees and wild roses.

Excitement grew among the passengers, as the sailors prepared an initiation ceremony for those on board who had never before traveled in these icy latitudes. The Old Man of the Sea, enormous, swaddled in all the pelts and furs of his shipmates, crouched at the topmast and began his climb down the ratlines, bellowing as he came. Heavy and unsteady in his gait, he grabbed a bucket and threw it at the heads of the novices. There was pandemonium. Some hid behind coils of rope, others fled belowdecks to find shelter among the hammocks, while still others took to the masts. The poor cat, an important passenger despite his green and scaly skin (it was he who warred on the rats in the hold), ran for cover among the legs of the crewmen. The chickens in their coops were put out of harm's way in the saloon or council room, which also served as the captain's mess. Finally, order was restored. And yet the long journey was far from over. Nearly a thousand miles still had to be covered before they would reach their destination: Quebec, a small city perched on a bluff of the Saint Lawrence, the capital of New France, whose Indian name referred to the abrupt constriction of the river at this spot.[12] Not only was arrival not imminent, but the most dangerous portion of the journey still lay ahead. Sailing around Newfoundland, into the Gulf of Saint Lawrence, and up the Saint Lawrence River presented more hazards than crossing the Atlantic. In order to steer clear of the many small islands that barely broke surface above the opaque water, and to avoid the shoals off Ile aux Morts, Baie des Trépassés, and Anse des Orphelins, accurate navigation was required, and a good bit of luck besides. Dreaded above all else was an encounter with sea ice — the word "iceberg" did not yet exist — because even large blocks were hard to see and to gauge in a fog. These great white masses, whose jagged outline reminded the passengers of cathedrals with countless gleaming turrets, drew a lively procession in their wake. Plankton clung to the underwater ice surfaces and attracted schools of fish, which in turn brought circling gulls and terns.

They soon could make out, lying at anchor on the Newfoundland banks, a number of large boats — known in fact as "bankers." The fishermen stood in barrels lashed to the deck, protected by large leather aprons and sheltered behind a sort of leather shield the height of a man. The hemp lines they cast over the sides carried five-pound weights of lead. When a tug was felt, they hauled in the heavy line hand over hand and brought the cod on deck. Each man cut out the tongue to keep track of his share of the catch. A boy then carried the fish to the header. The header's task, as his name implies, was to behead the fish and gut it. With a table next to him and equipped with a large knife, he also worked standing in a barrel, as the most practical way to avoid slipping and falling overboard. The header then tossed the fish to the next man, the splitter, who slit the fish open to remove the backbone and liver, which a boy caught on the fly and threw into a cask. The cod was then dropped through a hole in the deck. The salter, standing in the bottom of the hold steeped in the smell of brine, seized the fish and packed it away between two layers of salt. When the season was over, or when the holds were full, the bankers returned to their home ports — Le Havre, Saint-Malo, Les Sables-d'Olonne, Dieppe, La Rochelle, or Bordeaux.

As the ship proceeded toward Newfoundland, it sailed into the midst of hundreds of small boats, bobbing on the waves. Called shallops, they were light enough to be transported overseas in sections, and they could be rowed or sailed by three men. Unlike the crews of the bankers, the fishermen aboard the shallops slept ashore, returning to harbor each evening with their catch. And on nearing the coast, where a dark and spongy moss lay over the rocks and cobbles that lined the shore, huts could be seen at the head of every inlet. These primitive communities, the site of an intense and organized activity, were the realm of sedentary fishermen, working from fixed plants. Rather than true colonies they were outposts where a few men spent the winter — not necessarily the same ones every year — to keep the operation going and guarantee an early start the following spring. Although some men wintered at the stations, the fishery was still basically migratory. Women were few. At the time of La Salle's arrival, there were only a dozen families at Placentia on the west coast of Newfoundland, where Louis XIV had installed a civil government and a garrison in 1660.

The captain chose to go down the east coast of Newfoundland and take the southern passage around the island, rather than to set a course past Belle-Isle and down the coast of Labrador, which was often dangerous at this time of year. Making his way into an inlet, the captain struck the sails and ordered his men to lower lines over the side. Cod snapped hungrily at the bait, and the large slate-colored fish were hauled on board. There was something practically miraculous about the fishing: you could bring in 300 fish in three hours.[13] A swarm of terns began to wheel over the boat, so excited by the odor of fish that they began diving toward the deck in great numbers, clustering so thickly as to risk injury from the sailors. The cook, planting himself by a cauldron that had been anchored fast in the forward hold, now set to work. Soon officers and men alike were feasting on the delicate flesh — fresh cod, the first fresh food they had tasted since the month of July. The connoisseurs among them were especially partial to the tongue, the liver, and the head. Though they had taken aboard a side of beef, two sheep, and several dozen fresh breads, the passengers had been reduced long weeks ago to eating ship's biscuit (it took a mallet to break it), salt herring, and moldy dried beans and peas. Veteran passengers now began to clamor for a sort of sausage made from a hash of codfish hearts, the guts minced with lard, spices, and small pieces of the flesh.

There was not an Indian in sight. Standing figures could actually be seen on the heights along shore, but these were European fishermen watching for the arrival of herring shoals. It would have taken a practiced eye to make out the aborigines in the interior, protected by the damp and leafy woods. Contact between the two populations was in fact scarce. The Europeans stayed along the coast and did not attempt to occupy either the grasslands or the forests. The Beothuk — as the local tribe were called — came down to meet the fishermen at the beginning of the season. They came to barter with the pale little men who had eyes the color of the sea, to swap their furs and game for weapons, fishhooks, and cooking kettles before disappearing back into their villages. These short and peaceful exchanges were enough to decimate the Beothuk, however, since the least contact with Europeans caused measles and influenza, both fatal diseases to the natives. At the end of the seventeenth century, only a few hundred Beothuk were left.

The ship pursued its course, angling westward, and entered the vast Gulf of Saint Lawrence, practically an inland sea. The scale here was clearly different from that on the coast of Europe. Off the Gaspé Peninsula, which is swept by a warmer current, the passengers were finally able to see Indian dwellings, the famous wigwams, "huts consisting entirely of poles, which are covered with segments of the bark of birch trees, sewn edge to edge, and most often livened with a thousand different figures of birds, elk, otter, and beaver that the women draw themselves by means of an animal hair brush. The huts are round in shape and of a size to lodge fifteen or twenty persons, so light and portable that the savages roll them up like sheets of paper and carry them on their backs wherever they choose."[14] But even more fascinating to La Salle and his companions than the huts was the activity in the water. First there were the whales, a very gregarious species of black whale, traveling in schools of several hundred, whose jumps, rolls, and other acrobatics offered an unexpected diversion. These whales were particularly easy to hunt, being slow and unwary, and had the added advantage that their carcasses floated, making it easier to cut them up and tow them back to land. They had once been very numerous on the Atlantic coast of France, but had been so harassed by Basque fishermen that they had sought refuge on the far side of the ocean. The hunters, following their prey, settled thickly on the coast of the Gaspé Peninsula. In no time, the Indians caught on to the benefits of fishing for whales, but unlike the French who fished from a skiff with a harpoon, they adopted a much more sporting method: paddling with all their strength, they chased the whale down, jumped onto its back like rodeo cowboys, and held on while the whale leapt furiously as they tried to plunge a stake into its blowhole. Under the surface of the water, half seen and half guessed at, were the elongated bodies of white dolphins, "a fish in the form of a whale, virtually as large, white as snow, with the mandibles of a horse."[15] There were also an incredible number of salmon, and on the banks of the river there were seals of all sorts: hooded seals, gray seals with pure white pups, spotted Greenland seals. There were also porpoises, always described as hideous fish that looked like horses; and sea elephants, "large as Norman oxen, with webbed feet like a bird, an otter's head, and ivory teeth."[16] The males possessed a sort of flexible trunk they could expand to expel air. These extraordinary animals, measuring twenty-five or thirty feet in length and weighing several tons, lived in groups and grazed on the algae along the shores of the Saint Lawrence at low tide. The weight of their enormous bodies, which their flippered limbs could not support out of the water, and their placid natures, along with the fact that their flesh tasted like veal, made the sea elephant a species marked for destruction. Sea otters, playing in groups or floating on the calm surface of the water, also captured the passengers' attention. Finally, on the numerous islands that dotted their course, the travelers could make out large foxes, and sometimes also bear.

The ship progressed up the coast of the long island of Anticosti, on which whaling stations had been built for rendering blubber, then angled toward Egg Island, so called for the eider eggs that Cartier and his companions had feasted on there, and finally coasted along the northern shore of the Saint Lawrence, which was thought safer than the southern. Navigation on the river was extremely difficult, due as much to the countless small islands and ledges as to the clash that occurs twice a day between the river's natural current and the rising tide, causing powerful whirlpools and eddies. The captain made a stopover at Tadoussac on the mouth of the Saguenay River. A strong current of dark water issuing into the Saint Lawrence from a deep gorge, the river is savage and inaccessible, its shores barely softened by the white trunks of birches rising among the pines. The site had been occupied by Pontgravé in the first years of the century. He built a few primitive huts and left sixteen men to spend the winter there to wait for a harvest of furs from the Indians. The unfortunate men didn't survive the season, but the site, located on a traditional Indian thoroughfare, was too promising to abandon, and every spring traders journeyed there to buy furs from the native trappers.

At Tadoussac, the Saint Lawrence is still an estuary, measuring twenty miles across. The southern shore was low and half-obscured, even in fair weather, by banks of mist. The north shore, by contrast, rose steeply and was covered with magnificent forests. La Salle and his companions were astonished to see gigantic trees seeming to grow out of rock that had no visible soil cover. He was particularly amazed, as previous Europeans had also been, at the great quantity of fish visible in the transparent waters. "The Saint Lawrence is the river most abundant in every sort of fish that has ever been seen within the memory of man."[17] And there were not just fish. For as far upstream as the tidal current carried, a procession of marine animals accompanied the ship — whales, sea elephants, dolphins. They passed many islands, Ile aux Coudres, Ile aux Oies, Ile d'Orléans — where Cartier had been so happy to find an abundance of wild grapes growing that he first named it the Island of Bacchus — and each of the islands appeared welcoming, the trees filled with birds resting or regrouping before the start of the fall migration. Enormous turtles stretched out their wrinkled necks and dropped into the water without a sound. At a distance, a low canoe glided along, paddled by a man in a black robe squatting barefoot in the stern. And here and there, a reminder of familiar humanity, European houses dotted the green shore.

The ship made its way slowly upriver. The captain took care to stay well in the middle of the channel to avoid eel weirs, a sort of palisade erected in the sandy bed of the river by the local inhabitants. The eels, swimming downstream, came up short against the barrier, and the inhabitants went out at low tide armed with buckets and shovels to collect them. At last, at the tip of Ile d'Orléans, where the river narrows abruptly, the capital of New France appeared, Quebec. Its name was exotic, but the church towers, the pitch of the roofs, and the arrangement of the wharves brought to mind, as if a mirage, the distant homeland.

✤ 2 ✤

Clearing the Land
1667–1669

*H*E STEPPED ASHORE AND FELT SOMEWHAT DISAPPOINTED. The name Canada,[1] with its Indian sound, had stirred his imagination, but the place was tamer than he had expected. Leaving European shores, La Salle had thought to put civilization behind him; now, after an interminable voyage, he found himself disembarking at a small provincial capital where the rules of etiquette were subtly practiced. He observed with curiosity the worthies who descended from the Upper Town to greet the boat. At their head was the governor, Rémy de Courcelles, and beside him the provincial administrator, Jean Talon, who had organized the colony and was known to be Colbert's trusted ally. La Salle made his way toward a group of men dressed in long black robes, introduced himself to the Jesuit father superior, and was presented by Monsieur de Queylus to the Recollet friars. They pointed out to him the judge, the notaries, the engineers, the gunsmiths, and the three most prominent merchants in town. All of this small crowd took part in an endless dance, inclining their heads and bending their legs to one another, all the while keeping a close watch on the merchandise that was being unloaded, and pausing in their discussions long enough to bark out orders as to where a crate should go, or to inspect a bill of lading, or pocket their mail. La Salle pushed his way through the growing crowd to buy some apples from a man trundling a wheelbarrow full of them, and was startled to get back in change for his coin a grimy pack of playing cards. He then noticed other buyers offering beaver tails in settlement for somewhat larger transactions. Currency was in such perpetual short supply in Canada that barter was often used. The young man smiled as he bit into his apple: maybe Rouen was farther away than he had thought. He set out on a tour of the town.

Ironically, the fledgling city did not look new. The harsh climate had taken its toll on the earliest dwellings, and the battery emplacement built by Champlain at the river's edge had been worn away by ice until nothing was left of it but a ruin. Champlain's first residence, a central building flanked by two half-toppled towers, was in similar disrepair. La Salle crossed Market Square, a small group of wooden houses — the only stone building here was the new storehouse, where beaver furs were stacked before being shipped to France by the first boats that left in the spring. The storehouse, only built in 1663, was already starting to deteriorate. La Salle deposited his bag at the inn owned by Jean Gloria, a native of Dieppe, who had come to Canada as a servant of the Jesuits and elected to stay on after his term of service was up. He sauntered out again into the disorderly jumble of houses that made up the Lower Town. The crush in this part of town was oppressive as people bustled to put away the load of provisions come from France. The heights above beckoned to him, and La Salle set off toward them along a steep path known as the Breakneck. After a stiff climb, accompanied by a knot of children who scampered directly up the cliff face holding on to branches and tree trunks while giving Indian war whoops, he emerged onto a plateau dominating the Saint Lawrence.

He was now in the Upper Town, the official town where nuns, priests, and officers lived. A few steps from the ruined fort stood the convent of the Ursulines, surrounded by a palisade. Right next to it — but then all the buildings on this bluff seemed to be touching — were the provincial administrator's quarters, the courthouse, the *Hôtel-Dieu* or general hospital, and the Augustine convent, which abutted the Jesuit college. This college was the largest group of buildings within the settlement and consisted of a seminary, a school, a church, and a residence for Jesuits serving in the area. The traveler took some satisfaction in knowing that those gray walls would not close around him, and that he had to take orders from no one. Turning his eyes toward the superb and empty landscape, he gazed for a long moment at the great river below. But taking hold of himself, he clattered back down the path toward the wharves. There was not a second to waste in getting to Montreal, the farthest limit of French colonization, and the point of departure for any expedition into the heart of the unknown continent.

The ships coming from France stopped at Quebec. To reach Montreal one transferred to smaller, flat-bottomed river boats. At summer's end, there were always dozens of rafts on the river, half-submerged under the weight of logs that were being floated down to the wharves at Quebec to be cut in lengths and stacked for firewood — supplies always seemed to run low during the interminable winter months. The rafts, once unloaded, headed back upriver empty. La Salle made arrangements with a boatman and left as soon as possible for Montreal.

Quebec had the flavor of the old country, with its dignitaries and its shopkeepers, its streets where priests and housewives rubbed shoulders with the butcher, the baker, and the apothecary. But Montreal was purely a product of the New World. It was a dangerous town, situated at a crossroads of Iroquois war paths, and a rough one — it only dated back to 1642, and had virtually no amenities. Montreal was also a bizarre town. Although founded and run by priests of the Sulpician order, and christened Ville-Marie de Montréal in honor of the Holy Family, the town hosted trading fairs to which Indians came to sell their furs and, as a result, it attracted all the most intrepid and least scrupulous elements in the country. Behind Quebec were untracked forests, but the town fronted on the estuary, and faced toward the sea and Europe. Montreal, however, was surrounded on all sides by virgin wilderness, a rugged and inhuman country from which Indians at intervals erupted violently. The natives who appeared on the outskirts of Quebec were Huron converts, already to a large extent tamed and weakened. In Montreal, the inhabitants lived in fear of surprise attacks; furthermore, they had to endure the presence of the many wild Indians who camped on the banks of the river during their trading trips to town. They hauled their canoes up the shore, pitched their wigwams, and started cooking feasts whose stench was nauseating to the settlers. A young traveler, writing about his first visit to Montreal, noted in ironic tones that "the ladies walked with their fans before their eyes so as not to notice the nasty things hanging between the Indians' legs. Sometimes, however, they succumbed to these vile Cupids *meno per il gusto che per la curiosità*."[2]

The trading fairs were attended with a certain degree of pomp, at least on opening day. The Indians were fond of speeches and elaborate exchanges of gifts. The governor of Montreal listened, waited patiently for them to finish smoking their long pipes, and, at last, declared the fair open. Anyone who had the least thing to sell set up a counter along the exterior palisade and tried to find an interpreter. The fairs were rife with the sort of crazy juxtaposition that constituted the normal order in New France. There would be a crowd of Indians, naked as your hand, a feather or two pasted to their heads, armed with tomahawks, or bows and arrows, or brandishing the sorry firearms they had managed to acquire; then a group of Europeans, adventurers, or interpreters fresh from a stay with the Indians, who would be tanned and aggressive, hirsute, robed in animal skins; merchants from town and the outlying areas would also be on hand, maintaining a bearing consonant with the dignity and importance of their occupation; and finally the priests, with their long cassocks and grave demeanors. As night fell, drunkenness increased and the good folk barricaded themselves behind closed doors, afraid of the violence that the Indians and coureurs de bois were likely to wreak. At these times, the holy city of Ville-Marie, fortress-like with its narrow-windowed and thick-walled houses, was submerged in the greed of its European inhabitants and the excesses of its Indian visitors, until it seemed nothing but a sinister and dangerous outpost.[3]

In 1667 when La Salle arrived, the small town — Montreal and its immediate vicinity numbered only a few hundred inhabitants — was witnessing a period of tremendous vitality, even aside from its fairs. It was here that travelers to the interior stopped to transfer from river boats to canoes which, though often needing to be portaged because of the many rapids along this stretch of river, alone made passage to the Great Lakes possible. It took four to six men to paddle a canoe, and many young men traveled to Montreal looking for work. It was also here that inland expeditions, some of which lasted several months, were outfitted with supplies and equipment. The town was a hive of activity, all of it directed toward the interior, a fact that seemed exciting to La Salle. He found that the extraordinary mix of people — adventurers, Indians, merchants, as well as priests, who were both educated and energetic — was one that suited him to perfection.

A former Jesuit was an attractive prospect to the Sulpicians, as they were having trouble holding their own against the Black Robes (the name given to the Jesuits by the Indians), and the arrival of a vigorous and determined young man came as if in answer to their hopes. The threat of the Iroquois still weighed heavily on Montreal. Peace had been restored, but the inconstancy of the Indians was well known and rightly feared, particularly as their hostility was easily triggered by the vagaries of trade. Only a strong and resolute population could guarantee the safety of the colony. For this reason, the Sulpicians readily granted land to arriving immigrants.

In all likelihood, La Salle did not need his brother's intervention to obtain a grant of land. He was given several thousand acres west of the island of Montreal, at the level of Sault Saint

Louis, just above the falls that prevent boats from traveling up-river much beyond the city. The site entrusted to him was there-fore a strategic one, an outpost standing guard against Iroquois incursions. As for his acreage, it was virgin forest, densely over-grown with mixed pine and larch, with frontage on the boiling foam of the river and within earshot of the roar of the nearby falls. Of course, he could only reach his land by canoe. Until the end of the century, and apart from a few cart tracks around the cities of Quebec and Port-Royal in Acadia, there was no way of getting from one point to another without going by water. An Indian canoe was a necessity. It was made of birch bark, re-inforced inside with small hoops of white cedar, and solid enough to survive prolonged use, while also light enough to be portaged easily around rapids and rock-strewn shallows. La Salle, once he had learned to paddle crouching on his heels, became a tireless canoer. He set aside a 400-acre portion of land for his personal use, and offered the remainder to settlers in lots of about fifty acres[4] apiece, with no seigneurial rights to pay for four years. He was to name this fief Saint-Sulpice.

The spring following his arrival, La Salle started to put his land into production. He dug channels to draw off water from the marshy riverbanks, then organized a crew to clear the land, or, as the Canadian expression has it, "to make the land." Removing trees and clearing underbrush was such hard work that twenty men working full time managed to clear only about twenty-five acres a year.[5] Even then, the largest stumps often couldn't be pulled, there being no draft animals, and had to be left obstruct-ing the fields. The labor was exhausting and gave such slender and disappointing results that it is easy to see why a man might be tempted to put down his pick and shovel and take to a life in the woods. The work had no end to it because rocks had to be re-moved from the field all over again every spring. Successive freezes and thaws caused the stones to work to the surface. They were gathered and used to make boundary walls, or shore up eroding banks, or reinforce a path, or erect small buildings. Chipmunks (called *suisses* by the settlers because they reminded them of the striped uniforms of the Pope's Swiss guard) liked to make their burrows in these stone walls, and the great quantity of nuts they buried in them helped propagate nut-bearing trees. Eventually, these trees came to mark the boundary lines between properties.

A very simple first structure soon stood in the clearing. It was a house with narrow windows, of course made entirely of wood, using a Canadian technique called *pièces sur pièces* in which the wall planks are set horizontally rather than vertically. This method had the advantage of allowing the planks to be of varying lengths, and helped the structure stand up better against seasonal alterations in the wood. Also, the technique was simple enough that two men could raise a building on their own. La Salle moved onto his land at the spring thaw, and was quickly surrounded by his colonists. Unlike the inhabitants of the Saint Lawrence valley around Quebec, who preferred the freedom of isolated farms and refused to live clustered in villages, the population of Montreal, and especially those on the exposed part of the island, lived close to one another, sheltered behind an embankment fortified with a log palisade.

This new world, at once so hostile and so full of promise, required a period of apprenticeship, and La Salle's now began in that small, smoky house. The first thing a Canadian did on waking was to light his pipe to keep away the flies, mosquitoes, black flies, and other blood suckers that came in through the cracks of his hut to torment him. Men quickly abandoned their impractical European clothing for outfits more suited to life in the forest. On their feet they wore moccasins: these supple, unsoled boots, made of fine moosehide calfskin, were less apt to rip the bottom of a canoe. To protect their shins on forest outings they wore buckskin leggings ornamented with painted designs, porcupine quills, or variously colored moose hairs. La Salle bought himself an Indian raincoat made from the intestine of small seals, and a robe made of fur strips so thin they could be braided or knit. The Indian who sold it to him recommended that he always dry it very carefully, since a wet robe could freeze and its weight then make it impossible to transport. In the hot summer months, freezing weather seemed a long way off.

The warm months were almost magical for the plenty that was at hand, and La Salle was struck, as earlier visitors had been, with the miraculous ease of hunting on his land. In Canada when you set out to hunt wood pigeon, there was no need to spend hours concealed in a blind: you netted the birds by throwing an enormous hoop net over them as they roosted on the branches of a tree, or quicker yet you stunned them with a stick. There was an abundance of big game in the forest as well, but La Salle prudently had caches made, a sort of cupboard on piles where, when the cold weather started, frozen venison could be stored out of reach of dogs and wolves. The river teemed with fish. Rather than preserve fish in brine barrels, La Salle chose the Indian method of wrapping it in birch bark to dry it. He also learned to dry pine, willow, or serviceberry bark to make *tisane* — the trapper's tea — an effective cure for scurvy. As often as possible, he left his men to work his estate and went off to explore the forest. The absurdity of carrying a sword was quickly borne in on him. "One doesn't wear a sword in this country," he wrote a friend, "as it is an encumbrance when walking in the woods, and useless against the hatchets normally carried there — the savages have the strength to throw their hatchets thirty paces with such skill that they ordinarily bury the steel within the skull of anyone they designate."[6]

Hatchet in hand, more to clear a path in front of him than to kill enemies, who rarely showed themselves, La Salle learned to orient himself in the wilderness, not with his compass but by feeling with the palm of his hand around a tree trunk for the side with the thickest bark, indicating the north. Before long, he could identify the animals around him by their tracks and recognize the traces left by men who were invisible but whose presence he sensed. Covering his body with grease against the unbearable plague of mosquitoes, and having mastered the art of starting a fire in damp cover, he pushed ever deeper into the forest, growing bolder and more confident every day, and more intoxicated with the mysterious sound of the wilderness closing in around him. Month by month, his endurance increased. He trained himself to walk, to carry loads, and to fast without tiring. Like a true Indian, when he was gnawed by hunger, he would watch for the activity of woodpeckers around certain trees and would strip off the bark, uncovering galleries filled with large carpenter ants which he devoured by the handful.[7] From the first snowfall on, he could be seen head down, body leaning forward, gliding on his snowshoes, which he would maintain with care at every stop. With his wild hair, his deerskins, his watchful gaze and long supple stride, he soon seemed to have been born of a new race.

During that first winter he spent steeped in nature, he often had the feeling he would have to become a different kind of man in order to endure the hideous cold that gripped the land. The cold was all the more unexpected as the summers were surprisingly warm compared to France. One didn't anticipate such extremes in temperature. The only comparable winter that France saw during that period was the exceptional winter of 1709 when "a freeze, which continued hard for nearly two months, [made] the rivers solid within a few days right to their mouths, and the sea along the coast froze solid enough to carry wagons bearing the greatest loads."[8] Winter in Canada was announced by silence. The birds all but disappeared. The streams, rivers, and falls froze over. Snow piled up to heights inconceivable to a Norman who had never seen it except in the form of ephemeral flakes. In Montreal, six feet of snow could fall in two days. The Sulpicians had already warned La Salle by telling him of the hardships of "the winter of the great snow,"[9] when it had snowed from All Souls' Day at the beginning of November until the month of March without letup. It is one thing, though, to know that it is cold in Canada, and it is another to chop your cider with a hatchet, hear the crack of rocks and tree trunks as they split with the cold, and step out your door into a bitter wind that hacks at your face, draws tears from your eyes, and makes you teeter on the glare ice. La Salle never went out now without a long wool scarf with fringes, which he used to cover his mouth before speaking. According to a legend that goes back to the time of Cartier, words froze as they passed one's lips, and, in the spring, the air filled with the sound of thawing conversations. To protect his head he wore a beaverskin hat pulled down over his ears, and he bought triple-layered Indian mittens, an essential item, he was told, if he wanted to keep all his fingers. One morning he noticed that the edge of the river was starting to ice over. A few boats were still on the water, in defiance of the danger — at any moment they could be crushed by floating ice.

Most people ventured outside as little as possible, taking their cue from the bear and the groundhog, and passed the winter in lazy hibernation in their dens. La Salle on the contrary wanted to learn the ways of the forest in subzero weather. In winter, men hunted with traps rather than with a rifle. Once there was snow on the ground, the tracks of game were easy to follow. You could survive in the forest by setting snares for snowshoe hare, or by hunting moose, which, unable to move freely in the deep snows, were essentially defenseless. Fishing, practiced by chopping a hole through the ice, was also rewarding for anyone valiant enough to stand out on a frozen river or lake. The discovery of his own endurance encouraged La Salle to give his plans a more precise form.

A more ordinary man would have been happy with his present lot: an estate that promised considerable income; the free run of the woods; complete, blissful independence after years of submission. But La Salle was no ordinary man, and he was more than ever determined to reach and explore China. He had enough agility of mind to realize that exploration was expensive and that he would have to enter the fur and brandy trade in order to finance his ambitions.

The French had long envied the Spanish the gold and silver of Peru. Profits from the cod fishery were meager and prosaic by comparison. In the seventeenth century, however, for the simple and frivolous reason that hats made of long-haired felt were in fashion at the French court and in Paris, New France was the source of enormous profits. A young marquis who wanted to cut a figure in the world thought nothing of spending twenty to thirty livres on his hat, and the nobility all down the line would follow his lead.[10] The raw material for this headgear was beaver fur, preferably taken from pelts that had been worn and softened by Indians. Known as greasy beaver, these furs commanded the highest prices, and the French were in a better position to obtain them than the English or the Dutch. They alone had access, by the Saint Lawrence, the Ottawa, and the Great Lakes, to the heart of the continent and to the tribes able to procure the thickest furs. The fur trade, which was exceedingly profitable, was subject to a monopoly. Furs could not be sold directly in France; instead they were bought at fixed prices by a company with its headquarters in Quebec. Colbert's idea in designing the system was that traders would buy furs from Indians who regularly made the trip to the fairs at Tadoussac and Montreal. But the Canadians were neither as docile nor as well supervised as the Sun King's subjects who had stayed at home. Every strong and enterprising young man dreamed of going upriver to meet the Indians and bypass the official markets. (The Europeans did not hunt beaver themselves, since the Indians would have taken any incursion into their hunting grounds as provocation; besides, the furs had no value unless they had been worn and lubricated with fat by the natives.) The civil government was afraid that if the colonists were allowed to roam the woods freely and barter with the Indians they would quit the hard work of cultivating the soil, which was frozen six months of the year, and abandon any pretense of establishing a true colony. The authorities therefore took great pains to regulate individual trading parties. But to no avail. To live like Indians, with all the license and adventure this offered, and to return at the end of a few seasons wealthy men was too tantalizing a prospect for the settlers to forgo completely. The coureur de bois issue was never settled to Colbert's satisfaction. Once he got his bearings, La Salle often traveled up the Ottawa River to make contact with the Indians and each time came back with his canoe filled to the brim with beaver furs.

In order to make money quickly, however, one had to know how to tempt the Indians. Kettles, sewing needles, and glass beads no longer interested them after a century of trading. Firearms and alcohol, on the other hand, were still attractive commodities; and the coureurs de bois, encouraged by the merchants, had no hesitation about satisfying the worst proclivities of the hunting tribes. The brandy question was a source of heated argument within the colony. The secular colonists — the local governors, administrators, and the vast majority of settlers — wanted trade with the Indians and therefore wanted the right to sell them alcohol. In any case, they rarely felt the ill effects of the natives' drunkenness. The priests had a different set of concerns. They lived among the Indians and found their drinking bouts terrifying. Indians didn't drink for pleasure but to lose complete control of themselves. Intoxication helped them achieve a state of trance, something they found highly desirable, but which at the same time led them to acts of extreme violence. The Jesuits, although they were men of inordinate courage, hid in their huts or fled into the woods when the warriors returned to camp with brandy. "Never did the frenzied bacchants of times past do anything more furious in their orgies."[11] Any abetment of the Indians' drinking ran directly counter to the Jesuits' missionary purpose. They tried therefore to forbid the sale of brandy to the natives, but never managed to obtain the backing of the king or his minister.

To trade with the Indians one apparently had to give them what they clamored for with such insistence; and the competition from the English and the Dutch was too keen for the French to deprive themselves of a commercial advantage on the grounds of virtue. Consequently, the coureurs de bois continued to give drink to those who supplied them with furs. A cask of rotgut brandy cost 1,000 livres and held approximately 2,000 gallons. A pint cup could be exchanged for a pelt worth four livres. The arithmetic was fairly simple, and La Salle was quick to do it.

He lost no time. Within a few months he had learned to travel Canadian-style, which is to say by water, and to find his way in the woods, and he had grasped the mechanics of the barter system. But he would have failed his former Jesuit teachers if he had not undertaken the more arduous task of learning an Indian dialect.[12] This was an awkward project. French and the American Indian languages are of different families and there are no similarities between them to help bridge the gap. The Indian language tended to be nebulous, while French was precise; one was grounded in material objects, the other suited to abstractions; the natives had a hundred words for discussing a pine tree but marked distance or the passage of time with imprecise measurements. Their language, as a Recollet friar complained, "was sterile from the point of view of religion: one finds in it no terms with which to describe the Deity, or any of His mysteries."[13] And yet the French and Indians had to find a way to communicate. In the sixteenth century, Cartier had returned from his first voyage with the two sons of an Indian chief. Their conversations and mutual lessons had resulted in the first French-Iroquois dictionary consisting of about fifty words. On his subsequent voyages, Cartier left two French boys to spend the winter with the Indians. Not only did they learn the dialect, but one of them, Etienne Brulé, adopted the Indian way of life. In spite of his tragic end — he was eaten by the Hurons several years later, having proven "highly depraved and addicted to women"[14] — these exchanges continued and provided training for the interpreters vital to the colony. Later, the Recollet friars compiled dictionaries, as did the Jesuits and the Ursuline nuns after them. The task was further complicated by the number of dialects. Among Algonquin speakers, variations in the language were so great that each tribe would have needed an interpreter had there not been captives among them, often speaking several languages, who were happy to translate the speech of visitors — with some latitude for their own imagination. Early on in the seventeenth century, the French concentrated on the Huron language, for the good reason that the Hurons, who lived around the Great Lakes, were well-established in the role of middlemen and had imposed their language on many other Indian nations.

How is it possible to learn a language like Huron without real books, grammars, or manuals? Like the many French Jesuits who were unable to preach the gospel until they learned the language of their flock, La Salle was obliged to go to the natives for schooling. French interpreters absolutely refused to share their knowledge and in any case spent more time in the woods with the Indians than on the shores of the Saint Lawrence.[15] In Quebec, if one had a great deal of patience, it was possible to hire one of the Indians from the nearby missions. "I do conjugations, declensions, and some little syntax," wrote Father Le Jeune, "with incredible effort, as I was sometimes compelled to ask twenty questions to understand one word, so changeable and untalented was my master."[16] It also happened, as the Jesuits were to complain, that their native instructors slipped indecent words into the lessons, which the fathers would then go forth and preach in all innocence.[17] La Salle had the good fortune to engage two Iroquois who, with the coming of autumn, set up camp on his estate — a good illustration of the easy familiarity developing between the Indians and the French. While the English despised the aboriginal peoples, and let their contempt be felt, the French welcomed them and were accepted by them.[18] In the course of long evenings, of endless days when the snow piled up at the door and freezing winds kept them from going out, La Salle learned the Iroquois dialect and was soon able to ask the natives questions. He began to form an idea of the country's geography. The Indians described a river which they called the Ohio. It took nine months to follow the river's course down to its mouth on a large sea. La Salle concluded that it was none other than the river the Algonquins called the Mississippi, and the route to the Orient.

Two years after his arrival he felt well-prepared enough to start organizing his expedition. He opened negotiations with the Sulpicians to have them buy back the land they had given him eighteen months before. His concession had appreciated in value, since a portion of the land had been cleared and planted. The friars bought part of the original grant only, and the rest was sold to a man named Jean Milon. La Salle now possessed a capital of 3,000 livres. His next task was to obtain permissions from the civilian authorities. Freedom of movement did not exist in Canada as a right — there was an absolute prohibition against going into the wilderness, and one was not allowed to travel without a valid passport. Striking out into the woods without proper authorization was a sure way of getting into serious trouble. The coureurs de bois, of course, did as they pleased, but La Salle was not an adventurer who could be swayed by the profits to be made hunting. Riches did not tempt him. His ambition was directed toward glory, honor, and the joy of seeing borne out a theory he had been turning over in his mind for many years. His obsession with traveling to China was so strong that his land came to be called "Lachine," meaning "China" in French, which is why there is a section of present-day Montreal known by that name. La Salle wanted the right to explore in the king's name. He traveled to Quebec at the spring thaw to discuss it with the governor, the Marquis de Courcelles, and with the provincial administrator, Jean Talon. They listened to his petition with sympathy. La Salle spoke well, and his ardor and enthusiasm, balanced with his care in making preparations, impressed them favorably.

By his seriousness of purpose he won over both the governor and the administrator, who, despite the directives from their minister, found themselves agreeing with La Salle that the boundaries of New France should be extended. It seemed absurd to stake everything on agriculture in a country where the soil lay buried under a blanket of snow for six months of the year. Rather, they imagined New France as the depot from which all the riches from the unexplored interior of the continent would be shipped to France. Accordingly, Courcelles granted letters patent to La Salle authorizing him to explore the woods, rivers, and lakes of North America; he further provided La Salle with letters of recommendation for the governors of Virginia and Florida in case his explorations should lead him into their territories. Another expedition, this one aimed at saving souls, was preparing to leave Montreal at the same time, under the aegis of a Sulpician priest named Dollier de Casson. To La Salle's disappointment, Courcelles suggested that the two expeditions should join forces. In a tone that brooked no opposition, he pointed out that they were both going in the same direction. La Salle so disliked sharing the leadership of the enterprise that he would have preferred to go alone. Touchy about his independence, he was unable to see the benefit of having someone as vigorous and capable as Dollier along on his first voyage, nor did he recognize the value of Father Bréhan de Gallinée, an excellent cartographer. Father Dollier had not spent his youth inside the four walls of a seminary. As a cavalry captain he had won the admiration of Turenne, the king's most brilliant marshal, for his bravery and vigor. He was said to be "of tall stature and of such extraordinary strength that he was able to carry two men seated in his hands."[19] The winter before, a soldier had fallen through thin ice on the lake, and when none of his comrades would go to his rescue, Dollier had fished him out. Missionary though he was, he had very powerful arguments on his side. Kneeling in prayer at an Algonquin camp one day, he was noisily interrupted by an Indian. Without taking the trouble to rise from his knees, the good father sent the man flying with his fist, gaining the admiration of the assembled flock. He was also renowned for his knowledge of medicinal plants. The three men traveled to Montreal together, and La Salle must have let his disappointment show. In his account, Father Gallinée wrote, "It occurred to the Abbé de Queylus that Monsieur de La Salle might possibly abandon our Company, and that his temperament, which was known to be rather volatile, might lead him to depart at the first whim."

❧ 3 ❧

Monsieur de La Salle's Indian
1669–1671

DEPARTURE WAS SET FOR JULY 6, 1669. From Montreal, where he had bought a house after the sale of his estate, La Salle made final preparations.[1] The expedition numbered seven canoes: three for the priests and their seven crewmen, and four canoes for La Salle, who traveled with twelve men. They had no trouble finding boatmen because the governor had issued permissions for the men to join the expedition — proof of his very real support for the enterprise. La Salle hired his crew for fifteen months, until October 20, 1670, and promised them a salary of 400 livres. The Sulpician priests, who were hoping to make their base in an Indian village, knew how important it was to win any contest with the tribal shamans. They had accordingly convinced two surgeons to accompany them. Whether these Europeans were more effective at curing the sick than the native medicine men is open to question, particularly as the natives had no resistance to the germs the Europeans carried and contact with them was enough to kill the Indians by the hundreds. In any case, two practitioners of the medical art joined the outfit and stowed their lancets, scissors, cannulas, and splints with methodical care in the bottom of the canoes. The language problem worried Father Gallinée. It proved so difficult to find competent interpreters, however, that he settled for a Dutchman who spoke no French. La Salle was less concerned, expecting that he would be able to handle any encounter with the Iroquois himself. Besides, his Indian companions from the previous winter were accompanying him.

After a last look at the sketched maps the Jesuits had compiled, the party set off. All the men, with the exception of Father Gallinée, had a good idea of what travel on the Saint Lawrence meant. They knew that on this journey they would be navigating normally — in a boat — only in those places where the river widened into a lake. Such passages were short and sweet since the Saint Lawrence generally rushed through narrow gorges, more a torrent than a river. Here, the canoe was useless. One walked upriver through the boiling, foaming water, carrying one's boat. This mode of travel was not for the faint of heart. Father Gallinée found no peace of mind squatting in the bottom of his canoe "separated from death not by a finger's breadth but by the thickness of five or six sheets of paper."[2] He now had to learn to walk rapidly through swirling water without slipping on stones and without upsetting the baggage that was tied to his back by a strap that cut into his shoulders. He did not complain. The other men had to hold the canoe upright to prevent its contents from spilling out and, at the same time, choose the surest way although they were hardly able to see because of the veils wound around their heads against mosquitoes. They advanced slowly. As a rule, they traveled fifteen leagues or about thirty-five miles a day on still waters, a quiet lake for example, and much farther descending a rapid river. But all through this hard, lofty, and impenetrable forest, where the way seemed to be barred even at the edge of the trees, portages were the roughest challenge. Weighed down like mules, sweating, their breath coming hard, the men advanced cautiously, surrounded by clouds of insects, blinded by perspiration and by branches slashing at their faces, pulling themselves along when they came to cataracts by grabbing at trees anchored on solid ground. For a man who was not physically fit, it was hell.

In the evening, they looked for a spot where they could drag their canoes onto the spongy bank. They dried themselves around a fire and smoked a long, delicious pipe before starting to think about preparing food. Choosing the time and place for the night's bivouac was always a source of argument between La Salle and Father Dollier. Both wanted to establish their authority. Luckily, the group maintained its good humor, in part thanks to the abundance of game in these woods — the elk couldn't take flight in the thick brush — and to the miraculous ease of catching fish — one day they caught fifty catfish in a half hour. "One learns to do without bread, wine, salt, pepper, and condiments," wrote Father Gallinée, stirring a kettleful of sagamity gruel. Made mostly of cornmeal and water mixed with fish or game, sagamity was the Indians' main dietary staple. The corn was boiled prior to departure to make hulling the grain easier, and the cereal kept well, forming the major element in the travelers' diet. They were resigned to it. "The food is not appetizing," wrote one, "but it is surely very healthful as it maintains the stomach perpetually clear, and it is very diuretic as one urinates up to fifty times a day, so that if one ate nothing else one would never be the worse for it."[3] At night, some slept under an overturned canoe while others stretched a hide or netting over four stakes to make a sort of crib protecting them from mosquitoes. The canoes were always tied to a tree, like horses to a picket, to keep the wind from blowing them away. Crushed with fatigue, the man on watch had trouble keeping his eyes open.

Twenty-seven days after their departure, the travelers reached the shores of Lake Ontario. This enormous lake, a true freshwater sea, whose gray outline faded into the distance, had often been described by the Jesuits and other travelers. Dollier and La Salle headed south according to plan, gliding over the water so easily that they were able to hoist sail, and on August 11 they reached Irondequoit Bay, site of the present town of Rochester. A band of Indians, kinsmen of their guides, came quietly down to meet them and invited them to visit their village, which according to their chief was near the source of the Ohio.

Up to this point, La Salle had had contact only with peaceful Indians. He hadn't known the horror of the Indian wars, or the settler's constant fear of an Iroquois attack even while in his own fields. An Iroquois might stay motionless as a stump for days on end watching his victim. La Salle had never seen mutilated corpses or scalped heads; he had never heard the howls of captured companions. The Indians with whom he had bartered, unexpected though their behavior might sometimes have been, had never contrived any unpleasant surprises for him. On the contrary, he had enjoyed observing them. Leading a primitive existence on his own land, and during his trips into the woods, he had often been led to imitate the Indian arts of survival. And the Indians' extraordinary resistance to cold, hunger, and fatigue had evoked his admiration. He always felt irritated in the company of missionaries, who wanted only to change the way the Indians lived and thought. Their ideal would have been to convert all Indians into sedentary farmers. La Salle would have liked to transform himself into an aboriginal nomad, at least for the spell of his journey. On leaving the seminary, he had abandoned any desire to convert primitive men. He remained a good Christian, and an irreproachably moral one, who abhorred the debauchery commonly seen among coureurs de bois. But native life, at least the life of those still in a natural state, fascinated him. He believed that only through contact with the Indians could he acquire the local knowledge and the skill necessary to keep from being crushed by the fearful forces of nature. Right at the outset of this trip, however, he discovered a different reality and faced a painful trial that would test his ability to carry out his plan.

The travelers agreed to divide up temporarily. La Salle and Father Gallinée took a few men with them and followed the Indians, leaving Dollier and the others to watch the canoes. "We set forth accordingly," the father wrote, "ten Frenchmen with forty or fifty natives who obliged us at every league to rest for fear of overtiring us. About halfway, we found another band of

Indians coming to meet us and who made us offerings of food and joined us to return to the village."[4] Their village was much larger than any La Salle had seen near Montreal or Quebec. A thousand or so warriors lived in four neighboring clusters of longhouses. The dwellings were not wigwams but lodges with walls made of birch bark. From the start the visitors had difficulty making themselves understood. La Salle proved not to speak Iroquois well enough, and the Dutch interpreter was completely useless. The Indians, however, seemed glad to welcome the travelers and sent to a nearby Jesuit mission for an interpreter. The Frenchmen were given the largest house in the village. Women supplied them with firewood, children brought quantities of fruit, and several elders invited them to feast according to the customs of the country. The visitors were travel-hardened, or so they thought, but at the sight of large pieces of dog, offered to them in greasy wooden bowls, still coated with singed hair, they had trouble hiding their revulsion. As the welcoming feast went on, they turned down partly raw bear claws, at the risk of creating an incident. In these filthy, fetid shelters, crammed full of children, old men, and dogs sleeping under the same repulsive blanket, a new and sordid side of native life was revealed. However, La Salle needed the Indians' support and hoped to obtain guides there. Undismayed, he organized a round of talks with his hosts.

First there was an exchange of gifts. The French received necklaces of porcelain beads and offered in return kettles, axes, and knives and asked for a guide to accompany them on their descent of the Ohio. La Salle, impatient by nature, managed to remain impassive during long sessions in which endless speeches were followed by protracted silence. "The Indians assembled in our hut were about fifty or sixty of the most important elders of the village. Their custom is, when they come in, to sit down in the first vacant place they find, without regard to rank, and at once get a coal to light their pipes, which do not afterwards leave their mouths during the entire council."[5] The French weren't clear as to how their affairs were progressing, but their hosts' kind gestures and cheerful expressions reassured them. Things were to change as rapidly as if a gust of wind had suddenly brought clouds to darken the horizon.

One morning there was great excitement in camp. Some Indians, returning from an expedition to the Dutch, had brought back a cask of brandy. La Salle and Gallinée had been warned that under the influence of alcohol, Indians were prone to acts of extreme violence, but neither had ever experienced this. The spectacle they were now witnessing frightened them. Gone were measure, ceremony, and silence, replaced by frenetic activity. The men howled and shook their tomahawks; the women struck the bark walls with their clubs to scare off evil spirits; and in the smoky lodges, naked bronze bodies, wild eyes, heaps of food and vomit, accompanied by the barking of dogs, combined to form a hellish vision. It took no knowledge of Iroquois to understand the extent of their danger. In the preceding days, La Salle and his companions thought they had been staying with natives or *naturels*, natural men, in the expression of the day — men unmistakably imbued with dignity, living in harmony with the natural world around them. But the brandy episode seemed to have exposed their more cruel and barbarous side. The Frenchmen were further horrified when they were obliged to attend a torture session. The prisoner, a young man, had been brought back to the village after a skirmish in which a boy had been killed. The mother who had lost her son was offered the prisoner in reparation. She, however, refused to be consoled and, by choosing not to adopt the young man, condemned him to the horrible death the Iroquois meted out to their enemies.

The voyagers knew perfectly well that the Indians practiced torture, and the possibility of martyrdom often inflamed the missionaries' zeal. The story of Father Jogues, who had miraculously managed to escape his torturers in 1642, was known to every Jesuit in France and to every inhabitant of Canada. Besides, contemporary European mores authorized cruel punishments and savage executions. Agrippa d'Aubigné in his epic poem, *Les Tragiques*, published at the beginning of the seventeenth century, glorified the martyrdom of persecuted Protestants in precise and unbearable terms. He describes Thomas Haux at the stake, for example, engulfed by flames, signaling to his brothers "with the bones that were his arms."[6] Criminals and suspects alike were subject to interrogation by torture. Madame Voisin, a notorious poisoner, was tortured until she broke down and was subsequently burned at the stake. Madame de Sévigné's son, protesting the torture of women to a judge, received the following reply: "My dear sir, there are some indulgences granted to the women in deference to their sex." "How, pray, sir? Are they strangled?" "No, sir, but logs are thrown on their heads and the executioner's boys tear off their heads with iron hooks."[7] But to be seated as guests of honor, among old men and chiefs calmly smoking their long pipes, while a man was burned with slow fires, mutilated by frenzied women, showered with boiling water, all the while howling like a man possessed — this took superhuman callousness. And yet what other attitude could they adopt? After several days of madness, calm returned. La Salle and Gallinée took the opportunity to rejoin Dollier. None of the men seemed openly unnerved by the experience, yet Father Gallinée returned to France the next year and never set foot in Canada again. La Salle, for his part, was far too committed to his enterprise to falter at the thought of further perils, however terrible. The Indians might be dangerous, unreliable, and inhuman, but they inhabited the territory he was determined to explore, and he needed them. He came away from the episode more than ever convinced that he would be better off traveling alone. If faced by a village gone mad, at least he wouldn't have to worry about the reactions of his companions.

The French party resumed its journey, heading south, and crossed the Niagara River. Father Gallinée, as a geographer, would have liked to ascend the river and look at the falls, whose tremendous roar they could hear and whose site they located in the distance under a column of spray. But it was late in the season, and they needed to cover as much ground as possible before the onset of bad weather. They came to another village and there, after a few gifts and numerous parleys, they finally managed to barter for two natives who would serve as their guides. One of them, a Shawnee captive named Nika, attached himself to La Salle. Surly and often gruff with his companions, La Salle responded graciously to the Indian's signs of affection. They walked together side-by-side, one of them speaking and the other listening attentively, repeating each other's words aloud, and soon they were conducting actual exchanges. La Salle was a good student. Within a few short weeks he had acquired an adequate knowledge of Nika's dialect.

With their guides to lead them, the Frenchmen often camped in Indian villages, and at one of their stops, toward the end of August, they discovered a white man. His face looked familiar, and it turned out to be none other than Adrien Joliet. One of the strangest facts about this sparsely peopled continent, where a dozen Frenchmen ran back and forth like ants, was that it already seemed to be marked by stable thoroughfares. Given the logic imposed by the seasons and the use of rivers and lakes as roads, occurrences of travelers running into each other in this otherwise enormous solitude were not unusual.

Adrien was the brother of Louis Joliet, one of the great explorers of the period. Born in Canada, where their father, a resident of Quebec, manufactured sleighs, the Joliet boys grew up with a good education. Virtually all children in Quebec went to school — boys to the Jesuit college and girls to study with the Ursuline nuns. The result was that more than 80 percent of the Canadian-born population could read and write, an astonishing ratio for that time, especially considering that in France only one person in five knew how to sign his name. Another significant difference was that in Canada, an artisan's son who showed signs of intellect was quickly integrated into the ruling class. The Joliet brothers, who dreamt of nothing but voyages and exploration, were always protected by the Jesuits and were quick to win Talon's confidence. Louis was encouraged to pursue the various projects that eventually led to his travels on the upper Mississippi, and Adrien was commissioned by Talon to investigate the area around Lake Superior for copper deposits. He found no ore —

he would have had to search much farther north, around Lake Abitibi, where copper crops up abundantly in surface rock — but one never returned from an expedition in Canada entirely empty-handed. There was always something to discover, and Joliet captivated Father Dollier with his description of the numerous tribes living around Lake Superior — they had never been visited by missionaries and seemed ready to receive the word of God. This was invaluable information to Father Dollier. The Sulpicians were always at odds with the Jesuits, who had built missions all around the Great Lakes and showed little inclination to make room for their competitors. The priests Dollier and Gallinée were so enthusiastic at the prospect of a new mission field that they decided to abandon the exploration of the Ohio and head north. La Salle, who was probably delighted, argued that his state of health kept him from accompanying them — no European was entirely free of stomach ailments after a few weeks of the native diet. Father Dollier said Mass before an altar that was propped up on a pair of paddles and shaded by the sails of the canoes. La Salle took communion, and the men parted.

Finally La Salle was happy. He was now the master of his own enterprise and reasonably confident of his chances. He decided to spend the winter in the area before striking out into the unknown. Winter was always less severe on the Great Lakes than in the dark and forested area of Montreal, and that year it was especially mild. On the advice of Nika, his Shawnee guide, La Salle retreated from the windy shore and wintered a few miles inland with his men in a quiet village. That spring, he resumed his expedition and at length reached a large river flowing westward from the south end of Lake Erie. This was the Ohio, meaning "beautiful river," described to him so many times by his Iroquois tenants, a large, foaming, rapid river. It appeared from afar as a brilliant gap dividing the green mass of the forest. The men were heartened, and in their impatience to slip downriver toward unknown territories, they hastened their step.

But navigation on the Ohio was still at that time a figment of the imagination and would only become a reality some hundred

years later. The channel was clogged with rocks, gravel, tree
trunks and debris. Large alluvial deposits collected at the bends
in the river, and these shifting dams created dangerous and un-
stable stretches churned by eddies and falls. La Salle and his men
were therefore obliged to carry their canoes. With water up to
their waists if not their armpits, their feet torn, they were constantly attacked by swarms of horseflies and mosquitoes, and
faced the added danger of rattlesnakes among the rotting leaves.
It was impossible to walk along the river's edge. The banks were
so inhospitable that the Indians never camped there, instead
building their villages beside tributaries. In winter the river froze
into enormous ice blocks that battered against the rampart of
trees, and the rampart, though constantly renewed, regularly lost
portions to the massed weight of the ice. The fallen trees turned
the bank of the river into an impassible tangle of roots, trunks,
and branches. Not only were the banks impossible to travel, but
it was hard to find a place on shore to rest. On the few stretches
where the water seemed calm enough to launch the canoes, one
had to be on constant watch for snags caught on the river's bottom which, though hardly showing above the water, could rip the
hull of a skiff from stem to stern.[8] La Salle soldiered on, always in
the lead, pressing the pace, silent, indifferent to the murmur of
unrest rising behind him. The men grumbled. Progress was
hopelessly slow. La Salle, driven by his obsession, failed to notice
the resentment building and turning to hatred. Consequently, he
did not bother to offer explanations or even to note that his authority was being challenged. It was beneath him to watch for
whispered meetings, a hostile tone or look. More serious still, he
did not register how hateful the slow progress on the river had
become to his companions, and how tempting was the open
prairie that now replaced the forest on either side. He managed
to hold his band together until the falls at the present site of
Louisville, "a place where the river drops from a great height
into a vast marshland, below the point where it is joined by a very
large river flowing from the north."[9] But one night, at the end of
August, the guides and porters all disappeared. Desertion here

was equivalent to murder. A lone man could not make the return trip to the missions on the Great Lakes before winter, let alone reach Montreal. In fact, a lone man could not survive in the empty wilderness. But La Salle was unflappable, and Nika had not left him. The Jesuits were wrong not to have chosen him for a mission — a man of his fiber would have worked miracles. Checked in his forward thrust, La Salle found the inner strength to turn back on his tracks. He still had his musket for defense, his compass to tell direction, his hands to set snares, dig roots, and bait hooks, and he had his canoe. Thanks to Nika, his encounters with isolated tribes along the way were peaceful. The first snows descended on him just as he was reaching the Great Lakes. Dazzled by the white ground, he thought he was going blind. Indians found him and cared for him, applying pine needles to his eyelids, but although they tried to hold him back he insisted on returning to Montreal as quickly as possible. The citizens of that town were not easily surprised, but La Salle's appearance in the dead of winter, along with Nika — thin, wild-eyed, drunk with elation at having made the first descent of the Ohio and at having prevailed over distance, solitude, hunger, and cold — produced a considerable stir. La Salle betrayed no emotion other than impatience to begin again. The expedition had ruined him, however, and he once more needed money.

He went back to trading in the Montreal area. This was profitable and at the same time afforded him the chance to extend his knowledge of the woods and rivers. Furthermore, he would learn which of the Indians and Frenchmen might follow him to people the empire now starting to form in his mind. While hunting along the Ottawa River north of the Saint Lawrence with a band of Indians, there occurred another of those coincidences that are so surprising in this vast country — he ran into Nicholas Perrot. It turned out that Perrot was exactly the kind of colonizer La Salle wanted. From the Bourgogne region in France, the son of an officer of the peace, he had seemed destined to a tranquil existence when he suddenly took it into his head to go to Canada as a servant of the Jesuits. He adapted so quickly and so well to the climate of New France that the Jesuits sent him to winter in an Indian village to learn the different dialects. He not only mastered enough languages to become one of the best interpreters in the country, but he learned the ways of the natives and acclimated himself so thoroughly that he never encountered the least trouble in Indian territory in the course of his long career as a voyageur. He was always greeted with honor and generosity. These facts were of a kind to impress La Salle, and to encourage him.

In his travels, La Salle often met up with coureurs de bois, and though he was a man with a pronounced taste for solitude, and a deep distaste for familiarity, he made it his business to observe the ways of these young men and develop links with them. If he was to be successful in his plans, he would need their help. Their physical stamina was phenomenal. Since they had better nourishment than the Indians, who did not stockpile foodstuffs and who regularly suffered famine in winter and during their migrations, these young men often had greater endurance than the Indians themselves, were better canoers, and of a more amorous disposition. The Indians wondered at the sexual prowess of their guests. Virginity was not particularly valued in the woods; while married women were expected to be faithful, the Indians readily offered their daughters and sisters to the visitors, whose energy always astonished them. La Salle disapproved of these excesses but recognized the attraction of the Indian girls for young men living in a country where males outnumbered females by a factor of ten to one. The young in New France were herded into marriage at an early age, and no dalliances were allowed to those who failed to find a wife. For all their faults, however, La Salle admired the independence and courage of the coureurs de bois, and marveled at their great number. The flight toward the woods worked against Minister of Finance Colbert's plans — to develop stable roots for the region rather than to explore the expanding new frontiers — but counted favorably toward his own.

From the colony's inception, the French were torn between two ways of proceeding.[10] One was to establish a solid foundation by means of regular and unheroic toil: clearing, tilling, producing children, living a European-style existence in fealty to Church and Crown. This was Colbert's ideal, and he would happily have left the exploration of the unknown continent to the Jesuits. The other — and not even the most docile Canadian was completely immune to its attraction — was to spring forward, explore, put out feelers, go upstream, and, in so doing, live differently and slip the yoke of political and religious discipline, which was particularly restrictive in Canada where the clergy were powerful and determined to set a good example for the natives. Also, as the population was small, its members watched and reported on each other's doings avidly. There was a dichotomy between land and water. The land produced settlers who were sober and sensible, while the rivers carried away the boldest men toward the unknown, taking the most vigorous, the most energetic, and those best suited to developing and defending the colony. Hence the minister's fury. But all Colbert's raging determination to stop this drain of manpower from the central colony came to nothing. Young men continued to set out in spite of the threat of heavy fines, floggings, hard labor in the galleys, and even death, knowing that they could always resettle in New Holland or New England if the reprisals ever materialized. La Salle for his part knew that if the French were to extend their dominion in the New World, it would be thanks to these young men.

La Salle had abandoned the idea of finding China at the other end of the "Great River" or beyond the "Interior Sea." He understood that the rivers on this continent did not flow west but south, toward richer and more welcoming lands than the snow- and ice-covered country of New France. He now became more and more convinced of the need to find a practical route between the Great Lakes and the Mississippi. Clearly, following the Ohio was too hard ever to become a common itinerary. As soon as the ice melted in the spring of 1671, La Salle went down to Quebec for an interview with Talon. The administrator listened with interest and was favorably impressed. Despite being Colbert's man, he too could not resist the prospect of penetrating deeper into this surprising country. La Salle offered the argument that buffalo hides, which provided such good leather, would make excellent saddles and boots, and could replace beaver fur if the fashion in hats ever changed. Talon, who was obsessed with finding mineral deposits, approved the appropriation of lands containing such a plethora of riches. But hemmed in on one side by his minister, who minced no words in his instructions, and on the other by Governor Courcelles, a man of narrow outlook, he could do no more than promise his support. As with his earlier voyage, La Salle would have to finance the venture himself.

The great thing about this new country was that one could find money there. Once again the Sulpicians of Montreal came to his aid and lent him the capital to stock up on presents for the Indians and general merchandise. In the month of August, a bit late in the season but La Salle now had the confidence to take risks, he left in the company of his faithful Nika and six boatmen. From Lake Ontario they passed via the Niagara portage into Lake Erie, then crossed Lake Saint Clair (where Detroit is today) into Lake Huron. They traveled up its west coast, discovered another inland sea, Lake Michigan, and the beautiful harbor that, a century later, would become the site of Chicago. To La Salle, these deep waters were a revelation. Navigation was easy here, and real flat-bottomed boats could be used to transport heavy loads. The waters were generous as well — fish jumped and splashed; flights of ducks, swans, Canada geese, and teal settled noisily on the lake surface. Did the travelers reach the Mississippi? This question would long be debated by the respective partisans of La Salle and Joliet, though it seems of minor interest. Louis Joliet and Father Marquette traveled on the upper Mississippi in 1672. La Salle, if he reached it in 1671, made no effort to explore it. All that he had observed in the course of this expedition encouraged him in his general plan, but first he had to return to Quebec to convince the authorities.

❀ 4 ❀

The Governor's Ear
1672–1673

THE AUTHORITIES, AS LA SALLE HAD KNOWN them up to that time, were in fact several — power in New France being divided between the governor, the provincial administrator, and the bishop. In September 1672 the situation altered with the arrival of a new governor, who assumed office at the very moment that the great administrator, Jean Talon, and the bishop, François de Laval — a rigid, dominating man — were returning to France. The freshly named governor, Louis de Buade, Comte de Frontenac, lacked neither ambition nor self-assurance, and was immediately to impose a new regimen.

It was enough to see him disembark — and the whole town was at the jetty for his arrival — to understand that a ray of the Sun of Versailles had come to tickle the inhabitants of the coldest of Louis XIV's colonies. After ten weeks of boredom and discomfort on the crossing, it was rare for a passenger not to be staggering as he set foot on shore — and it was usually a dirty, thin, and wobbly foot at that. When twenty guardsmen, resplendent in their uniforms, marched down the gangway and lined up to form an honor guard, and an imposing man strode with sure step onto the pier and saluted the assembled populace, a shiver of admiration ran through the crowd. It was not surprising that the Comte de Frontenac should have panache. His innate pride was nourished by the ancient ties that linked his father's family to the Bourbons and the influence wielded on his mother's side by two generations of the Pontchartrain clan. Born in the seraglio, he understood the importance of style and manner.

The energy he radiated was not an affectation. Frontenac, though already fifty years old and an old man by the standards of the time, had arrived on these distant shores because he believed that fortune and glory awaited him here. This thankless posting, in a treacherous country hardly more peopled than a desert, exposed to assault from the Indians, the Dutch, and the English, was one he had actually sought. In fact, he had intrigued to obtain it. At a time when living far from court was the despair of many good and able souls, Frontenac had wanted to leave the kingdom. And it is easy to understand why. A tumultuous marriage, financial ruin followed by a declaration of bankruptcy, and the feeling that he had been unfortunate in his various ventures (a painful admission for a man filled with a sense of his own importance) all justified him in turning his thoughts to an unknown land, a virgin country with an undefined frontier, which for almost two hundred years had been servicing Europe's appetites. For La Salle, going to Canada had represented a start in life; for Frontenac, it was an opportunity to start over.

He was born in 1622 in the chateau of Saint-Germain-en-Laye where his father, a playmate of King Louis XIII, held the post of governor. His father died a few months after his birth, but the child was not left entirely unprovided for. A godson of the king, he had the support of his mother's family, and drew wealth from the property of Palluau-sur-Indre and from Ile-Savary, a handsome Renaissance castle near Loches. The boy received a good education, since he regularly attended classes at a boy's college (a relatively rare occurrence at that time). Then, as befitted a young nobleman, he embarked on a military career.

The Thirty Years War was in progress, and fighting had spread through Europe from north to south. Frontenac campaigned for more than ten years — in Holland, Italy (where he received a wound in the arm that he would feel all his life), and finally Spain, until the signing of the Peace of Westphalia in 1648. On his return to Paris, he moved back into the family town house on the Quai des Célestins. There he fell in love with a neighbor, Anne, the only daughter of an officer of the state council, a certain Neufville de La Grange. The young lady was superb. She had the imperious beauty of a goddess — a portrait of her as Minerva still hangs at Versailles — and she was witty, cultured, and endowed with iron determination. Her father, a choleric and irresolute man, unable to handle her himself, had, on the death of his wife, sent Anne away to be reared by a female relative, Madame Bouthilier. As the wife of a superintendent of finances, this lady was able to use her contacts to get information on her ward's suitor. The report was not good. The young man had squandered his inheritance. Money slipped through his fingers, and he was said to be a bad lot. At this news, Anne's father called a halt to the courtship and explained himself in plain language to a friend: "I saw as clear as day that, far from having twenty-five, or twenty thousand livres income, he did not even have five."[1] Where once he had been so flattered by the young count's interest in his daughter that he agreed to serve as the lovers' go-between, carrying their love letters, he now became adamantly opposed to the liaison and, little suspecting his daughter's stubbornness, locked her away in a convent.

As befitting a soldier, Frontenac refused to be outflanked by the enemy and took the offensive. He arranged a meeting with his beloved in front of the church of Saint-Pierre-aux-Bœufs, which had the rare privilege of administering the marriage sacrament without parental consent, and married her on a Wednesday in October 1648. Enraged, her father remarried in turn, planning to sire another child so as to disinherit his insubordinate daughter once and for all. He married a widow, Françoise d'Ableiges,[2] who had already led quite an eventful life: her father had been madly in love with her and had arranged the assassination of her husband in order to kidnap her to the Château de Dieppe, where he held her prisoner, and where she would have spent the rest of her days had not Queen Anne of Austria ordered her release. She now found that she was married to a man who had one thing on his mind, which was to make her pregnant. After six years of trying, he succeeded, and a second daughter was born to him in 1654. He had in the meantime fallen out irrevocably with his son-in-law. The unfortunate Frontenac lost the first of a long series of court battles and was enjoined not to touch a sou of the fortune his wife had inherited from her mother without first obtaining the consent of Neufville, his father-in-law.

The couple's domestic life started to sour. The young countess took pleasure in appearing at court and in town, but her husband grew irritated that he could neither build as he wanted at Ile-Savary, nor live the life of a great lord in Paris. He was unable even to dispense liberal gifts and rewards to the men of his regiment. Frontenac had thought that he was marrying a girl who was rich and in love, insubordinate to her father but submissive to her husband. He was forced to recognize, however, that the beautiful Anne had as yet no access to her money, appeared constantly impatient to get away from him, and was no more concerned about his wants than she had been in the past about her father's. The time was one of political revolt. In the atmosphere of freedom, she dropped her husband, who was always busy redesigning his walkways and shoring up his walls at Ile-Savary, to join the ladies-in-waiting of the king's cousin, the Grande Mademoiselle. These ladies played the part of Amazons for several months, spiritedly taking the side of the opposition Frondeurs, but the civil war ended in victory for the king[3]. And as neither the king nor Mazarin forgot past insults, Mademoiselle was made to pay for her boldness.

The Grande Mademoiselle was exiled from Paris, and fled to her chateau at Saint-Fargeau near Auxerre, followed by her ladies-in-waiting. The fun was over. The castle had the gloom of an abandoned dwelling. The drawbridge was broken. One had to enter on foot into this "old house where there were neither doors nor windows, and where grass was growing knee-high in the courtyard." Mademoiselle was brought into "a very ugly room with a post in the middle."[4] It was cold. The ladies, their daring exploits forgotten, jumped with fright at the slightest creaking. They all slept in the same bed for reassurance. The days dragged on. They grew listless, and quarreled to dispel their boredom. Questions of precedence assumed such importance that when the Comtesse de Fiesque, one of the ladies-in-waiting, suggested that she invite her friend Mademoiselle d'Outrelaise, it was opposed by Mademoiselle. The young lady "would likely prove an embarrassment, as she was not of a station to eat with [Mademoiselle] nor to ride in [her] carriage." After a great deal of negotiating, Mademoiselle d'Outrelaise was invited; she charmed the entire company and Madame de Frontenac in particular. The two developed such a tender bond in fact that Monsieur de Frontenac would lose his place.

He only rarely came to Saint-Fargeau. It was a house full of women, run by a spinster who dreamed up the most irritating domestic arrangements, and it exasperated him. Hadn't Mademoiselle arranged during one of his visits to install his wife and himself in a study that was separated from her bedroom only by a door that wouldn't close? Another time she had put their bed in a room with three other women. He rarely came as a result. Besides, his affairs were in such disarray that he was often obliged to stay in Paris. He remained attached to his wife, however, and believed he was free to visit her whenever he pleased. It once happened that he turned up unannounced. "At his arrival," Mademoiselle reported, "his wife was taken by surprise, and her astonishment was apparent to all, as it was succeeded by no feelings of gladness. Rather than looking after her husband, she ran and hid, crying and uttering laments because her husband had said he wanted to stay with her that night. I was surprised to see her declare her aversion so strongly, one I had never suspected before. The Comtesse de Fiesque went and remonstrated with her, telling her that she was obliged in all conscience to go with her husband. This only made her cry harder. The countess brought books to Madame de Frontenac, in which she showed her the truth of all she was saying. Finally the situation reached a point where I sent for the parish priest and his holy water to exorcize her."[5] Frontenac, who knew nothing of this, had leapt hotly into bed, and the next morning, unsurprisingly, was in a foul humor. There was a scene. Mademoiselle, shocked and alarmed, decided it was her duty to protect Madame de Frontenac from the violence of her surly husband. She had misunderstood the lady. Madame de Frontenac did not want to sleep with her husband, it is true. But she was not going to be filed and forgotten at Saint-Fargeau now that her sentence of exile had expired and she was free to enjoy the festivity and brilliance of Paris. As for Frontenac, he never importuned her again. He turned to a young beauty, Madame de Montespan, with whom he fell madly in love. The news of this romance traveled far enough that, several years later, when the beautiful Athénaïs abandoned herself to the arms of Louis XIV, a fit of retrospective jealousy was attributed to the Sun King to account for the pleasure he took in posting Frontenac abroad.

While love flourished, debts piled up and lawsuits started to multiply. Monsieur de Neufville died and left his fortune to his younger girl, including the share that belonged by rights to his elder daughter. Further lawsuits were brought, but nothing came of them. Finally Frontenac went bankrupt and turned all his assets over to his creditors; his wife managed to obtain a division of property and bought back Ile-Savary out of her own money. Under circumstances as humiliating as this, Frontenac did the only honorable thing for a gentleman: he petitioned to rejoin his regiment, which was then fighting the Turks in Hungary. Leaving his financial problems behind, and an acerbic wife who made him keenly aware of his shortcomings, he happily resumed his place in the brotherhood of arms. In June 1669, he was offered a new adventure. Louis XIV authorized him to take a commission as lieutenant general with the forces of the Republic of Venice, which was then hopelessly mired in its twenty-five-year conflict with the Turks.

The war was being fought in Crete along a very limited front. The Turks occupied the whole island except the town of Candia, a fortress on the coast with free access to the sea. In its battle against the Infidel, Venice had France's sympathy, but neither Mazarin nor later Louis XIV wanted to take sides openly for fear of provoking the enmity of the Ottoman Empire. Young French officers fought for Christianity nonetheless, either by reporting directly to the Venetian captain general, Morosini, as Frontenac did, or by joining the ranks of a small French army under the command of the Duc de La Feuillade.

Frontenac traveled to the port of Toulon, where expeditions rallied for this new crusade. Wearing lace and ribbons, their hats stuck with feathers, young men climbed aboard long galleys with high gilded sterns. The voyage lasted several weeks, full of laughter and song, after which they landed amid the horrors of a city that had undergone a long siege. Ditches full of water surrounded Candia, making it impossible to mount rapid sorties and catch the enemy by surprise. There was no adequate fodder or stabling for the horses; the infantrymen were weak with hunger and fainted at the slightest effort. And the newcomers, champing at the bit, were forced to settle into the quagmire of this interminable war. Accounts of the siege, which survive in Venice today, have the monotony of bulletins from World War I, and an asphyxiant gas, developed by the Turks, was actually used, just as in World War I, adding further horror to a bloody conflict.

In 1668, slight hope remained of freeing Candia. It is unclear whether Frontenac had been able to weigh the chances of success before signing on. At any rate, he landed to find the Venetian camp discouraged and hardly inclined to follow a freshly arrived officer, impatient to plunge into the fray. Besides, he was French. Despite the fact that he served in their army, the Venetians welcomed him without enthusiasm. The allies looked on each other with distrust, and the atmosphere in the besieged town was deteriorating. The French lost a hundred men in a courageous but

poorly planned sortie, and began preparations for their with-
drawal. The Venetians were furious at being backed into a costly
and dishonorable defeat. Frontenac was in the wrong place at the
wrong time. Morosini accused him of having delivered secrets
from the Venetian war council to the French. He defended himself angrily against the charge, but was obliged to return to France
in October 1669. Too proud and too mindful of his good name to
swallow the affront, he submitted an explanation and a complaint
against Morosini to the doge and the Venetian senate before leaving; he even made a spectacular entry to the doge's palace in an
attempt to obtain reparation. But in spite of a strong faction in
Venice hostile to Morosini, Frontenac was not able to gain reinstatement to his office as military counsellor to the Republic.

There was nothing left for him but to return to Paris and
molder away in mortifying idleness as his wife's dependent. The
beautiful Anne had taken quarters in the Arsenal with
Mademoiselle d'Outrelaise, in an apartment put at her disposal
by Maréchal Richelieu. The ladies had come to be known as "the
Divines" for their wit and charm, which was appreciated in the
highest society. "They insisted on incense, being goddesses, and
it was their life to discover who would lavish it on them," Saint-
Simon was to write in his memoirs. But Frontenac had "no desire
to die of hunger as a mortal by the side of a goddess."[6] When the
governorship of New France fell vacant, he went after it with all
his might. He mobilized all his influential supporters, not least of
whom was his wife, and defeated the other candidate, the Comte
de Grignan, who was Madame de Sévigné's son-in-law. In a con-
soling letter to her daughter, she observes that "it's a sad thing to
reside in a new country, and to leave the world one knows and
loves to live in another clime, among people one would be
ashamed to associate with in this."[7] It was Frontenac, therefore,
who boarded a ship for freedom, independence, and, so he
hoped, fortune. This was the man whom La Salle was traveling
down the Saint Lawrence to meet.

The only things they had in common were imagination, a
dogged will, and a talent for making enemies. La Salle, despite

having to obtain permissions and raise money, ironically enough had more freedom of action than the governor, who was theoretically in Canada to carry out his minister's instructions. But the leash from Versailles to Quebec was a long one, and Frontenac, who saw himself more as a viceroy than as a governor, conducted a program of stubborn independence that was not without its subterfuges. Whenever he embarked on an undertaking that flew in the face of Colbert's stated wishes, he was careful to keep it quiet until the month of November, after the last boats for France had already left. The news of his doings would then reach Versailles only the following autumn, and an official rebuke could not be expected until the following spring. Playing his cards carefully, he could buy himself eighteen months of peace.

From the minute Frontenac arrived, La Salle understood that this was to be no ordinary governor, and one had only to see him with the Indians to be convinced of it. His first official act had been to call together the inhabitants of Quebec to pledge an oath of allegiance to the king. A few Hurons wandered out of their huts, which were built on a piece of land near the seminary, hidden by a palisade "made of whole trees,"[8] and attended the ceremony in the large Jesuit church. The handsome appearance and eloquence of *Onontio*,[9] as they called Frontenac, impressed them so much that they asked him to repeat his speech the following day in front of all the Hurons from the neighboring missions. He did so with delight. Convinced it was good for the Indians to see him as a kind and openhanded father, he took pleasure in assuming the role, which he soon learned to perfection. His audience applauded him loudly and "took the oath after their custom." Another step taken soon after arriving in office was to send Louis Joliet and a Jesuit, Father Marquette, to explore the upper reaches of the Mississippi. This augured well for his ongoing interest in sending expeditions out across the continent.

La Salle was not ready, however, for the enthusiasm Frontenac showed his proposals. The governor's ambition had two sides: the first, public and glorious, was to consolidate France's power

in America; the other, secret and somewhat ignoble, was to en-
rich himself personally. La Salle's plan was so grandiose that
Frontenac could present it as a great national project, while at
the same time it suited him for private reasons. It was difficult for
him to be open to his entourage or to Joliet, an ally of the Jesuits,
about the complexity of his intentions. La Salle's isolation, on the
other hand, and the fact that he belonged to no faction inspired
Frontenac to confidence. And so friendship grew between the
two of them, one still a young man (La Salle was not yet thirty)
who had seen nothing but the inside of a seminary and the vast
open spaces of the New World, and the other a veteran of
Europe's wars, a courtier moving in the highest circles who, now
past the age of fifty, was about to discover the forests of North
America, Indians, and the headiness of unimpeded horizons.
The two men spent the long evenings of the winter of 1673 not in
the governor's palace, whose leaky roof let in the wind, rain, and
snow, but in a nearby house that was clean and dry. From their
Canadian wing chairs, which are as much windbreaks as they are
seats, enjoying pumpkin pies brought to them by the nuns, they
took the time to develop their opinions in front of the great map
of North America drawn up by Sanson.

La Salle was convinced that the Mississippi flowed into the
Gulf of Mexico, and Louis Joliet's reports would confirm his
opinion. If the French could gain possession of the land adjacent
to it, they could create a vast empire which would cut the
American continent from north to south, confine the English to
the region east of the Appalachians and the Spanish south of the
Gulf of Mexico. As colonizing such a vast area was unthinkable,
they would have to build forts at distant intervals to hold down
the new possessions. This would allow commercial activity to proceed. At this, Frontenac pricked up his ears. The plan delighted
him, and he in turn explained his views to La Salle.

Drawing on a project that had been sketched out originally by
his predecessor, he proposed building a fort at the eastern tip of
Lake Ontario that would serve both military and commercial
ends. Built on one of the main Indian war trails, it would be an

obstacle to the Iroquois if their hostility toward the colony ever revived; it would also give the French a major commercial advantage by making it easier to barter with the fur-selling tribes before they could trade with the Dutch or the English. Another agreeable feature of the plan was that the governor-count stood to grow rich from it, as he would be in direct control of the fort and its occupants. Frontenac possessed a genuinely decisive character, a trait La Salle appreciated, being himself impatient. The plan was no sooner hatched than Frontenac began to implement it. The two men agreed that it would be unnecessary to reveal the full extent of their projects: the establishment of a fort in that area would be an unwelcome prospect to some. The inhabitants of Montreal depended on the fur trade for their livelihood and would bristle at the idea that the fur-supplying tribes would be intercepted farther upriver. At Trois-Rivières, Quebec, and Tadoussac, the merchants were not eager to have the governor meddle in the Indian trade. Frontenac, who could be skillful, simply announced that he wanted to make his presence known in the region, as a show of power to the English, the Dutch, and the Iroquois, and was therefore undertaking a tour of inspection of his realm that would lead him as far upriver as Lake Ontario.

La Salle was sent ahead to prepare a meeting along the lake shore with the Indian chiefs. They too might be alarmed at the construction of a fort in their territory. Frontenac was astute enough not to exclude the clergy from his plan. As the Jesuits were constantly traveling between their various missions, no one had a better knowledge of the movement of the Indians, their mood, or the measures they were taking. The governor arranged for Father Fénelon, who knew the lake shore, to accompany him. For his interpreter, he chose Charles Le Moyne. A native of Dieppe, where his father was a surgeon,[10] Le Moyne, like many others, had entered the service of the Jesuits as a *donné*. After spending four years in contact with the Indians, he had not only learned the Huron language but had shown a degree of courage that was unusual even in Canada, where intrepidness and valor were the order of the day. The expedition left Quebec at the end of the planting season, so that any settlers wanting to join them would be free to do so, and Frontenac arrived in Montreal on June 25, 1673. The colonists, hoping to discourage him, painted the darkest possible picture of the upper reaches of the river (frightening travelers in this way was an old Indian ruse). They warned Frontenac against obstacles to navigation "that the majority of people assure [him] are more difficult and more dangerous than those faced by the Argonauts."[11] The governor was not unduly worried. He organized his stores of food, his 120 canoes, his 400 Canadians, and about fifty Hurons from the missions. The Indians were glad to accompany him and proved very useful to the enterprise, not only because of their matchless woodcraft but because they were unusually obliging.

Frontenac had been present when the grand style of Louis XIV was born and he knew how effective ceremony and etiquette could be; his genius was in adapting it to the woods and to Indian life. He had two flatboats built, on which he mounted six small cast-iron cannons recovered from the ruins of the fort of Quebec. He judged it "appropriate for the sake of the Indians to daub them in red and blue with the sort of ornament the painters of this country, who assuredly know less than Monsieur Le Brun, are capable of drafting; this produced an admirable effect on the barbarians."[12] His flotilla ready, he set off, taking good care to let it be known that he was "delighted" by their upriver progress. Unlike La Salle, Frontenac knew how to make himself liked by his men. He had learned in the army how to give his troops encouragement and infuse them with the desire to overcome obstacles. In the psychological climate he was able to create, difficulties only knit the little band more closely together rather than driving them apart. And troubles were plentiful. The rains came down so heavily that the biscuit went moldy and the stores ran short. Then, in the suffocating humidity, the plague of mosquitoes became unbearable.

> The greatest torture, compared to which the rest is a game, but which passes all belief, such as one could never even imagine in France unless one had experienced it, are the mosquitoes, the

cruel persecution of the mosquitoes. The Egyptian plague, I believe, was not more cruel. There are no-see-'ems; there are black flies, which are a very small fly, whose sting is so sharp or rather so burning that it seems as if a small spark had fallen on the part that is stung; there are gnats, which are like black flies except that they are even smaller, hardly visible; they attack the eyes particularly. There are wasps; there are horseflies; there are, in a word, *omne genus muscarum*. But one wouldn't mention the others if it weren't for the mosquito. This little animal has provoked more swearing since the French have been [in New France] than there had been swearing until then in all the world. A swarm of mosquitoes sets out with the traveler in the morning; then, as one passes a stand of reeds or goes through willows, as almost always happens, another swarm will fly furiously at the canoe and won't be shaken off. We are obliged to wave our handkerchieves continually, which doesn't frighten them at all; they fly a small way off and return to the attack immediately. Our arms grow tired before they ever do. When we land for dinner, from ten o'clock until two or three, there is an entire army to contend with. We make a smudge — that is, a large fire that is afterward smothered with green leaves — and we must stay in the thickest of the smoke if we want to avoid the persecution. I don't know which is worse, the remedy or the evil. After having dined we may feel inclined to take a little nap at the foot of a tree, but that is absolutely impossible: our rest time is spent fighting mosquitoes. We climb back into the canoe with the mosquitoes, and when the sun sets we land with them. Then we must do battle against not one army but many. We are eaten and devoured, they enter our mouths, our nostrils, our ears. They cover our faces, hands, and bodies. Their stinger passes through cloth and leaves a red mark on the flesh that swells on any who haven't developed a tolerance to the stings. After eating our supper hastily, we are impatient to burrow into our bedding. But however adroitly you squirm under the canvas, there are always two or three that enter with you, and it only takes two or three to make you spend a bad night.[13]

Mosquitoes weren't the half of it. Above Lake Saint Louis, there were fallen trunks in the stream bed, which obliged the canoes to work out from shore and travel against the strongest part of the current. But nothing ruffled the governor's good disposition. At the end of these hard days, instead of sinking down in front of the fire and being waited on, he organized games of ninepins to distract the men. They liked it that he shared their hardships, staying out in the rain for hours once to see that their food stores were safely put away, and no request from him was too difficult. Even the Indians went to work when the count asked them to, and he so strongly regretted his inability to address them in their language that he announced his intention of learning Huron.

His enthusiasm was contagious. While La Salle was always absorbed in his own thoughts and never allowed his emotions at natural phenomena to appear, the naturalist in Frontenac peered through the soldier. He never tired of observing the forest: he was learning to recognize the white pine, a large, round tree with hard wood, sometimes two hundred feet tall — its cone had tasty seeds that were eaten by elk and pecked at by a bird with lavender plumage and a black beak. He learned to tell balsam fir, which has a flat, flexible needle; white spruce, with its pointed crown and low branches that were browsed by deer; and big maples, which grew more and more common as they progressed farther west. They cut into one of them so that he could taste "its sap, which is sweeter than barley water and more pleasant to drink."[14] He marveled at the luxuriant vegetation, at the taste of raspberries and blueberries, which they scooped up by the handful. Attentive even to the smallest details, he had a drawing made of a flower that reminded him of lilies-of-the-valley in his native Touraine. One day he stopped the canoes to catch a goose with beautiful plumage; it was difficult because the bird kept diving underwater to escape its captors. But he managed to persuade his men to build a cage for the bird, which he intended for the king's menagerie at Versailles.

His confidence in the project increased as they drew near the lake. The banks of the river became more regular, to the point where he easily imagined "making paths for men or horses to haul [the boats] with far less difficulty than they tow them up the Rhone."[15] Even the woods were more open. One could go stag hunting here, he wrote in his report; lighthearted, he already saw "the fine dwellings" that would one day be built; and with a little labor the more difficult places in the river could easily be made navigable. When they finally reached the entrance to the lake, where La Salle had summoned the Indians to meet them, Frontenac stopped to set the stage for his show. Wanting to dazzle the woodland Indians and convey the pomp, prestige, and dignity that attended his king, Frontenac miraculously managed to mount a balletic court entrance in the middle of the American wilderness.

The Iroquois, gathered at Cataracoui on a point of land between two sheltered bays, saw 120 canoes approach them in formation. On a flatboat, surrounded by his entire military retinue in uniform, sat the Comte de Frontenac. The second boat bulged with the governor's honor guard in full regalia, and behind them were the notable men of the colony. A canoe from Trois-Rivières flanked the governor on his right, and on his left were the Hurons and Algonquins. Four hundred soldiers in their musketeers' tabards followed behind. A drum beat out a continuous roll, in accompaniment to the clinking of weapons. Bringing up the rear were carpenters and workmen, and the whole procession glided slowly over the water in perfect order, band playing and banners flying. Even the whites in Canada had never seen such a splendid display.

On landing, the troops pitched their tents. A mast was quickly erected, and the flag of the king of France, a gold fleur-de-lys on a white ground, was hoisted with impressive ceremony. As night was approaching, Frontenac inspected the grounds and retired, not wanting to show any eagerness to engage in talks. The next day, the soldiers formed columns again and performed maneuvers. Long sails were stretched in front of the governor's tent, and the Indian elders came to sit at the council fire Frontenac had built in token of respect for their traditions. Without a word the old men lit their pipes, handsome ones of polished stone in the shape of birds, and impassively puffed billows of blue smoke into the air around them.[16]

Frontenac then spoke to the Indians. Exuding authority and exhibiting a mixture of dignity and good-naturedness, he addressed the old chiefs, many of whom were bent with age and disfigured by wounds, by calling them his children. Le Moyne translated his words of peace and goodwill emphatically. With inimitable naturalness, Frontenac adopted one of the most deeply rooted Indian customs and broke off his speech at intervals to distribute ceremonial gifts. At the first intermission he gave out rifles, biscuits, wine, and brandy to the men, and dried prunes and raisins to the women; at the second break he made a gift of twenty-five heavy coats, as many shirts and stockings, and five packets of marbles. At nightfall, Frontenac invited one of the chiefs to dine with him; known as Totonsheti, the man had the reputation of being friendly to the Dutch, but his usually stern expression had given way to an unaccustomed smile.[17] Any fears Frontenac might have had that the Iroquois would react negatively to the construction of the fort were quickly laid to rest.

The first show that Frontenac presented had been intended as entertainment; the second, which was to build the fort in record time, was meant to instill in his Indian audience awe and respect for the clear superiority of the French. In fact, the operation would have impressed even Colbert for its efficiency and economy of means. The site engineer, Raudin, had thought of everything.[18] It was no simple enterprise. To install five hundred people in the middle of the forest was something of a stunt, yet the tents were pitched, the men fed, the tools unloaded swiftly, all without apparent chaos. Raudin traced the outline of the fort on the ground according to a plan previously drawn up. Then each man set to work: first the virgin land had to be cleared. Once the trees had been felled, the carpenters sawed them for boards; some men dug the ditches, others erected the stockade. The operations went so smoothly and quickly that the Indians were dumbstruck, and many of the French themselves were surprised at the results. The fort, begun on July 12, was finished on the nineteenth; even more astounding, the men had cleared twenty-five acres around the structure. But this was not enough for Frontenac. Seeing the vast expanse of the lake, "an infinite area, yet easily navigable,"[19] he was struck, as La Salle had been, by the need to develop a fleet adapted to this "inland sea," and he gave orders to build a large vessel, a kind of flatboat for transporting large quantities of men and supplies.

At the same time, he continued his diplomatic endeavors, and every night Le Moyne invited different Indians to dinner; they, feeling perfectly safe, would arrive with their wives and children, and the women would dance for the company in thanks for the favors that Frontenac lavished on them. The governor waited until the fort was well along before convoking a great assembly; there he spelled out the commercial advantages of an alliance and, pointing at the practically finished fort, the officers, the soldiers, and the boats mounted with guns, he observed that "if your father can come so far, with so great a force, through such dangerous rapids, merely on a visit of pleasure and friendship, what could he do if you awakened his anger and he was obliged to punish his disobedient children? He is the arbiter of peace and war. Beware that you offend him."[20] The following day, the Indians answered by inquiring at what price the French planned to offer their goods. They eventually asked for a political alliance against the Andastes tribe, promising in return to respect the freedom of the Hurons and Algonquins, and agreeing to Frontenac's proposal to adopt several of their children.

Frontenac had scored a clear success. La Salle had not put himself forward, but he knew that he could now count on the governor. They decided to return together, leaving a handful of men to guard the fort. The governor sent a message to Montreal asking for a year's supplies to be sent out: hens, pigs, cows, and all the merchandise necessary to open a trading post.

❈ 5 ❈

A Divided Colony

1673–1675

THE CURTAIN FELL SLOWLY ON THE FESTIVITIES, as the French did
not all leave at once. Frontenac preferred to stagger his men's return to the colony. He himself was among the last to go, waiting
for a messenger to bring word that the resupply convoy was on its
way to the fort before embarking. He arrived in Montreal on
August 1, 1673, and his reports to Colbert show him to be burst-
ing with satisfaction. "Everyone here agrees that it was the
biggest thing that could possibly be done for the advancement of
religion, the security of the colony, and the increase of trade."[1]
He congratulated himself, and rightly so, on the little time it had
taken him to conduct the operation, and on the "miracle" of not
having lost a man or a canoe. The king would no doubt be grateful that the cost was low. Thanks to help from the colonists, the
expedition had only cost 10,000 livres (Frontenac had loaned the
sum himself after borrowing it from two Montreal traders, Bazire
and Jacques Le Ber, a relative of La Salle). The river navigation,
described to him in such daunting terms, had proved so feasible
that he projected "within a few years time making communications between Montreal and the fort as easy as they are between

Quebec and Montreal."[2] As for the Indians, he boasted of "having instilled in them all a great deal of respect, fear, and friendship [and of having] so won them over that at present there were no wild Indians who were not on our side." And as there is little glory to be gained from convincing people who lack merit, he stressed approvingly the degree "of eloquence, skill, and subtlety with which their delegates all spoke [to him], and [were he not] afraid of ridicule [he would say] that they reminded [him] somewhat in their manner of the Venetian senate, although their furs and blankets could hardly match the robes of the magistrates of Saint Mark."[3] Frontenac had left the site in the hands of a certain Sieur de Brugière and retired with La Salle, for whom the fort was only the first link in the chain of a long undertaking. They agreed between them to allot the proceeds from the following year's trading to the governor's two main creditors.

Logically, they should have gone quietly back to their business, one to focus on the various problems of the colony, and the other to make plans for the next move. But Canada was not a country guided by reason, coherence, or even good sense. Rivalries seemed to thrive in the brutal climate and, instead of being defused by compromise, tended to explode into fierce brawls. You would think that a handful of men, set down on the frozen earth thousands of miles from family and homeland, who had barely recovered from the bloody attacks of the Iroquois surrounding them, and who had constantly to be on guard against the wiles of the English and the ambition of the Dutch, would compensate for the external violence of their world by maintaining a great inner calm. Such was not the case; the internecine quarrels of the Canadians were astounding for their diversity and violence, and always shocked newcomers. The people of Quebec thought the Montreal population capable of any treachery to protect their profits from the illicit trade with the Indians. Montreal's inhabitants were proudly conscious of being an outpost of the colony, and despised the councillors, inspectors, and other functionaries who claimed to govern them. Nor did the clergy provide an example of serene generosity: the Jesuits,

Recollets, and Sulpicians competed for native souls in the bush and for royal favor at court. These strains had the effect of making the colonists unusually independent for that time: they were quick to rebel against the provincial administrator, the bishop, or even the governor. Colbert wrongly thought that Canadians could be governed the way Picards were governed in Picardy or Normans in Normandy. Frontenac, with his abrupt behavior, was to show himself perfectly attuned to this surprising environment.

The merchants in Montreal foresaw that both the newly built fort and the powerful partnership between Frontenac and La Salle would bring them financial loss. They knew firsthand of La Salle's skill and success at trading; Frontenac's power alarmed them, as the governor held control over regulation and could ban all travel in and out of the colony, effectively shutting down trade with the Indians. How could you engage in barter without venturing into the wilds? The fact is neither Frontenac nor La Salle enjoyed much popularity in Montreal. It could even be said that Perrot, the governor of Montreal, saw them as disloyal competitors and resented them all the more as he had managed his affairs very nicely until then without benefit of supervision. Perrot became governor after marrying Talon's niece, and owed his fortune to an excellent scheme. On an island west of town, which is called Ile Perrot to this day,[4] he had installed a partner to intercept the Indians on their way to the Montreal trading fair. Perrot therefore was able to buy furs before the other merchants, and did so in such quantities that he was forced to build a warehouse on the island to store them all; he could also be persuaded to shut his eyes when any soldiers deserted to roam the woods illicitly. His business further prospered thanks to the fact that it took two weeks to reach Montreal from Quebec, putting him virtually beyond the jurisdiction of the capital. His insolent confidence, however, made him enemies at home. The Sulpicians, for instance, who held the right to choose the local governor, now regretted having let Talon guide their choice. Frontenac learned all these details from La Salle and, wanting to weaken a rival, decided to play his official card: was it not his mission after all to discourage the coureurs de bois? As it happened, it suited him. He gave orders for the judge in Montreal to arrest two of the most notorious illicit traders, who were openly in cahoots with Perrot. The governor of Montreal in turn threatened the judge with prison if he obeyed. Frontenac sent three of his guardsmen to proceed with the arrest. Undeterred, Perrot had Frontenac's men imprisoned. Once his anger cooled, however, he had second thoughts about making enemies with a man so much more powerful than himself, and had the prisoners released. As for Frontenac, he also had time to rethink his position. His first impulse had been to launch an attack on the "insurgents." But his twenty guardsmen could not carry it out alone, and the peaceful colonists in the area of Quebec would be few to volunteer for an assault on the roughnecks of Montreal. Another consideration was that the king might not be pleased to learn that the governor was using the meager troops at his disposal to fight his own subjects. Frontenac finally thought it advisable to enlist the good offices of Father Fénelon as a mediator.

Father Fénelon's uncle had been the governor's companion-in-arms at the siege of Candia, and Frontenac had been struck by the priest's curiosity and openness of mind during that summer's expedition to Lake Ontario. Besides, Fénelon himself was delighted at the chance to iron out the situation. He convinced Perrot to accede to the governor's summons to Quebec and offered to accompany him. Perrot, now fearful that he had brought the wrath of the Crown on his head for dealing brutally with its emissaries, decided not to wait until spring to comply; he put on his snowshoes and set off on the two hundred mile trip down the ice-covered Saint Lawrence. There were still few horses in Canada at this time. The first horse arrived by ship in 1647, to the great wonder of the Indians. (Unlike what happened in South America, where the Indians fled in terror at the sight of Spanish horsemen, the natives of Canada immediately admired and coveted these speedy, docile, and winter-hardy animals. It is commonly thought that it was the appearance of a centaur — a man welded to his galloping mount — that caused the earlier terror.

But the appearance of a poor nag, made weak by its long sea journey and carefully being led from the slippery deck onto the pier, held nothing to inspire panic.)[5] Horse raising progressed with desperate slowness, however, and after twenty-five years there were barely thirty horses in the entire colony. Only at the end of the century would there be enough horses to make the trip regularly along the frozen paths beside the river, and for the colonists to hold harness races on the holidays.

Perrot and Fénelon made the journey on their Indian snowshoes, stopping at nightfall to stay with settlers along the way. Traveling in stages was not difficult because the households on this part of the trip were never grouped together in villages but spaced out along the river to provide natural stopping places. The river served as the main artery, in winter as well as in summer, since by traveling on it one avoided having to slog across land through snow and mud. All the properties, which consisted of long strips of land, had frontage on the river. Each lot had only three boundaries: its narrow frontage on the Saint Lawrence, and the line on either side where it joined the neighboring properties. The long ribbons of land extended back into the uncleared woods behind, and no one took the trouble to determine just how far. Only in the eighteenth century were lots belonging to a "second tier" plotted out behind the first line of properties. The colonists between Montreal and Quebec were often former officers who had chosen to settle in Canada and had received large land holdings in return. Their presence survives today in the names of the towns and villages sprinkled along the river: Sorel, Saint-Ours, Varennes, and Verchères, for instance, were all officers in the Carignan regiment. At that time there were no villages, and the fact distressed Talon, who wanted his colonists to live clustered together as in France. But the immigrants remembered village life in France without fondness and saw that their very isolation protected them from supervision by the bishop, the provincial administrator, and the governor. Besides, the ingenuity of Canadians had eliminated one of the basic reasons for villages as they had so much time during the endless winter months for tinkering that they hardly needed the services of specialized tradesmen.[6] Thanks to the way land was divided up, a traveler could be sure of finding shelter every ten or twelve miles along the river; and as travelers were few and hospitality a matter of course in these parts, the welcome was likely to be warm. The settler's wife, often dressed like an Indian woman in a short leather skirt and knee-length scarlet leggings, wearing shoes made of caribou hide and filled with hazel catkins, would set before the travelers a steaming bowl of pea soup. In winter, peas were the Frenchman's sagamity gruel, the one dish served at every meal: the peas, dried in the sun and stored in underground cellars, kept better than any other vegetable. When arriving on a Saturday, Father Fénelon would offer to celebrate Mass the following day, and the settlers would hastily gather their nearest neighbors. Because clergymen were few, settlers were unable to receive the sacraments regularly, and Mass was always a joyous occasion in their monotonous lives. The mistress of the house would open a barrel of salted eels or thaw a meat pie to celebrate the church service. The priest and Perrot would afterward resume their journey down the solitary frozen river, barren of all animal life except for snowshoe hares, so white they looked like fat snowballs.

Immediately upon their arrival in Quebec, Perrot and Fénelon reported to the governor's palace. Perrot was unable or unwilling to make an apology, and the old antagonism resumed. Frontenac, as irascible as ever, took offense and placed Perrot in a room used as a prison; Fénelon was ignominiously ordered to return to his prayers; and a new governor, La Nouguère, a veteran of the Cretan campaign who had followed his commander to New France, was dispatched to Montreal. But La Nouguère had been appointed without consultation with the Sulpicians, who owned the site of Montreal. Bitter quarreling flared up again, with such passion that it threatened to break the colony apart. Everyone took sides. La Salle, of course, did not waver, despite the fact that his brother and his Sulpician sponsors were siding against Frontenac. When Fénelon preached a sermon on Easter day attacking temporal power as then manifest in Quebec, La Salle exited noisily from Mass to protest the outrage. From that moment, La Salle had sealed his alliance with the governor.

The first boats in the spring of 1674 began to arrive at this point. The mail they brought from the minister was not meant to please Frontenac or to strengthen him in his current situation. Colbert regretted to learn of the construction of Fort Frontenac and said so frankly: "It is not His Majesty's wish that you should make long journeys up the Saint Lawrence River, nor even that the colonists should occupy as wide an area in the future as they have in the past. On the contrary, His Majesty wishes you to work unceasingly and during all the time you remain in that country toward concentrating the colonists more closely together and gathering them into towns and villages that they may defend themselves more easily. His Majesty considers it far more appropriate to His Service that you devote yourself to a thorough clearing of the most fertile lands, and those nearest to the sea coast and communications with France, and to populating them thoroughly, rather than pushing discovery far into the interior, to parts so distant that they can never be inhabited or owned by Frenchmen.

"There are two cases where this general rule may be excepted: the first, if the countries you claimed for France were necessary to the commerce and trade of the French and their discovery and possession by another nation might disrupt the commerce and trade of the French. The second case is if the country you discovered brought France closer by communicating with a more southern sea than does the entrance to the Saint Lawrence."[7]

Frontenac expected this reprimand. In fact, he had taken every precaution to present the minister with a done deed. And besides, it could be easily demonstrated to Colbert that establishing Fort Frontenac was justifiable under the very exceptions he had specified. The problem was that Frontenac found himself once again shouldering an enormous financial burden. No one would reimburse him the 10,000 livres he had advanced to construct the fort. He risked once again being ground underfoot by his creditors.

La Salle, as anxious as his protector over the turn events had taken, once again journeyed upriver to inspect the fort. Business was prospering under the competent administration of Le Ber and Bazire. Indians were already arriving in large numbers to offer their pelts; it was possible to attract even more. La Salle shut his ears to defeat. Once back in Quebec, he made the following proposal to Frontenac: he would return to France and petition the king for the land holding at Cataracoui, where Fort Frontenac was located, and for a title of nobility. He would undertake to reimburse Frontenac, meet the expenses of the seigneury, and (it went without saying) make the governor a partner in any subsequent profits. The plan was reasonable in every respect. Frontenac could not grant him the Cataracoui land himself; La Salle would have to go to France for it. And the title of nobility was necessary because it gave the holder an exclusive right to local trade, a source of enormous benefits if managed well. Titles of nobility had a different meaning in Canada than in France. A Canadian nobleman's title came not from the land but from the king, and the title gave him no power over the tenants on his seigneury. The tenant's obligation to provide feudal labor that provoked such resentment in France was nonexistent here, as was the prohibition against hunting and fishing that imposed such unfair hardship on French peasants. Here, a seigneur's house might be no larger than his vassal's, and the notion of a feudal castle, its full weight supported on the backs of villagers, was foreign to Canada. Finally, the seigneur was not descended from an ancient family accustomed to wielding virtually absolute authority over its dependents. Relations between seigneur and tenant were consequently much warmer and closer than in France. A nobleman could not be stripped of his nobility in Canada for exercising a profession incompatible with his rank. One met noblemen who were pursuing careers as surgeons and interpreters, while others were notaries, judges, or pharmacists;

and almost all engaged in trade.[8] In France, a nobleman was forbidden to engage in commerce but, in Canada, the seigneur controlled all the commerce on his lands. The only question, when his fief was at such a great distance from the centers of population, was to determine how far these lands extended. This explained La Salle's interest in acquiring a title, and Frontenac's enthusiasm for the proposal as soon as he grasped its subtlety.

What is strange is not so much that the plan was well conceived but the extraordinary rapidity with which it was put into execution and the prodigious transformation that took place in La Salle. The man who had roamed the forests and followed unknown rivers dressed like an Indian in animal skins, trying to read the intentions of Indian chiefs, was now preparing with virtually no transition to cool his heels in Colbert's anteroom wearing a powdered wig and lace ruffles at his neck. Frontenac added a note in his dispatch to the minister: "I cannot close, Sire, without recommending to you the Sieur de La Salle, who is crossing to France, and is a man of intelligence and ability, more capable than anybody else I know here to accomplish every kind of enterprise or discovery one might entrust to him, as he has the most perfect knowledge of the state of this country, as you will see, if you are disposed to give him a few moments' audience."[9]

La Salle sailed in November 1674. His Indian guide, Nika, who accompanied him, spent the entire journey on deck, feeling that the wind and cold were preferable by far to being shut up in the depths below. The same ship was carrying Perrot, Father Fénelon, and Frontenac's secretary back to France. During the long idle days on board, their equanimity returned. Perrot and Fénelon, who could hardly guess what sort of reception Colbert had in store for them, gradually lost their haughtiness, and La Salle, who was preoccupied with his own undertaking, was not anxious to revive old quarrels. Besides, once back in France they would all be Canadians together, and all were equally curious about the changes that had taken place in their homeland. Would concern over the war with Holland, declared in 1672, allow Colbert the time to deal with their petitions and settle their differences? They worried unnecessarily: their arrival coincided with Turenne's victory at Turckheim; and they did not realize the extraordinary efficiency of Colbert's administration, which made it a rule to examine every case brought to its attention. La Salle stopped in Rouen where his family welcomed him warmly. The boy's success was enough to make them proud — he had left with hardly a sou seven years earlier, and now was returning with the full support of Canada's governor general to call at Versailles, where he was expected. Nika astonished them, although there had been Indians in Rouen before. The Shawnee youth spoke French well enough to make himself useful, and people very quickly stopped noticing him as he followed La Salle like a watchful shadow. No sooner had the drapers clothed him respectably than the traveler was off to Paris, trailing Nika, and enjoying once more the speed and comfort of stagecoach travel. His old companion Father Gallinée was in Paris to welcome him, eager to celebrate La Salle's success and show him his beautiful map of the Great Lakes. He recommended La Salle to his Sulpician friends and inquired to find him lodgings. La Salle took quarters on the Rue de la Truanderie, in the parish of Saint-Eustache. Then came the test: Colbert was making him wait. The minister may well have wondered what La Salle wanted, this large and exalted young man who flew into a rage whenever a secretary or a valet counseled him to be patient. Finally, La Salle was given an audience. Keep it short, he was told, because the minister is extremely busy. La Salle was at his best when forced to be concise: he spoke clearly but with feeling, and offered a well-argued brief. He made his case.

On May 13, 1675, the king granted him Fort Frontenac, the surrounding islands, and "four leagues of territory along the rivers and lakes to a depth of one half league with all rights to fishing and hunting." In addition, the king accorded him the right to trade and to continue his discoveries to the south and west, and, "in consideration of the good and admirable report made to us of the actions he has performed in the country of Canada," the king conferred the rank of nobility on "his dear and well-beloved

Robert Cavelier," who took as his coat of arms "a greyhound argent on a sable field under a gold six-pointed star."[10] In return, La Salle engaged to reimburse Frontenac the 10,000 livres originally spent to build the fort. La Salle would rebuild it in stone, maintain a garrison there equal to the garrison at Montreal, with enough workmen to clear and farm the surrounding land. He would grant concessions to all who wished to settle there, according to the custom of the country, and he was required to draw as many Indians there as possible and "to give them land to cultivate and build villages on, to teach them trades and incite them to a life more like our own." Finally, he promised to build a church as soon as the population reached one hundred and to maintain one or two Recollet friars in the meantime "for celebrating Mass and administering the sacraments." The financial conditions were burdensome. Anyone other than La Salle would have counted on making quick profits from the fur trade to meet his obligations, but this bold explorer and fearless voyager did not treat his debts lightly. A great lord might do so (just think what schemes Frontenac would have launched under similar circumstances!), but La Salle acted soberly, as his merchant ancestors would have done. He returned to Rouen, where he borrowed a portion of the money from his relatives and arranged for them to guarantee the loans he might receive from other merchants in Paris. He was so successful that he left for Canada with a capital of 45,000 livres. From now on, he took the trouble to keep meticulous accounts,[11] in which every expenditure was recorded, from the repayment of the 10,000 livres owed by Frontenac to his creditors, to the wages paid the tailor and the baker, to the cost of burying the fort's carpenter.

The return journey turned out to be interesting enough in itself. The ship was carrying the formidable bishop François de Laval; the new provincial administrator, Jean Duchesneau, who was to make Frontenac's life so difficult; and Father Hennepin, who several years later became La Salle's travel companion. It is hard to imagine that the bishop took much part in the conversation of his fellow travelers. He was returning to Canada, where he had labored since 1659, after an absence of three years. François de Laval was already fifty-nine years old. His ancestry was superb — the Lavals were descended from Gui de Laval, son of Matthieu de Montmorency, the high constable, whose ancestors owed their rank as first barons of France to the fact that a forefather had been baptized with King Clovis I at Rheims in 496 A.D. From his background, from his excellent education at the hands of the Jesuits, and from an exalted sense of his mission, he drew such enormous pride as to be almost humble. "I do not say he is a saint, that would be inaccurate," wrote Mother Marie de l'Incarnation, superior of the Ursuline order, "but he lives in saintly fashion and as an apostle. The country holds him in admiration."[12] Laval wanted to wield supreme authority in all matters over everyone, and had been at loggerheads with each governor of Canada in succession, even the most conciliatory. It was said that the bishop's doctrine, which was the Jesuits' as well, was that "matters will go well for the Christian religion in New France only when the governor is a puppet of the Jesuits, or when the bishop has become governor."[13] Needless to say, the saintly man spent little time on deck socializing with the young explorer and ex-Jesuit novice, who in turn had little interest in the conversion of souls. Furthermore, La Salle was a close associate of the current governor, a man who would never willingly allow spiritual authority to encroach on secular power.

Duchesneau, the provincial administrator, was of a different breed — the breed of servants. The qualities of a top-ranked civil administrator that had made for greatness in Talon were utterly lacking in Duchesneau.[14] Retiring and attentive, this notable from Tours who had no money belonged literally to Colbert ("I am beholden to you," he had written to the minister at the close of a flattering letter), and he had been posted to Quebec primarily to keep an eye on Frontenac. Clearly, the governor was starting to provoke distrust in high circles, as Duchesneau's appointment demonstrates. Colbert had not forgiven Frontenac for acting independently, and had dealt the fractious Perrot only pro forma punishment, sentencing him to three weeks' imprisonment in the Bastille before sending him back to Canada. Duchesneau, who was closely attuned to his master's outlook, certainly took care to have no contact with La Salle, or even to show interest in his voyages and explorations, a taboo subject for a protégé of Colbert. Of the ship's company, only Father Hennepin, a Franciscan missionary, was left. La Salle's adventures and personality so enthralled Father Hennepin that he stayed at La Salle's side throughout the journey. A brash talker, he told how as a young monk in Artois he had been sent by his superior to take up a collection in Calais and how he arrived as the herring fishermen were returning to port. "I hid myself behind tavern doors while the sailors were telling of their voyages. The tobacco smoke made me very sick to the stomach; but, notwithstanding, I listened attentively to all they said about their adventures at sea and their travels in distant countries. I could have passed whole days and nights in this way without eating. More and more, I found my earlier inclinations reinforced."[15] Always fascinated by voyages and discoveries, and burning with the desire to explore new horizons, he had repeatedly implored his superiors to send him to Canada.[16] As chance would have it, Father Hennepin made the crossing with La Salle, who so convinced him of the importance of creating a mixed French and Indian community around Fort Frontenac that Hennepin decided on the spot to follow him to the shores of Lake Ontario. During the voyage they managed to argue violently over a trifle. A group of young, marriageable women was travelling with them, all highly attractive, since Talon had specified that it was necessary to send girls who were "without physical flaws and had nothing about them that might provoke distaste."[17] The young women decided one day, being robust and gay, and tired of the boredom and idleness of life on shipboard, that they would climb out on deck, push back the ropes and chicken coops, and start dancing to the music of a flute played by one of the officers. Father Hennepin wanted to intervene in the name of morality. La Salle accused him of being a killjoy and a "pedagogue." The priest grew livid and pointed out that "the term, as everyone knows, refers to a foolish and impertinent man," and suggested that the twelve years La Salle had spent instructing in Jesuit schools fitted him perfectly for that title as well. La Salle turned pale with rage, but the shores of America were approaching and everyone was reconciled. The girls were placed in the custody of the Ursuline nuns; the bishop paid his visit to the Jesuits; Duchesneau called on Frontenac; and La Salle, Father Hennepin, and Nika dropped their bags at the inn.

❖ 6 ❖

A Canadian Seigneur
1675–1678

LA SALLE ARRIVED BACK IN CANADA with his pockets full, the wind in his sails, and his head teeming with ambitious projects. What he found waiting for him were slanderous insinuations and low tricks, and he was forced to recognize that, in spite of Canada's vast countryside and wide-open future, its inhabitants were sadly narrow-minded. Frontenac's wrangling with Perrot, for all its tragicomic aspects, reflected the fragility of the colony's social fabric, and La Salle's troubles were to highlight the pernicious use some colonists made of their supposed virtue.

In Quebec, he was invited by the king's tax collector, Bazire, to lodge in his handsome house in the old town. Bazire's wife, an attractive woman and deeply devoted to the Jesuits, received him with exceeding amiability. La Salle was too obsessed with his great project to pay attention to women and had in any case retained the chaste habits of his youth, but he couldn't help noticing that "[his hostess] pressed her attentions on him more and more familiarly, until it appeared to him that the woman was trying to excite passion by seeming to feel it."[1] One evening, the lady "took his hand and placed it upon her breast" and assumed

such postures that he was obliged "to flee in order not to suc-
cumb [but] he turned the situation into a joke and withdrew before she had time to recover."[2] He found the husband spying on
the other side of the door. La Salle, who was virtuous but not
stupid, understood that they had laid a trap for him. The most
troubling aspect of the incident was that Madame Bazire belonged to an association called the Sainte Famille, which consisted of pious ladies of Quebec, who had sworn on the Holy
Bible "an oath to tell all that they knew of good or ill about the
persons in their acquaintance,"[3] and who gathered for this purpose every Thursday "behind closed doors" in the cathedral of
Quebec. These fierce guardians of public morals formed "a sort
of Inquisition against all who were not in step with the Jesuits." La
Salle made no effort to disguise his dislike of the Black Robes.
The ladies of the Sainte Famille were so resolved to tarnish his
reputation that they ignored their first setback and tried a new
tack. After La Salle had left for Fort Frontenac they started a
rumor that he had seduced a young woman and was living in sin
on the banks of Lake Ontario. They took care to have the rumor
reach La Salle's brother, a particularly damaging development
since the various loans coming from France for La Salle went
through the Abbé Cavelier's hands, giving the Abbé therefore
power to cut off his younger brother's funds. The priest leapt
into his canoe with the intention of restoring his brother's house
to order but on reaching Fort Frontenac was relieved to discover
that morality was still in place: the three married women were
carrying on no dalliances, the Indian girls in their wigwams were
receiving no one on their leafy beds, and the governor of the
fort, assisted by two Recollet friars, was setting a most scrupulous
example of moral behavior.

One wonders why La Salle provoked such antagonism. Of
course, he nettled not only the fur traders in Montreal but also
the Jesuits, and his strategy had such far-reaching consequences
that it was likely to alter the fate of the colony. Canada had
reached a new stage of development in the last few years. Until
1674, the French had basically known only the basin of the Saint

Lawrence, a river closed to navigation six months of the year. The Spanish, for their part, were not aware that a river draining into the Gulf of Mexico could be traced back to the northern part of the continent. The Mississippi and its powerful affluents, the Missouri and the Ohio, linked the French empire to the Spanish and might have increased the riches of these colonies tenfold, yet they remained unknown to the Europeans. The Spaniards, being absorbed in making profits from the fabulous wealth of gold and silver in South America, paid little attention to the Mississippi. To the French, on the other hand, a warm water port with year-round access was of vital importance. Everything changed in June 1674 with the return of Louis Joliet, who, with Father Marquette, had traveled on the Mississippi. They had left from Michilimackinac, "Turtle Island," which lies between Lake Michigan and Lake Huron. They followed the northern shore of Lake Michigan and took the Fox River to the Wisconsin and the Mississippi, which they descended to a point below its confluence with the Ohio well into the country of the Illinois. They turned back before reaching the Gulf of Mexico, but established strong evidence of a southern access route to the colony. The economic importance of this news was so great that the search for a Northwest passage to China and the treasures of the Orient was at that time abandoned. Fortunately so, as this famous passage through the Arctic Ocean, when finally discovered in 1909, proved to be slow, toilsome, and impractical, and was never actually used more than a few dozen times.[4]

In La Salle's mind, the hypothesis that there existed a route to the Gulf of Mexico was transformed into a certainty, and justified his efforts to anchor New France in the area around the Great Lakes. The Jesuits did not object to exploration or even to trade with the Indians when these operations were under their control, but La Salle's activity struck them as scandalous. They had managed, at the cost of unceasing effort, to create a long string of missions around the lakes. There were some on Lake Huron, Lake Michigan, and Lake Superior. They occupied the strategic passage between Lake Huron and Lake Superior at Sault Sainte

Marie, and the passage at Michilimackinac between Lake Michigan and Lake Huron. They had establishments at La Pointe, on the far west end of Lake Superior; around the Baie des Puants, known as Green Bay today, at the source of the Fox River in the northwestern part of Lake Michigan; and even in the far north where Father Albanel had reached Hudson Bay. All these missions were similar: a chapel, flanked by a house or two and protected by a palisade, with a few acres of cleared land around it. There, with the help of their apprentices or their salaried workers (religious fervor had somewhat abated in France after 1660, and the clergy now often had to pay their servants), the Black Robes hunted, fished, explored, traded with the Indians, and tried to make them into Christians.[5] The Jesuits were intelligent and energetic; for thirty years they had had the field to themselves as evangelists, colonizers, and discoverers. Now, they were confronted with La Salle, a man whose considerable influence was backed by the governor, and felt their power and monopoly threatened. In fact the Jesuits were not keen on having neighbors at all: for one thing, they set a bad example for the Indians. When Frenchmen, freed of the supervision of their families and overjoyed at the sheer number of available Indian women, ran gaily from hut to hut on "torch runs,"[6] the display of their admirable vitality never failed to astonish the natives and demoralize the Black Robes. Furthermore, the priests believed that while they themselves maintained trade within permissible limits, the Canadians would give free rein to their greed, make the Indians drunk, and destroy the native way of life without rebuilding it on a Christian model. The clergy also harbored some resentment against the secular powers in France. Had they been obliged to choose whether to be ruled by the pope or by the king, they would have chosen the pope, whose authority was less burdensome and more distant. They had grown accustomed to handling business in their own way, and the arrangement suited them. With colonists settling nearby, the watchful eye of the government would now turn toward them. Frontenac, exceeding all bounds, had tried to require them to have passports issued for every trip they took, as though they were lowly settlers.[7] And he had denounced their activities. "To speak frankly," he wrote his minister, "[the Jesuits] are as much concerned about converting beaver as they are about converting souls."[8]

The Jesuits were exasperated that Fort Frontenac, with its great potential, should be governed by a man who, though a product of their schools, was now insultingly independent. La Salle's energy seemed dangerous as well. Earlier, they had accused him of being a visionary. But now that "by means of extraordinary care, effort, and expense he had achieved his aim and done what no one had ever done before, believing it impossible, he [had] become the target of their envy and dislike."[9] Where did this man draw his devilish energy? The original fort made of boards and palings had disappeared and was replaced by a stone fortress, built of rocks "polished naturally by the action of the water on the lake shore,"[10] and protected by four bastions. Its ramparts were seventeen feet thick and extended a distance of 800 yards, a heroic feat under the circumstances. Nine small cannons defended the square, and the men had dug a large ditch around the periphery for added security. It is a wonder that he was able to organize the transports for this undertaking and compel men to take part in so considerable an effort. When Frontenac visited him in September 1676, he found a mill and a bakery, a well for water, a forge, land under cultivation, and a garrison consisting of two officers, a sergeant, and twelve soldiers. Storehouses containing provisions of arms, ammunition, food and trade goods stood next to "large and handsome quarters."[11] Nineteen workmen — gunsmiths, carpenters, and masons — were employed around the fort. A surgeon was on hand to bleed the sick, and there was no shortage of patients as both whites and Indians readily sought the treatment. A servant of the Jesuits, Simon Baron, had introduced the technique in 1637, and the Indians had adopted it enthusiastically: "He bled more than two hundred patients, up to fifty in a single day. All and sundry offered him their arms: those who were well had themselves bled as a precaution, and those who were sick thought they were halfway cured after seeing their blood flow."[12] Finally, there was the *Frontenac*, a large flat-bottomed brigantine, and two covered barks were moored in front of the fort. The boats were extremely useful "because a few men may transport a great many goods in ships of this sort and they are not obliged to go out at night as one must with canoes, which expose those who are forced to sleep on land to the surprise of the barbarians."[13] The master of Fort Frontenac, using a broad definition of "local trade," was able to ply a highly profitable coastal trade on Lake Ontario. The Jesuits responded by exerting their influence in Quebec to obtain an edict from the sovereign council prohibiting traders from entering Indian territory. This did not stop La Salle. He managed to attract enough Iroquois to settle an Indian village at the doors of his fort, and all trade was routed through them. La Salle was not contravening the edict, but he was still undercutting the influence of the Jesuits. In addition, he was gaining considerable popularity among the Indians. "He knew the Iroquois were not the barbarians they were claimed to be, and hoped not only to live with them peaceably but to draw them to himself by various means."[14] The Indians actually took part in erecting the ramparts, and at the end of a day's work the French and the Indians often went to the sweat lodge in the native village together. The sweat lodge was "the best of their medicines," according to Father Le Jeune, who described their method in detail. "They shut themselves in an oven where they raise a small tent, very low to the ground, surrounded by bark and entirely covered by their animal hide robes. They heat five or six stones which they put into this oven, and enter it naked. Inside, they sing incessantly, striking the walls of their steamroom gently. I saw them emerge dripping with sweat, after which they run to the river, throw themselves in, and rub themselves from head to foot."[15] The Indians' presence also provided entertainment for the colonists. Their lacrosse games were great sporting events. They raised two posts, separated by a considerable distance. The players (there were always a great many of them) divided into two sides and, using a sort of racket with a long curved handle, tried to send the ball as far as their opponent's post. A violent game, it always ended in a feast at which many were nursing their wounds.

It would be wrong, however, to suppose that relations between the two groups were especially cordial. The French worked hard and were surprised to discover that the Indians did nothing, the men in particular, except to hunt and fight wars. Even when they were living in a village, the Indians did not see the point of providing for the future. When food was available, which is to say on their return from the hunt, they wolfed it down in incredible quantities; when food ran short, they went hungry. Alternating between feast and famine, they seemed not to know any middle ground between gorging and fasting; the Europeans meanwhile economized, spreading the bounty of the seasons evenly.

The few French families at Cataracoui lived not in the fort itself but on farms along the lake shore. The cattle, poultry, and pigs originally brought from Montreal had already reproduced the following summer. The settlers had suffered setbacks the first year when a grasshopper invasion destroyed their grain and vegetable crops. (Even today, grasshoppers can descend on the area in such large numbers that they cover road surfaces like a second layer of asphalt, and, when they take flight, rise like a flying carpet and hammer the roof and sides of a car like a hailstorm.)[16] On the advice of the Indians, they dug trenches and lit fires in them, into which they swept the grasshoppers. Once the insects were roasted, the Indians picked them out and ate them, finding them delicious.[17] The following year, harvests were good, and La Salle's description of his territory is moving in its enthusiasm: the country around the Great Lakes

> is nearly all so beautiful and so fertile, so free from forests and so full of meadows, streams, rivers, fish, game, and venison, that one can find there in abundance and with little effort, all that is necessary for the support of powerful colonies. The soil can produce everything that is grown in France and with the same methods. Flocks and herds can be left to pasture freely in the countryside all winter; there are even wild cattle which, instead of hair, have a very fine wool that may answer for making cloth and hats.[18]

In his optimism, based on the climate's being much milder than in Montreal and the soil much richer (the future would prove him right), he passed over in silence the plague of mosquitoes, mayflies, and other winged creatures that made travel on the lakes so unpleasant during the summer's heat.

The fort's activities as a whole were bothersome and infuriating to the Jesuits. Whether La Salle took proper stock of the priests' upset is uncertain. If he knew of their irritation, he made no mention of it. This indifference to what did not directly concern his projects is reminiscent of his attitude toward his men on the descent of the Ohio when, in what nearly proved a very costly mistake, he contemptuously failed to reassure and comfort them. That he inspired hostility is shown by the fact that an attempt was made to murder him. "Monsieur de La Salle found himself poisoned by a salad to which hemlock had been added, which is a poison in those countries, and also verdigris. He was sick almost to death, vomiting continuously for forty or fifty days afterward, and he recovered only thanks to his extremely healthy constitution. The man who gave him the poison was called Jolycœur, one of his servants. He could have had the man killed, as he confessed to the crime, but he only had him shackled and imprisoned."[19] Either for lack of proof, or to avoid being drawn into a struggle he was unsure of winning, or yet again because he needed the knowledge and experience of the Jesuits, La Salle decided not to make an issue of it and accuse the Jesuits, or let any suspicion of the crime fall on them: "Nevertheless I am bound," he later wrote in a letter to the Prince de Conti, "to do them the justice of saying that it was not at their instigation that the poison was given to me."[20] He had no intention of becoming mired in a useless quarrel at the very moment when he had learned some news that was of the highest interest to him. It concerned his rival, Louis Joliet.

Joliet had returned from his expedition on the Mississippi by a different route than by going back to Green Bay. From talking with the Indians, he had gleaned enough to leave the Mississippi where the Illinois joined it; this river led him easily, "with no guide other than a compass"[21] to the southern point of Lake Michigan, where Chicago now stands. This shortcut was extremely useful, the northern route being much longer and more difficult. The new route also offered a tantalizing prospect of settlement — the country neighboring it was much more fertile than the frozen shores of the Saint Lawrence, and the Indians living there seemed peaceful. Joliet had announced to Father Dablon, the Jesuit superior, that the discovery of the Illinois River was probably just as important as the discovery of the Mississippi, because "in consequence the French could easily go to Florida, there being only one portage to make at the point where Lake Erie falls into Lake Ontario, a distance of perhaps a half-league. One could easily build an outpost there and make another bark for Lake Erie."[22]

Joliet's ambition, naturally, was to found a colony in the Illinois valley. He had just married and was thinking about settling down rather than continuing his voyages. He had excellent relations with the Jesuits and also had the support of Charles Aubert de la Chesnaye, a native of Rouen who became one of the richest men in the colony (he shared with Bazire the role of tax collector for the king). Joliet was consequently in an excellent position to obtain the confidence and financial backing of the commercial class of Montreal and Quebec. Before colonizing the area, however, he needed to obtain the king's authorization. He thought that he was taking the right step by having Duchesneau look after his interests, and the provincial administrator undertook to submit Joliet's petition by mail in 1676. But Duchesneau had no power at Court. He watched over the governor's activities with hypercritical zeal but, where a Talon would have drawn up a large-scale development policy, Duchesneau's energy was spent in stupid and unending quarrels with Frontenac. The answer, when it arrived back on August 28, 1677, was no. "His Majesty does not wish to grant permission to Sieur Joliet to settle in the country of the Illinois with twenty men as he requests. The inhabitants of Canada must be made to multiply before any thought is given to other lands."[23] Frontenac was relieved to learn of the king's refusal and quickly made arrangements to spend several weeks with La Salle. There, in the wilderness of the woods, they hatched a diplomatic strategy.

Joliet was skillful in a canoe but maneuvered poorly on land, and Duchesneau was incapable of giving him useful advice. The king and Colbert had always stated that they did not want the colony to expand. They dreamt of a colony along the lines of New England, where dogged farmers stayed put to scratch at the soil, build up communities, clear away forests, and consolidate their foothold on the coast, instead of roaming the woods and rivers like wild men. The governor had orders to drill men in the village square after mass, but villages were nonexistent — the requirement was absurd. Colbert, who had always been so severe, so sober, was starting to rave. Canadians refused to take part in this archaic form of discipline, and for good reason. In a war against the Indians, military exercises in the traditional French style were worse than useless. One had to know how to travel on snowshoes, hide behind a tree trunk, make out a footprint on moss or snow — marching in parade formation was irrelevant. Often, the soldiers who arrived from France, disconcerted by their unorthodox enemy, elected to guard the farms while the settlers took their place on the campaign. Frontenac was too much of a courtier to contradict the king on military matters, or on the subject of exploration. The trick was to present the issue in a different light, and La Salle agreed completely. Why walk straight toward defeat, when a detour or two could lead to victory? A Norman who had been schooled by the Jesuits could hardly be opposed to the art of compromise. All they needed to do, the two men agreed, was to ask permission to search for the mouth of the Mississippi, with no mention of trading or colonization, and simply obtain authorization to build forts wherever necessary. Above all, La Salle decided to return to France himself to make sure that the petition would be accepted. With a light heart, he paid his sixty livres for the one-way trip (the return cost only thirty livres, the price of a good hat) and embarked for France on October 24, 1677.

La Salle was no longer the young unknown that Colbert had kept waiting for days on end outside his office. His reputation was good. Too reserved to have many friends, he still had his supporters. Seignelay, Colbert's son, valued and supported him, as did the Prince de Conti, grandson of the Grand Condé and husband of Louis XIV's illegitimate daughter by La Vallière, who received La Salle on the recommendation of his Sulpician friends. La Salle could be brilliant when he was called on to persuade. And though he sprang from distant and fascinating lands, where he was accused by the Jesuits of being as mad as a hatter, he demonstrated such precision of thought, such workmanlike habits of mind, and such soberness — all traits pointing to his bourgeois origins in Rouen — that his audience was reassured. He was a unique kind of bourgeois, however, since he preferred glory to wealth. By simply staying at Fort Frontenac, he could have amassed a considerable fortune in a short time. What made La Salle appealing was the unusual co-existence in him of a passionate imagination and a strict sense of reality. Through Gallinée, he became friends with the Abbé Renaudot, a relative of the Prince de Conti, and a man with wide access to the court at Versailles and Parisian society — Boileau at one point dedicated an epistle to him. The abbé has left an intellectual portrait of La Salle that suggests the austere charm of the young explorer. "All of my friends who have met him find him a man of great intelligence and good sense. He speaks on a subject only when he is questioned about it, and his words are few and very exact. He distinguishes perfectly between what he knows with certainty and what he knows with some element of doubt. When he doesn't know, he frankly admits it, and although I have heard him say five or six times the same things for the sake of several people who had not heard them yet, I have always heard him tell it the same way. In short, I have never heard anyone speak whose words carried a greater mark of truth."[24]

Before making his appearance at court, La Salle went to visit Madame de Frontenac at the Arsenal, where she still had her handsome apartment. Living separate lives had greatly improved relations between the Frontenacs. They had become friends again, and the governor conferred a good deal of responsibility on his wife — she received his salary in his absence, took care of his business interests, and did a thousand things for him. During the ugly squabbles with Duchesneau, the countess had made a call on Colbert to clear her husband of guilt. She was a woman of intelligence, influence, and judgment, and Frontenac rightly believed that she would be a useful guide to La Salle in the sophisticated jungle of Versailles.

At last, his case well-prepared, his backers solidly behind him, La Salle met with Colbert and gained all he had asked for. Louis XIV granted him the right to build and operate as many forts as necessary, and gave him a monopoly on the trade of buffalo hides (which La Salle had not requested), in the interest of discovering a route to Mexico. But La Salle's work was not yet done. He had won the battle, but the decisive issue of the war still lay ahead: the state would not be financing the expedition. It was one of La Salle's main recommendations, as far as Colbert was concerned, that he cost the treasury nothing. The explorer now turned fully to business matters. In his small quarters on the Rue de la Truanderie, to which he had returned, he organized his files, juggled with numbers, estimated the salaries of his men and the cost of building boats. Cousins from Paris, the Plets, who were shopkeepers on the Rue Saint-Martin, advanced him 11,000 livres and managed to convince a notary that the enterprise was solid. "His brothers and relatives spared no effort in making it possible for him to respond to the King's bounty."[25] The title of nobility that young Robert had acquired made all the difference in Rouen. Advancement certainly came quickly in New France, the merchants thought; in their eyes, a title was a lofty and unreachable beacon.

He immediately hired shipwrights and assembled a supply of anchors, sails, rigging, and ironmongery — all goods that could not yet be bought in Canada. He made the return crossing with that rarest and most wonderful thing, a friend, a true one. The Prince de Conti had a protégé that he did not know what to do with, Henri de Tonty. Abbé Renaudot suggested that the prince introduce him to La Salle. The two men took to each other immediately. Tonty was born in France, the son of a Neapolitan financier who moved to Paris in 1650. (It was Tonty senior who devised the form of borrowing called a *tontine*, originally to save Mazarin from financial ruin. The scheme was favorable to lenders and still existed in Balzac's day. A group of people pooled their capital into a fund from which they received income during their lifetimes; at the death of any of them, the income was redistributed among the survivors.) Tonty did not follow in his father's footsteps, instead choosing a career as a soldier. He served for several years, until his hand was blown off by a grenade. His arm was fitted with an iron device, which he learned to use to good purpose, but he was nonetheless obliged to resign his commission. He sought advice from the Prince de Conti, who directed him to La Salle. The two men got along so well that they left together for La Rochelle, where they boarded ship. The voyage brought them closer, and Tonty was so useful and energetic from the moment they landed that La Salle thanked the Prince de Conti warmly: "His honorable character and amiable disposition are well known to you, but perhaps you would not have thought him capable of doing things for which a strong constitution, an acquaintance with the country, and the use of both hands seemed an absolute necessity."[26]

La Salle's return to the colony was triumphal. Jesuit hostility had failed to prevent his great stroke, as bold as it was unexpected, of obtaining Colbert's support and Seignelay's (who would succeed his father in 1683). With Tonty at his side, as well as another young nobleman who wanted to take part in the adventure, La Motte de Lussière, La Salle was assured of having a close-knit team around him. He could always count on Frontenac, and even the merchants in the colony were starting to support him. With his backing in place, he wasted no time in preparing for the expedition. The first thing he needed was a boat, a big boat, to sail the lakes with.

❖ 7 ❖

The Sound of the Great Waters
1678–1679

COLONIZATION FACED A HURDLE that was practically insurmountable to anyone without superhuman strength and will — there were no roads or navigable rivers. Normal routes ended at Montreal. Beyond that point, transporting goods and livestock became a heroic endeavor. Imagine the effort it took to lash a cow to a raft, float it down the swirling current, hoist it up an embankment covered with brush, and afterward persuade it to step back onto the boat once the falls had been passed. Think of the exhaustion and the anger of porters, who felt none of the romantic enthusiasm that sustained explorers and missionaries, as they staggered under the weight of their loads. The main anchor of a small vessel weighed 450 pounds, and a sensible captain would insist on having two. That a distant outpost like Fort Frontenac was essentially self-sufficient did not solve the problem. At every forward advance the basic equipment had to be transported on men's backs all over again, starting from Montreal. Canadians had grown used to this constraint and didn't balk at river travel, but its dangers were real nonetheless. Joliet overturned his boat, as Frontenac reported to Colbert, "within sight of Montreal and he thought to drown there, having virtually completed a voyage of 1,200 leagues. All his papers were lost, as well as an Indian boy he was bringing to me from those lands, whose loss I greatly regret."[1] Transportation was a nightmare for anyone wanting, as La Salle did, to sail on the Great Lakes. Their configuration, in fact, makes it impossible for a boat to pass from Lake Ontario to Lake Erie.

Thanks to the Jesuits, the geography of the region was well known. The Great Lakes are like steps in a staircase, the highest being Lake Superior, "similar to the ocean in having neither bottom nor shores,"[2] and next to it Lake Michigan. (The name comes from an Indian word, transcribed as "Mitchiganon" by Father Dablon, but French Canadians always called it Lake Illinois.) These two lakes flow into Lake Huron,[3] the first through the rapids at Sault Sainte Marie, a jagged rocky stretch of water impassible to boats, and the second through the straits at Michilimackinac. Lake Huron runs gently into Lake Erie by means of a long navigable channel that widens to form Lake Saint Clair. Up to that point everything is fine, and "one can sail a bark from the bottom of Lake Illinois for a distance of four hundred leagues,[4] right to the end of Lake Erie, where navigation is interrupted."[5] The last step down is a long one: in fact a drop of more than fifty yards. Lake Erie does not flow into Lake Ontario at all, it plunges into it headlong at Niagara Falls. La Salle was familiar with the spot. "The falls are of unbelievable height and have no rival on earth. The Niagara River is only an eighth of a league across here, but extremely deep and so rapid that it sweeps away any animals that try to cross it, and not one can resist its current. It plummets from a height of more than 200 feet and its fall consists of two sheets of water and a cataract with a steep-sided island in the middle; its waters foam and boil awfully: the roar is continuous, and when the wind blows from the south side we hear the noise fifteen leagues away."[6]

This obstacle was enough to dash any hopes of navigating freely on the Great Lakes. Not that the falls would stop a group of men from passing — it was possible in spite of the dangers to climb the cliffs, even carrying Indian canoes. But the falls blocked the way to heavier boats. As La Salle could not set aside the considerable sums he needed to finance his expedition without trading on a large scale around the Great Lakes, he had to own a large bark. To conduct trade from a canoe in these fresh water seas would be absurd. Certainly, nothing could replace the canoe for rapid travel: in a following wind, the Europeans would hoist four yards of sail onto a little mast and whizz like an arrow; in winter they attached a skate blade to the keel and where the ice was smooth slid even faster. But to move large loads — and La Salle was planning to bring back large quantities of pelts — he needed a real boat. He would therefore have to build one above Niagara Falls. Transporting the anchors, the rigging, and all the hardware would be rough work. So be it. Conquering Canada would take strong muscles and equal determination. He had proven before that it was possible to perform tasks that people thought impossible. All his men had to do was follow his example. La Salle and his traveling companions, Tonty and La Motte, had carefully worked out their plans during the long voyage so as not to lose a moment on arrival in Canada in September 1678. Now his friends urged him on.

But La Salle was exhausted when they landed, and so ill that he had to spend several weeks in Quebec. La Motte left for Fort Frontenac alone, with orders to send out about fifteen men with seven or eight thousand pounds of merchandise. Other than the obligatory brandy and firearms, they would offer the Indians clothes, as bright and multicolored as possible, thread for sewing, spyglasses, blankets, and boxes full of small nails. They were to trade on the shores of Lake Michigan and if possible make friends with the Indians on the south end of the lake, so as to pave the way for La Salle's departure toward the Mississippi. La Motte would take his little band of carpenters and blacksmiths and go with Father Hennepin to the mouth of the Niagara River. La Salle, unlike the coureurs de bois, would never make even a temporary encampment without a priest to hold religious services, keep a log, and serve as cartographer. The advance party had the responsibility of building a fort and picking a site above the falls where the ship could be built. La Salle and Tonty would push on and join them as soon as they could reach Fort Frontenac, bringing the necessary equipment.

Preparations were hampered, however, by the distrust of the Iroquois, to whom the undertaking had never been adequately explained. The Indians were justifiably uneasy about the construction of a fort at the foot of the Niagara River. For one thing, they were accustomed to traveling freely to Albany, where all the trading for the city and colony of New York took place, and to New England. La Salle reached Fort Frontenac on December 16, to learn that the Iroquois already had gone to their winter hunting grounds, and that La Motte, too inexperienced to assert his authority and calm the Indians' suspicions, had done no more than "build a house fortified by palisades."[7] Although it was Christmas Eve, La Salle boarded the brigantine with Tonty and a dozen men. They carried a cargo of tools and supplies for the shipbuilding crew, as well as merchandise to placate the Indians. The following day they anchored at the mouth of the Genesee River (where the city of Rochester is today) and made their way to an Iroquois village. They took the opportunity to buy corn from the Indians and explain to them that there was nothing to fear from the activities of the French. La Salle had dealt with the men of this tribe before and was disagreeably surprised to find them in an ugly mood. As here too most of the warriors were away hunting, it was unlikely that they would attack, and La Salle was not unduly concerned. Reaching for his pipe, he took a seat in the village headman's lodge and, by promising that all their hatchets and firearms could be repaired at the shipyard forge, he managed to persuade the chief to loan him several young men to hunt and keep his workers supplied with meat.[8] The deal struck, he boarded ship and sailed for the Niagara River. Tonty had received his first lesson in Indian diplomacy.

La Salle left the brigantine at the mouth of the river, followed an Indian trail for a mile or two, and found the big fortified cabin where his men were huddled. To his disappointment, work on the shipbuilding site had not yet started, as La Motte had been too intimidated by the Indians to risk provoking them. La Salle took matters in hand and put the men to work.

First they had to select a site, and for that they had to climb the walls of the gorge enclosing the falls. An enormous pine tree, nicknamed "the Indian ladder," whose regular branches they used as a staircase, helped them to inch their way up what Chateaubriand called "an otter path."[9] They clutched at vines to keep from slipping and to steady themselves in the deafening roar of the water foaming below them. At last, hearts pounding and breath coming hard, they emerged onto the plateau.

At the entrance to a large stream, the Cayuga, La Salle (who was the first to recover his wits) found what looked like a suitable location, near a small island. Nika and the two Iroquois from the village showed the men how to build bark shelters against the rain and wind. The technique consisted of felling a certain kind of elm tree and stripping off the bark, being careful to remove it all in one piece, if necessary pouring boiling water over the trunk. One hoped for a sheet large enough to make a small tent.[10] The Indians then left on a bear hunt, not for food so much as to provide bearskins for the men. At this time of year, the hunts were organized as drives: the hunters, armed with sticks or hatchets, walked through the forest whacking trees and hollow trunks. From time to time, a big groggy bear, waking with a start from his hibernation, would lumber out of his den and fall into the ambush. Father Hennepin built a bark chapel in the same native style and, accompanied by two workers who knew how to sing the Gregorian chant and "some others acquainted with the rudiments,"[11] he intoned the Holy Mass.

The consolations of religion did not dispel the men's anxiety. In the murky light of winter, with the gray water in front of them and the mute and menacing forest behind, the men — many of them newly arrived from Europe — found their surroundings depressing. The food was disgusting and bizarre. Bear paws, fresh haunch of stag, squirrels, and porcupines: what really scandalized them was having to eat these foods without bread. Besides, as Father

Hennepin, who looked after the men's morals, took pains to note, "the Flemish, Italians, and Normans all had different outlooks. It was very difficult for us to harmonize so many temperaments."[12] Then, at the very moment La Salle had finished organizing the work, a catastrophe occurred. La Salle had left the brigantine anchored at the mouth of the Niagara, and he had warned the pilot of the sudden storms on the lake. Winds sometimes built up such powerful waves that mounds of water ten feet high crashed onto shore. The pilot, also newly arrived from France, did not take this seriously and was rash enough to sleep ashore with his sailors. The bad weather came up, the anchor failed to hold and the boat splintered against the rocks. Except for a single anchor, all the equipment brought from Montreal with such pains was gone. Supplies and trading goods alike were lying at the bottom of the lake. The whole operation had to be performed all over again. La Salle put Tonty in command of the construction of the vessel and La Motte in charge of the buildings at the foot of the falls — this cluster of huts received the somewhat pompous name of Fort Conti. As the season was too far along to use La Motte's boat, La Salle set out on snowshoes for Fort Frontenac with two men. A dog hauled their meager baggage. The only food they brought was a sack of wheat. They traveled through the frozen forest, gliding on the icy edge of the lake, sleeping in snow caves, snaring hares for food, and being guided by flocks of ravens to the remains of a doe or an elk not yet devoured by wolves. Their two hundred-mile journey so weakened them that for the last two days of it they had not even the strength to hunt.

La Salle did not return to the Niagara camp during the winter. His creditors were so shaken by the news of his mishaps that they "had all his property in Quebec and Montreal seized, even his secretary's bed, and it was awarded to them at the price they named — even though Fort Frontenac alone could repay his debts twice over if he were ever to die while away on his discoveries."[13] He consequently had to spend time in Montreal to put his affairs back on a solid footing.

Meanwhile, at the site above Niagara Falls progress was being made on the construction of the boat. Enough tools and rigging had washed up from the lake for the men to continue their task. The landscape, assuming they ever looked at it, was enchantingly transformed. The vapor billowing from the falls coated every twig with ice. Trees sparkled in the sun. Brittle bushes snapped at the least breath of wind. The sides of the gorge bristled with giant stalagmites making it impossible to climb them, except for the neighboring Indians who came and lurked, close-lipped and menacing, around the alien shipyard. One of them attacked the blacksmith, who defended himself with an iron bar reddened at the forge. A squaw boasted to Nika one day that her men would set fire to the big wooden carcass that was taking shape. A watch was organized around the clock. In the circumstances, it is not surprising that, in spite of the wilderness and isolation of the site, the carpenters were often on the point of deserting. Tonty, however, was a military man like Frontenac, and like him was able to inspire his men with the courage and desire to finish the task. He was afraid of nothing, and his valor was reassuring. If an Indian came too close, he knocked him down with a blow of his iron hand, leaving the poor man spitting teeth. At that rate, it didn't take him long to win the Indians' respect. He was wary of their tricks though, and had the bark launched as quickly as he could to avoid the risk of its being set on fire.

The finished bark was fifty feet long and sixteen wide, had two masts and a capacity of forty-five tons.[14] It was christened the *Griffon* in honor of the Comte de Frontenac, whose coat of arms included a winged lion. To give a relative idea of its size, the smallest merchant vessels of the day had a displacement of two hundred tons. The completion of the bark in such primitive conditions was nothing short of miraculous, and brandy flowed like water. Father Hennepin gave the blessing; the men sang a Te Deum and the Indians gathered on the banks, "four fingers over their mouths in sign of stupefaction,"[15] to examine this monster armed with five cannons. The anchor, so heavy that it had taken four men to drag it up the falls, filled them with awe.

Spring was returning, and the men's mood grew sunnier. They went to the trouble of sculpting a griffon with an eagle above it on the stem of the boat. The sap of the sugar maple made a delicious drink. Wild roses, beautiful orchids, and lilies brightened the clearing, and life shimmered again. Birds came back in large numbers. The swallows formed a big white cloud as they hawked for prey at the falls, diving abruptly just at the lip of the cataract. Once again, the insects buzzed. The plague of flies and mosquitoes had started again, but how could you not be amazed, as Father Hennepin had been, at finding tree trunks entirely covered with butterflies, their colorful wings fluttering? How not enjoy the great flocks of eagles, geese, and ducks? The birds landed on blocks of ice that were still floating in the river during the early season; they seemed to be playing, drifting toward the precipice and taking off a moment before reaching the falls. Birds that were slow, or that were lulled by the mist rising off the water, and swans that tended to sleep on the river were sometimes swept over. The men from Fort Conti would find them at the foot of the falls, flung by the current onto the rocks and into the crevices, from which they gathered them, clinging to branches so as not to fall in. Some mornings they would discover the broken body of an elk or a bear.

Once the ice had melted, the lake could again be sailed. La Salle's brigantine had foundered, but the boat that had brought the men to the Niagara River in the autumn was still intact. La Motte, who was suffering from an ulceration of the eye and who, according to Father Hennepin, "had never been able to endure the rigors of a hard life,"[16] took eleven men and sailed back to Fort Frontenac. La Salle had sent orders for them from Montreal. The vessel was to turn around with a new crew and carry fresh supplies and trade goods to the Niagara camp. Once everything was transported past the falls, Tonty and his men were to load the *Griffon* and make their way as quickly as possible to the south end of Lake Michigan where they would find the traders La Salle had sent to trade there the previous year. The plan was then to send the *Griffon* back with a cargo of pelts.

Tonty would stay among the Illinois and prepare the way for La Salle's arrival.

Unfortunately, Tonty could not manage to get the *Griffon* up the Niagara River and into Lake Erie. The force of the current made maneuvering under sail too dangerous. Chateaubriand, who traveled to Niagara a century later, wrote that several miles above the falls, "the water shot past with the speed of an arrow. It did not boil, it slid down the rock in a uniform mass; its silence before falling formed a contrast with the falls."[17] The men were afraid. Tonty realized the need to act fast and he lost no time in calling on La Salle for help. La Salle responded immediately. "Considering that there was no help for it and not wanting to scotch a voyage prepared with such labor and expense,"[18] he decided to go to Niagara. To prevent his creditors from confiscating any more of his property, he signed his title to Fort Frontenac over to one of his lieutenants, La Forest, "for the space of a year."[19] He arrived at Fort Conti at the beginning of August 1679 with three Recollet friars, all of them Flemish like Hennepin. One of the priests would stay at Niagara and the other two accompany La Salle on his exploration. One of these was Gabriel Ribourde, who, though more than sixty-four years old, was so enthusiastic about the site that he climbed the gorge four times in a row while helping to transport the trade goods.

Twenty-five people embarked on the *Griffon*. An accurate list was drawn up by the head carpenter, Moïse Hillaret, showing twenty-one Frenchmen including La Salle's valet L'Espérance (the name means *hope*), three Recollet friars, and the faithful Nika, still at La Salle's side. Arms, trade goods, and provisions were stowed in the hold. And "against the will of his men," — because even at several leagues' distance from the falls, the prospect of being borne down by the current was terrifying — La Salle brought the *Griffon* to the head of the Niagara River, sailing when the wind was stronger than the current, and poling the bark or hauling it from shore where the going was more difficult.

Of irresistible strength, authority, and intelligence, La Salle had once again conquered the elements and in so doing managed to lift his men over the hurdle of their very natural timidity. One almost wants to end the story here. The miracle boat is disappearing toward the west, all sails deployed, the fleur-de-lys billowing in the wind, the air filled with the sound of a thanksgiving hymn as the crew join in a chorus. The men are finally hopeful again, the days clear and serene. Sailing conditions were so favorable that they covered more than one hundred leagues in three days, rejoicing to see beautiful open country where large numbers of does and bucks gathered, and bear so fat they could hardly walk. These made very good eating: Father Hennepin, a connoisseur, pronounced their flesh "more delicious than fresh pork."[20] The imagination of the party was so fired by the many familiar trees — walnut, chestnut, plum, apple and several hardwoods fit for building — that they already envisioned the shore lined with settlements. On August 10, they were at the entrance to the strait (in French: *détroit*) connecting to Lake Huron, where the town of Detroit was founded in 1701. Their epic was far from concluding; in fact it was just beginning. La Salle would have to confront once more the violence of nature and the passions of men, the worst of the New World and the worst of the Old, with no abatement of his furious desire to triumph.

They made their way through the strait easily, the current seeming as "strong as the tide at Rouen, for, as the banks were very fine, the Sieur de La Salle sent a dozen of his men ashore to haul the boat in harness along the shore for half an hour."[21] By contrast, their progress up Lake Huron was arduous. The winds were against them, they had trouble finding good anchorages, and they constantly had to take soundings from the bow of the bark, for fear of rocks in these uncharted waters — the wind stirring the lake had made the once-transparent water opaque. A terrible storm battered the *Griffon*, whose creakings and groanings grew so alarming that "although the bark tipped until the rail was in the water, the men threw themselves on their knees to ask God's help." La Salle, powerless to right the ship, promised a chapel to Saint Anthony. Only the pilot, Luc, instead of praying cursed La Salle for having brought him to perish "on a paltry lake, when he had known glory on the oceans." The wind, however, calmed and a week later they landed at the Jesuit mission in Michilimackinac, the island commanding the passage between Lake Huron and Lake Michigan.

The mission was a microcosm of Canada. Its population included Jesuits, Indians (for the most part Huron and Ottawa refugees displaced by the Iroquois and the Sioux respectively, who were converts more from policy than conviction), coureurs de bois, and other adventurers. The arrival of the *Griffon* had the miraculous effect of uniting this disparate population in a common feeling of amazement. Neither whites nor Indians could believe that they were actually seeing a sailing ship, a large two-master, rising above the horizon on a lake where the only vessels had been frail canoes. The Jesuits and inhabitants of Canada never thought it possible to reach the northern shores of the Great Lakes except by ascending the Ottawa River and portaging to Lake Nipissing and the French River. The alternative was to follow the northern shore of Lake Ontario to the present site of Toronto, strike inland to Lake Simcoe, an enormous portage, and from there paddle down to Georgian Bay on the north shore of Lake Huron. The bark's appearance could only be a mirage. When the first men recovered from their surprise, they were struck with fear. These were members of the advance party La Salle had sent out the previous year to trade on his behalf with the Illinois in Green Bay.[22] These brazen souls, convinced that La Salle's dreams would never materialize, had installed themselves at the mission and were trapping for their own profit. Six of them had fled north to Sault Sainte Marie, taking with them 4,000 livres' worth of goods. La Salle went ashore. His first act was to arrest the four ringleaders and put them in irons.

Having shown that he was in charge, he produced a waterproof case lined with a resin-coated fabric of woven reeds and carefully took out a crimson cape trimmed with gold braid, which he threw over his shoulders. One has to marvel at the extreme importance these men gave to clothing as an element of the scenario — the priests never showed themselves to the natives, for instance, except wearing their black cassocks. La Salle, attired in his cape, led his men in marching order to the bark-walled chapel, where the Jesuit father celebrated Mass. Firearms were laid down outside the consecrated ground and left under a sergeant's guard — the stack of muskets, bows and arrows, and hatchets underscoring the motley nature of the place. For a moment the heterogeneous assembly joined in prayer. There were the Black Robes; the Recollet friars wearing gray; the crowd of seamen and artisans wrapped in skins and torn blankets, no longer looking like Europeans nor yet like natives; there were the coureurs de bois with blank and expressionless features, worried that the arrival of La Salle, backed by the governor and equipped with the extraordinary *Griffon,* augured stiff competition; and there were the Indians, decorated with headdresses, their faces streaked with paint and their arms tattooed — all standing silently.

After Mass, the Indians flocked to admire the "floating fort," their birchbark canoes surrounding it like so many pilot fish. Determined to reclaim his men and his merchandise, La Salle sent the indefatigable Tonty after the deserters with orders to bring them back from Sault Sainte Marie. Meanwhile, he intended to push on toward Green Bay. So as not to waste time waiting for Tonty, La Salle left word that they should meet at Saint Joseph, a place near the entrance of a river at the south end of Lake Michigan. In Green Bay, La Salle was lucky enough to find the remnant of the advance party that had stayed faithful: they had amassed for him 12,000 livres worth of furs. The chief of the tribe hosting them still remembered Frontenac's kindness during the great gathering of 1674, and felt great affection toward the children of Onontio.

La Salle now experienced the luxury of making a decision not forced on him by the violence of the elements, but suggested instead by reason. Thanks to the *Griffon,* he was in the position of a man who, having never owned anything but a bicycle, is suddenly offered a truck. Naturally, he decided to use it. He had the furs brought aboard, planning to sell them, as well as a quantity of

goods, tools, and utensils that were too heavy for the canoes —
these would be unloaded at Michilimackinac, where La Salle
could have them picked up later. The pilot would take the furs to
the Niagara River where a boat from Fort Frontenac would be
waiting for him. There, the furs would be transferred. And the
Griffon would come back to Michilimackinac to receive new instructions. This left La Salle at Green Bay with four canoes and
fourteen men — sawyers, cabinet makers, house and ship carpenters — and only a minimum supply of firearms and trade
goods. He kept the portable forge, which was useful not only for
making essential repairs but also for securing the goodwill of the
Indians. It is worth noticing that La Salle used the Jesuit network
to transmit his orders rapidly, just as Frontenac and every other
administrator had done. In this particular case, an Indian carried the message to Father André, the superior of the
Michilimackinac mission, who in turn sent either a Canadian or
an Indian by the northern route back to Fort Frontenac. Without
the Jesuits, who had a virtual monopoly on the "postal service,"[23]
La Salle would never have been able to convey his orders from
the head of Green Bay back to his fort. He would have preferred
some alternative to using the Jesuits to transmit messages, but
"the expense of sending a special messenger would amount to
more than a hundred ecus." With an untried route, a second
message would have to be sent as a backup and even a third,
which La Salle did not have time for.[24]

He made his way with lighter baggage toward the foot of the
lake, avoiding skirmishes with the different Indian bands along
the route, thanks to his calm and his long experience of their
customs. They seemed peaceful, but were always capable of unexpected behavior. La Salle and his men did experience storms
of extreme violence. Once, off "a high, steep coast" where "the
waves broke extraordinarily," he was obliged "in order to land
safely, to leap into the water with his three men, and, all three of
them together lifting the canoe and its load, carry it to shore, in
spite of the waves that sometimes washed over their heads."[25] La
Salle was not given to exaggeration. Many travelers have de-

scribed the terror of these waves, swollen by the wind and barreling unobstructed down the lake, until the horizon is lined with snowy hills of foam hurling themselves at the cliffs. To limit the load in their canoes, the men carried no extra stores, but finding food was hardly a problem in this game-filled country, on a lake where sturgeon were stranded by the hundreds along the shore following a storm and Indians were unaggressive. The expedition's task was made easier by the calumet given to La Salle by Frontenac's friend, the Pottawatami chief. "This calumet," La Salle wrote,

> is a kind of long pipe for smoking whose head is made of handsome red stone, highly polished, and whose stem, which is two-and-a-half-feet long, is made of quite a strong reed decorated with feathers of all colors mixed and arranged very cunningly, with several tufts of women's hair braided in different fashions. Each nation adds to it according to its customs. Such a calumet is a passport of safe conduct to all the allies of the tribe presenting it, all of them convinced that great evils would befall them should they violate the calumet's protection.[26]

La Salle and his men could therefore enter villages in all security to buy Indian corn. On October 28, 1678, they arrived at the foot of the lake and found themselves in a country that was even more beautiful and more temperate. According to his custom, La Salle landed and went to explore the woods, leaving the canoes to be watched by the crew. He picked grapes that were ripe and tasty, which the Recollets made into communion wine. They then proceeded up the east coast of Lake Michigan towards Saint Joseph where they would meet Tonty.

A look at the map shows that La Salle was only a few hours' travel from the mouth of the Illinois, the river he would eventually follow. He had no way of knowing this, however. When Joliet's canoe capsized in the Lachine rapids, the returning explorer lost all his sketches. The map that he subsequently drew was erroneous. It located Saint Joseph right at the bottom of the lake, and gave only an approximate picture of the river systems around Chicago. These mistakes would cost La Salle a great deal of unnecessary effort, obliging him to reach the Illinois by following the long and difficult route along the Kankakee.

To his great surprise, Tonty was not waiting at the rendezvous. This did not disrupt La Salle's plans unduly because he had decided to wait for winter to go into Illinois country, a course dictated by prudence. Winter was the hunting season, when "these peoples divide up into family or tribal groups. Once reunited with the Sieur de Tonty, who was to bring him twenty men, [La Salle] could safely make himself known to the first band he should meet. These he could win over by treating them well and by giving them presents; and he could pick up some rudiments of the Illinois language from them. By such means he could easily enter into an alliance with the rest of the nation."[27] And La Salle, to "distract his men with some useful occupation" during the weeks of waiting, suggested that they build a fort and a storehouse to protect the *Griffon* when it should return with its load of trade goods, and to serve as a defense in case of need.

La Salle's men did not like the Indians, hated portages through the mosquito-infested woods, could not stand sagamity gruel, and the winter cold dismayed them. But they were consummate craftsmen, and when La Salle proposed a task they understood, they set about it willingly. They worked every day except Sundays and holidays, when the entire troop attended divine office and heard the sermon that Father Gabriel and Father Louis took turns delivering after vespers. In two weeks they had felled trees and cleared brush from an area "the length of two gunshots," and built an earthwork forty feet long and thirty feet wide, that was reinforced against musket fire with squared-off joists and beams. The whole area was surrounded by a log palisade twenty-five feet high. Tonty finally arrived on November 20. The *Griffon* had never returned to Michilimackinac. None of the natives they had talked to along the lakeshore had heard any news of it. La Salle feared with good reason that his bark had been shipwrecked. This new catastrophe left him unshaken — throughout his life he showed so little interest in personal gain that it could seem he had never broken his vow of poverty. Resolving to strike out toward the Mississippi, he embarked on December 3, 1678, with thirty men and eight canoes. As they ascended the river, its grassy banks were already filming over with a thin layer of ice.

❊ 8 ❊

The Illinois Prairies

1679–1680

 $\mathcal{D}$ URING THE TEN YEARS HE HAD been traveling the rivers and
woods of New France, La Salle had acquired an exceptional mastery of distances. In the next three years, 1679 to 1681, he would
establish forts hundreds of miles apart on Lake Ontario, Lake
Erie, Lake Michigan, and on the Illinois River, which flows south
from present-day Chicago. He would cross the distance between
them several times, traveling with the speed of an Indian, on foot
or by canoe, with a single companion or in a group. Aside from
the mobility that he had learned from contact with the Indians,
he was familiar with their customs to such an extent, thanks to
Nika, that he allowed himself to act in a way that no other
European would have dared. One day he had the audacity to take
captive a native whose tribe had stolen trade goods from him; he
judged that this was the quickest way to have his property restored, and he turned out to be right. Another time, he lost his
way while hunting deer and wandered too far from camp to return by nightfall. He saw a fire glowing in the distance. He
walked toward it, and when he got there lay down next to the
coals, not caring that the Indians who had made the camp might

be surprised to find a visitor there, and slept until dawn. His easy rapport with the Indians now allowed him to have more varied relations with them, not just of peace or war.

His plan on leaving the fort was to go up the Saint Joseph River (which the French called the Miami because of the Indian tribe living on it), portage to the Kankakee, and winter on that river, a tributary of the upper Illinois. He expected to complete his preparations for the descent of the Mississippi while in Illinois country, where he proposed to construct both a fort and a boat. Matters were complicated by the fact that he was venturing into unexplored territory, toward the unknown Illinois Indians.

On the approaches to the Kankakee the ground grew spongy, and the men were surprised at the difficulty they had walking on these "quaking bogs."[1] A modern traveler writes that these quag-mires are covered with thick red moss and have the approximate consistency of a rubber mattress.[2] Ponds and pools had over-flowed, flooding the entire area, and an amphibious vegetation rose from the large, broken expanse of water. A river, picking its course between three lakes (southwest of the present town of South Bend), wound lazily around the reeds and the rushes, its current almost imperceptible. It was so narrow at first that the travelers could leap across it. They put their canoes onto this slip of a stream, strapped down their bundles methodically (a pre-caution that was so necessary they did it automatically), and, pushing more than floating, set off. From a distance, it looked as though they were paddling on dry land.

Imperceptibly, they crossed the natural boundary from the watershed draining into the Great Lakes, the Saint Lawrence, and the Atlantic Ocean to the Mississippi watershed emptying into the Gulf of Mexico. The men did not notice it, because the transition occurs extremely gradually. "The slow river flowing in a big swamp,"[3] as the Indians called it, was so stagnant that they sometimes wondered whether they were going up it or down. Moorhens rose heavily from the mire, as well as ducks and a few late geese that had missed the departure of the main migration; perch and pike teemed in the black waters, whose edges were now starting to ice over. Meanwhile, the river had grown so much that it was soon "as wide and as deep as the River Marne." Although the current moved more strongly, the river made so many detours that the travelers' rate of progress hardly increased, and "having plied our paddles an entire day, we sometimes found that we had not advanced two leagues in a straight line."[4]

La Salle and his men were entering the prairies, a vast open country of tall grasses, interspersed with large trees, and support-ing a rich population of game. They were not exactly aware of it, however, because all around them, as far as the eye could see, the land had been burnt. The Miamis set enormous fires in the course of hunting buffalo. Using a technique that was primitive but terribly effective, "the Indians," La Salle wrote, "set fire to the grass around the herds except at a few places where they station themselves with bows and arrows. The buffalo, in trying to avoid the fire, are obliged to pass in front of the Indians, who some-times kill two hundred in a day." The waste of America's natural resources had already begun at this date. It is true that the Indians knew how to use all the parts of the animal, and, when they had time, dried the buffalo's meat, tanned its hide, and even removed its hooves, which they attached to small paddles to make a sort of music.[5] But hunting by fire, which was practiced on a large scale, forced them to abandon the major portion of the carcasses to wolves and ravens. This echoes the senseless slaughters of the nineteenth century, when sportsmen shot at herds from railway coaches, for the pure pleasure of killing; and also the insane hunts where buffalo were killed just for the tongue, which was considered a great delicacy, and tons of un-used meat were left to rot. The explorers did not see the buffalo on their first descent, but they could guess at the size of the herds from the sight "of paths trampled, like our paths in Europe, by the passage of so many cattle."[6] They also discovered a huge bull mired at the river's edge, which gave them an accurate glimpse at the size of American cattle: it took twelve of them to haul it from the mud.

Finally, on January 1, 1680, after traveling for a month, they reached a large Indian village on the Illinois between the present towns of Ottawa[7] and Marseilles. Much larger than the villages in northern Canada, it numbered "460 huts in the shape of long arches, covered with double mats of flat rushes, so expertly woven that neither wind, nor snow, nor rain can penetrate them. Each lodge has four or five fires, and at each fire there are one or two families living together on good terms."[8] No sound came from the village. All the inhabitants of this ghost town had gone hunting. La Salle was disappointed to find no old men or women who had stayed behind, as he had been counting on buying corn. He knew that if he searched around the lodges he would find caches full of grain under the leaves and twigs, but he hesitated to help himself. The Indians were improvident, but even so kept enough grain to plant on their return from the hunt and to subsist on until harvest time. Taking these reserves would smack of insult. However, La Salle knew that it would be foolish to continue on a winter journey without food, especially as game would be scarce so soon after the fires, and he finally decided to take "thirty minots of Indian corn,"[9] leaving some trade goods in payment, before continuing down the river. One morning, sniffing the air like a large animal, La Salle scented smoke. He stopped his men to prepare for the encounter. A show of force might be necessary. He lined up the eight canoes abreast, weapons at the ready, and when the party had fanned out across the current they floated silently downstream. La Salle saw the Indians first — at the present site of Peoria — and gave a yell "according to the custom of the Indian nations" to ask whether they intended peace or war. "At first, the old men, women, and children fled through the woods [and] the warriors ran for their weapons, but in such confusion that, before they were aware, the canoes had landed."[10] At the sight of the calumet, which La Salle held up like a flag, calm was magically restored. A round of mutual pledging and feasting followed, during which the chief and La Salle spoke through an interpreter. The French wanted permission to spend the winter in the area. Before entering into the details of his plans, La Salle played his trump card: he had the blacksmith demonstrate the portable forge. La Salle knew the chief would be unable to resist the prospect of repairing his hatchets without having to travel a long distance, and would hate the idea that this miraculous invention might go to another village. The atmosphere grew friendly. The Indians were naked, had their noses and ears pierced, and their hair cut to the width of a thumb, but, according to Tonty, "they were very like the French in disposition."[11] La Salle assured his host that, if he were allowed to build a fort, he could be counted on to help in case of an attack. He then announced his intention of "constructing a large canoe that could travel down the river as far as the sea." This would have the great advantage of providing the Illinois better access to "the material necessities" which it was so hard to bring them from New France because of the trackless forests, the many dangerous rapids, and the vast expanse of the Great Lakes.

The two camps seemed in perfect agreement, and "the day passed in mutual satisfaction."[12] The French were extremely happy to hear from the Illinois that navigation on the river was easy, and that the sea was only twenty days distant by canoe. On the following day they were disabused. A party of Miamis arrived. The Miami nation were middlemen between the Indians of the Great North, who supplied large quantities of furs, and the colonists in New England. The idea that the French might install themselves in the Illinois valley and, acting as competitors, siphon off some part of their trade displeased them, and they decided to break up the new alliance. They informed the Illinois that La Salle had always had excellent relations with their enemies, the Iroquois — which was perfectly true — and that he was certain to bring arms to the Indians south of them. In consequence of their hospitality to the French, the Illinois would be caught between pincers. Though primitive in some respects, the Indians, particularly those who dominated trade, were capable of making sound political assessments and acting accordingly.

The Illinois chief, shaken, looked for a way to go back on his promises, at the same time wanting to avoid giving offense to La Salle by his abrupt change of heart. He hit on the stratagem, in use since the days of Cartier, of terrifying the Europeans with his description of what lay around the next bend in the river. At a second feast, he drew a horrifying picture of the country to the south, although it contradicted everything he had said the previous day, and spelled out in detail "the great quantity of snakes and monsters found in the river, [adding] that the river was full of cliffs and rapids, that the current was so strong that it carried one along helplessly, that these rapids and falls led to a chasm that swallowed up the river, and no one knew where it reemerged from the earth."[13] La Salle was not unduly disturbed by the inconsistency. He was used to it. Besides, Joliet and Marquette had passed this way and, more importantly, they had returned. But La Salle knew that it was useless (and probably dangerous) to contradict the Illinois. Drawing partly on the grand style of his century and partly on the Indian code of honor, La Salle only said "that they were afraid that they should reap but little glory on this voyage, as it offered only rare occasions to show courage and overcome difficulties." To intimidate his hosts and counteract the influence of the Miamis, he added: "We have been sent by a great captain, the greatest of all who rule beyond the sea. We walk with confidence in the power of his might."[14] This was language that the Indians understood and respected. Unfortunately for La Salle, his crew understood it less well.

Six of his men were so frightened that they decided to desert, a decision "in which there was more peril than in all the hardships and difficulties described to us by the Indians."[15] La Salle particularly regretted losing the sawyers he needed to build his ship, as sawing logs lengthwise to make boards was a highly specialized skill. He summoned the remainder of his party and cautioned them to let the Indians suspect nothing — there was no point in exposing their flank by a show of weakness. He announced to his hosts that he would go several leagues down the river and construct his fort on the south shore (between Pekin and Kingston Mines) at a place that was "easy to fortify." He started without further ado. Always careful, he installed a safety device to protect them until the stockade was built. Following a ruse devised by

Radisson, the Hudson Bay explorer, he strung threads unobtrusively in the grass around the site and hung little bells from them. Anyone trying to slip into the perimeter would be discovered when he set off the chimes. Radisson had perfected his technique in the lonely wastes of the Far North: with a tube made of birch bark, he scattered gunpowder in a furrow traced in a circle around his shelter. If ever a group of Indians started circling too close, he would toss a coal from the fire into the furrow. Immediately, an eery ring of flame would leap out of the earth. It worked every time. But La Salle did not need magical defenses. The Illinois left him to construct his fort in perfect peace. They were neither taunting nor aggressive. Their nature led them to other forms of diversion. "Large-bodied and licentious, they are very passionate toward women," writes Tonty, "and even more so toward boys. They become almost effeminate from soft living and indulgence in pleasure. Either from the influence of the climate or in consequence of their perverse imaginations, one finds many hermaphrodites among them."[16]

Once again, the workmen did impressive work. In the space of six weeks they built an imposing fort, surrounded by a stockade twenty-five feet high; its posts were a foot in diameter, sharpened to a point at the top, and sunk three feet into the ground. The fort was further protected by "two large and deep ravines," which they extended with a ditch and lined with *chevaux-de-frise* — wooden sawhorses with projecting spikes. In order to protect the enclosure as well as possible given its large size and small garrison, La Salle housed his men in two of the flanking angles, assigned the Recollet friars to the third, and placed the forge in the fourth. He and Tonty installed themselves in huts in the center of the square. The walls were of unpeeled logs, and the roof of woven branches. Two squared-off chunks of wood covered with green boughs served as beds. Fires were lit on two stones placed in the center of the floor, and the smoke escaped through a hole in the roof. La Salle and Tonty often sat down to meals with the priests, but they did not eat with the men. "I have never taken my meals with any except those with whom I may."[17] It was La Salle's way of not losing caste.

But in naming his fine castle in the wilderness, La Salle decided to call it Crèvecœur, or Heartbreak. It was the first sign of a crack in his armor, a dark foreboding, and it is all the more surprising for coming at a time when his courage, his intelligence, and his endurance seem inexhaustible. He had clearly mastered the art of getting along with the Indians in a wide array of circumstances. While traveling thousands of miles, he had met a great variety of them and had always managed to pass freely in their midst, either by force or diplomacy; Indian chiefs respected him; and the presence of Nika, who was quiet, steady, and unshakably loyal, helped him to go forward into the unknown. Nothing was too hard for him, nothing discouraged him. He was able to survive the winter in the frozen forests, but at the same time he was an agronomist, an engineer, a merchant, and, if the occasion called for it, a courtier. The forts he left along his routes were not huts but solid edifices, potentially the cores of villages and nodes of long-term settlement. But how was he to succeed in an enterprise of this scope without the unconditional support of his men? In fact, he could only count on Tonty, d'Autray (the son of Jean Bourdon, a native of Rouen like himself and an important merchant, who became attorney general of Quebec and had an interest in mapmaking), Etienne de Boisrondet, a Parisian, who was full of enthusiasm, and, once again, Nika. In the American wilderness it was practically impossible to keep men from deserting. Conditions were rugged — but then, it was no simple matter to flee from the Great Plains to New England. There was also the dread of the unknown, which could suddenly come over the men, and greed for the possibility of the riches spread before them, which drove them practically mad. They were necessarily subject to harsh discipline as well, and this sometimes led to revolt. La Salle demanded no more of others than he did of himself — just the opposite. In hard spots, he always walked in the lead in order to clear the trail[18] and face possible enemies. But he set a punishing pace and imposed strict rules of conduct: "I have no special food, clothing, or shelter, which are the same for me as for my men, [but I refuse to] give them free rein. Neither honor nor inclination would let me stoop to gain their favor in such a disreputable way; and besides, the consequences would be dangerous, and they would have the same contempt for me that they have for all who treat them in this fashion."[19] On the grounds of caution as well as principle, he allowed no relations with Indian women. His men resented this, and the coureurs de bois, who freely indulged in every excess, were constantly before them as examples. La Salle was under no illusion as to the conduct of his men, and he was conscientious enough to learn from the Indians how to treat venereal diseases. They recommended taking seeds of the mistquil, a tree bristling with large thorns, and the remedy was effective though somewhat violent.[20] La Salle pondered the difficulty of preventing desertions, which "occur in the most disciplined armies, where punishment is a great deterrent. It would be very difficult to keep them from it in a country that provokes much weariness, and where men of this sort are soon disgusted, as they lose hope of partaking in the debaucheries that sweeten the lot of soldiers in France."[21] "We need faithful men," he continued, "inured to fatigue and toil and skilled in trades we cannot do without. Libertines and children of good families are entirely unfit."[22] A suitable man "need not be greatly educated, but he must like neither gambling, nor women, nor fine food, for he will find none of these with me."[23] "I will not tolerate blasphemy, drunkenness, lewdness, or any license that is incompatible with proper order, without which one cannot succeed, and finally, I am a Christian and do not want to bear the burden of their crimes."[24] Along the Illinois La Salle realized how hard it was to meet the combined challenge of America's great size and the frailty of human nature. For the first time he doubted his own infallibility.

However, he gave no outward sign of his momentary dismay, and a lucky encounter rallied the party's spirits. La Salle worried that the description of the terrible dangers on the Mississippi would make a strong impression on his men, particularly on those new to Canada. He could think of no way "to remove the terror that lingered in their minds" without having his optimistic comments sound false. While hunting, however, he met a young warrior who had just come from the south. La Salle offered him one of the four turkeys he had shot. They squatted on the ground to chat while the turkey cooked in the Indian's kettle. Handing him a bit of charcoal and some bark, La Salle encouraged the young man to draw a map and tell him the names of the different nations along the Mississippi and the rivers that flowed into it. The Indian confirmed that there were no cascades or rapids on the Mississippi and described the obstacles of "sandbars and mud" very accurately. La Salle thanked him and gave him a hatchet "to shut his mouth, which is an Indian expression for advising secrecy."[25] Then, happily anticipating the effect these revelations would have, he went to the Indian village taking the most fearful of his men with him. There, in front of all the inhabitants, he described the unknown lands in vivid detail, naming all the various tribes and tributaries. The Indians covered their mouths in token of their admiring surprise and confessed that they had hidden the truth from La Salle "because they desired to have him always with them." This admission "gave the French back their courage," and they were further heartened by meetings with other tribes. When the natives learned that there were Frenchmen in the area equipped with a forge, they came often to the fort to have their tools repaired. La Salle liked to say that a blacksmith "turned more steel into beaver than the Jesuits turn natives into Christians,"[26] and he always took care that the Indians were well-received. He made them his allies by giving them needles and awls for piercing leather, which he drew from his large store of presents. When, as often happened, the French did not understand the Indian language, their visitors would communicate with drawings, and each time they confirmed that the river was perfectly navigable. An Indian chief who had traveled a hundred leagues out of the west to visit them displayed a horse's hoof hanging from his belt; this caused great celebration among the young men of La Salle's party, who could already see themselves galloping down the road to fortune, for the visitors unanimously boasted of the great quantity of beaver and other fur to be found in the Mississippi country.

The good news only heightened La Salle's disappointment at being unable to build a boat. It would be impossible to transport this wealth of furs without one. And if the Indians' hostility were ever aroused, La Salle confided to Tonty, and they were forced to flee, a vessel able to hold thirty men could offer them protection. La Salle eventually decided to try sawing planks himself with the help of a "willing-hearted" man. Luckily, the deserters had left one of their saws, an impressive tool, more than a yard long, which it took two men to handle. La Salle had often seen the operation performed. He ordered two large sawhorses built, both considerably taller than himself. Then they chose a large oak and chopped it down without much trouble — every Canadian grew up handier with an ax than with a fork; they cut the limbs off carefully and put the trunk on the sawhorses. La Salle took a position on top of the log and his assistant below it, next to one of the trestles, and they started sawing the tree lengthwise, cutting it into even planks. When a second man volunteered, and seemed to manage well enough, La Salle decided to construct a bark, but not one so large as "to frighten the men with the great number of planks."[27] The hull was completed on March 1. But what good to them was a boat that had no sails, rigging, or anchors? The *Griffon* was to have unloaded all these items at Michilimackinac. In order to lose as little time as possible, La Salle decided to set off on foot for Lake Michigan, intending to work out the details of his plan according to the news he received of the *Griffon*. In fact, he meant to return to Fort Frontenac and Montreal to collect the trade goods he was expecting from France and to calm his creditors, who would be alarmed if he were absent too long.

With the boldness of great captains who do the opposite of what would seem reasonable to the common run of men, La Salle now spread out his forces rather than regrouping them. He sent Father Hennepin and two men down the Illinois with instructions to follow the Mississippi upstream toward the north, if possible. Consulting at great length with Tonty on the division of their forces, he decided to retrace his steps towards Lake Michigan taking only five men with him: Nika, La Violette (who had been with him since 1675), Hunaut, Colin, and d'Autray. Tonty was to stay at Crèvecœur and guard the fort.

Each of the three groups was to face a different hardship. Hennepin and his party would run into the Sioux and be captured. Just as they thought they were about to be tortured and killed at the stake, they were miraculously saved by the arrival of the French explorer Duluth, traveling with one of La Salle's former soldiers from Fort Frontenac, Jean Fafard. The rescued party went up the Mississippi as far as Wisconsin and rejoined Lake Michigan via Green Bay. Father Hennepin, whose thirst for exploration and missionary work was quenched once and for all, was happy to learn that he had been recalled to France. He hurried off toward Montreal and Quebec, where Frontenac detained him for a dozen days, wanting to hear a full account of his adventures. Once back in France, Father Hennepin wrote his memoirs which, as they were republished in successive editions, became more and more fantastic. By the edition of 1698, the last to be published during his lifetime, he had discovered the Gulf of Mexico. La Salle never had the chance to read them, but is unlikely to have been offended if he had. From the first meeting he had spoken good humoredly of his companion's imagination: "He is sure to exaggerate everything, it is his character. He has even written to me that he came within an ace of being burned at the stake, although he was never in any danger of it, but he thinks it more honorable to act in this way and what he says accords more with what he wants than with what he knows."[28] Tonty, as we will see later, was forced to flee when the Iroquois invaded the Illinois valley. And La Salle faced the hardships of a spring journey through country lying under Iroquois threat and would be forced to lead a manhunt against men formerly in his employ.

Every season had its drawbacks when traveling the American backcountry: the advantage of crossing frozen rivers and

streams in winter hardly made up for the cold and the difficulty
of hunting; in summer, the heat and mosquitoes weakened even
the strongest men; and autumn, though wonderfully suited to
making trips, was all too brief. But nothing compared to the
hardships of a spring journey. La Salle realized it immediately:
"The river was sheeted with ice too weak to walk on but too solid
to be broken for the bark canoes to pass."[29] The biggest threat
was what he called "false ice," which gave way underfoot. A fall
could mean drowning in the rapid water below. If on a cold
night the stream froze over again, the surface would be so un-
even that walking was awkward and progress slow. As the
weather warmed, the river carried large sheets of ice, which
were dangerous to the canoes, and which the men had to hack
at with their axes. Along the banks, the travelers sank up to their
waists in snow too soft to support their snowshoes. The canoes
were useless, and finally became so cumbersome that they decided to hide them and continue on foot through bogs,
marshes, and torrents. Everything contributed to their suffering: the rain and the sun melted the snow, weighing down sleds
and snowshoes, and making their march even more difficult.
Man and beast stuck in the mud as though it were quicksand —
sometimes they killed a deer or an elk that was unable to free itself from the heavy muck. They took twenty-four days to reach
Fort Saint Joseph and walked 180 miles.

If La Salle had held any hope of seeing the *Griffon* again, the
news at the fort quickly disillusioned him. Nobody, either
Canadian or Indian, had seen the bark. There was no point in
proceeding to Michilimackinac. The lake's black surface was covered with melting ice, too weak to carry a man. Yet La Salle refused to rest or wait for the ice to melt, as it would shortly, and set
off on foot the next day across the peninsula toward Detroit on a
route that whites avoided and that Indians feared. Five or six nations, one more terrible than the next, inhabited the peninsula,
waging constant war on each other.

The route was made harder by the lack of marked paths. In his account, La Salle wrote: "Thorns and brambles tore all our rags and we were hardly recognizable, our faces were so bloodied."[30] To cross a river they would assemble a raft out of branches bound with rushes. Every night they dried their clothes and made themselves new moccasins, as the ones they had never lasted more than a day. Carrying too much already to further burden themselves with food — a traveler had to have a set of spare clothes, a kettle, an axe, a gun, and powder and lead — they nonetheless brought large amounts of leather to protect their feet in the Indian style.

To avoid the risk of meeting hostile Indians, La Salle took a gamble: he and his men used their guns to hunt despite the fact that it would signal their presence to every band of Indians in the woods. As though carelessly, they left the carcasses of butchered animals behind them, hoping to pass for a powerful Iroquois party, so sure of their strength that they traveled without bothering to take precautions. To complete the masquerade, they posted charcoal drawings of human figures on tree trunks at regular intervals to represent their prisoners, and drew scalplocks to indicate the number of their scalped prisoners. The Iroquois, in fact, advertised their feats with hieroglyphics of this sort.

The exhaustion of two men, worn out by trudging through vast flooded marshes, in weather so cold their clothes had to be thawed in front of the morning campfire, since, "having been drenched when [they] took them off, they had frozen stiff as sticks,"[31] obliged the party to stop and build a canoe. La Salle and Nika boiled enough water to lift the bark from a large birch tree and built a canoe-stretcher, stiffened with floor plates and reinforced at fragile points and at the seams with peeled elm bark, which served as a sort of tar. La Salle considered the canoe so sturdy that he boasted it could perform "a journey of four or five hundred leagues in weather that would endanger a good shallop." But he had no need to go so far. His compass had not misled him, and suddenly the stream they were following came out into the strait joining Lake Huron and Lake Erie.

La Salle once again split up his forces. As the lake was navigable, he sent his two weak men to Michilimackinac, hoping against hope that they would find some news of his boat. He, with Nika and the other two Frenchmen, crossed the strait on a raft. Strong headwinds prevented them from traveling on Lake Erie, however, and they followed the northern shore of the lake on foot. Two men — Nika, who had always been so vigorous, and another Frenchman — were overcome with weariness at the hard progress through the woods, drowned in rain and runoff. Having come down with high fevers and an inflammation of the chest, they were spitting blood. La Salle gave them his last potions of *orviétan*, a harmless mixture of vegetable pulp and honey, brought at great expense from Europe. With the last well man, he put together a new canoe, loaded the sick aboard, and crossed the lake to the Niagara River.

By way of reward for this horrendous journey of more than six hundred miles, he arrived at the fort to find it had burned to the ground. All the living quarters were gone and only the storehouse was still standing. In addition, he received disquieting reports about his business interests. The ship bringing him a cargo of merchandise from Europe had foundered in the Gulf of Quebec; the *Griffon* lay at the bottom of Lake Michigan; his creditors were setting up a hue and cry of distress. La Salle left the men who had come with him, all three "completely done in," and gave orders for them to return to Fort Crèvecœur as soon as possible with canoes full of arms, ammunition, and trade goods. They were to go by way of Michilimackinac and pick up the men they had left at the site of Detroit. He for his part would leave immediately with three new men, in driving rain, to cross the last seventy leagues separating him from Fort Frontenac. At the level of tiredness at which he must have been operating, he was no longer drawing strength from his muscles but from his nerves; his endurance was all mental. An obsession as intense as his was only a step from madness, and nothing is more moving than La Salle's awareness that he could easily skid from one to the other:

"I have to prove to you that I am not mad,"[32] he wrote on arrival to one of his creditors in Paris.

After all the effort, the weariness, the disappointments, he was finally welcomed at Fort Frontenac with a smile. A woman waited for him, to console and encourage him. Her name was Madeleine — Madeleine de Roybon d'Allonne. She was born in France, at Montargis. No longer in the first flower of youth, she was just three years younger than La Salle. Why she came to Canada alone is unclear, unless it was to find a husband. Her minor title of nobility was on a scale with La Salle's, and he had given her some land around the fort. There was no question that he was interested in her, but he could not very well marry just as he was preparing to leave on his great voyage. The topic intrigued people enough for one of his creditors in Paris to ask about it. "I am told," La Salle answered, "that you have been uneasy about my supposed marriage. I shall not make any engagement of the sort until I have given you reason to be satisfied with me. It is a little extraordinary that I must render an account of something that everyone may do quite freely."[33] Perhaps, but then everything concerned with La Salle was extraordinary.[34]

One would like to think that his desire to see her was partly responsible for the insane energy he showed on this frightening voyage. Mademoiselle d'Allonne knew La Salle well enough not to keep him from turning to his affairs immediately. He had to find money. His creditors had in fact seized his pelts at Fort Frontenac, with his brother's help, and sold them for their own account in Montreal. But La Salle was not yet beaten. He embarked in his canoe and surprised the merchants in Montreal by arriving there and confronting all who had intrigued against him. His ability to communicate his own conviction was so great that he found new lenders. And it was difficult to resist him. Canadians recognized endurance when they saw it, and they knew that shipwreck was a mishap that could happen to any of them. La Salle's exploits were impressive enough that they agreed to refinance him. Besides, the potential payoff was too attractive not to accept the risk. In barely a week he had collected the funds he needed and returned to Fort Frontenac, where Mademoiselle d'Allonne showed her trust by lending him 2,141 livres.

He was prepared to leave on July 22, 1680, when three men arrived by canoe bringing disastrous news. They were inhabitants of Fort Frontenac who had heard from coureurs de bois in the Niagara area that Fort Crèvecœur had been abandoned. While Tonty was away helping the Illinois to fortify a certain rock, the blacksmith, the carpenters, and the wood-cutters had vented their rage on the fort and left it in ruins, first taking all the tools, firearms, and food. Following the course La Salle had taken, they went on to ravage the fort at Saint Joseph and the storehouse at Niagara. There were about twenty mutineers. Eight of them were heading toward Albany, and the others were paddling up the lake in three canoes to murder La Salle, which seemed the surest way of avoiding punishment. His colonists had returned as quickly as possible to warn him. La Salle, it now turned out, knew how to play cops and robbers.

He left with nine men in two canoes to wait in Quinte Bay, which was hidden behind a point of land. Four men stood watch. They signaled the approach of two canoes, traveling fairly distant from one another. When the first one was about to pass the point, La Salle charged out to meet it. He stood balanced in the canoe while his men paddled furiously, his gun leveled at the traitors. When they saw this, the deserters gave themselves up without a struggle. The second boat followed suit, offering no resistance either. La Salle's party brought "these rogues" back to the prison in the fort and set out again to intercept the third canoe. The last set of deserters, however, were on the alert and managed to land with their guns and hide, each behind a tree, ready to fire. La Salle wanted to avoid a frontal attack. As dusk came on and he considered surprising the enemy from the rear, the mutineers made a break for their canoe. There was a short chase; the pursuers came within gunshot. La Salle ordered the deserters to surrender, but they refused. Guns were fired on both sides. Two traitors fell dead into the water; the three others went to join their comrades in prison. La Salle stayed icily calm. He finished his preparations for departure and, without waiting for the governor to arrive, left on August 22, 1680, with a new crew of workmen, heading for the Illinois valley. Since everything had to be started over, he started over.

❖ 9 ❖

Indian Territory

1680–1682

THE EXPEDITION AUGURED WELL. La Salle had received fresh financing, and his new company numbered twenty-five men. Among them were the shipwrights and sawyers essential to his plan, a surgeon, and La Forest — the administrator at Fort Frontenac, whose experience and energy had always served La Salle well. The route was better known now. And La Salle's firm hand with the deserters had impressed and reassured his men, who sang as they paddled vigorously toward the south, full of confidence. La Salle, though, seemed preoccupied. Warnings had reached him from all sides that there was trouble brewing once again among the Indian tribes. The rumors were to prove well-founded, and the year 1680–1681 unfolded under the sign of the Indian. La Salle would not play the part of explorer so much as of ambassador to the Indian nations.

The threat once again came from the Iroquois, who were more warlike and had a stronger political organization than any other Canadian Indians. They occupied the area south of Lake Ontario where the states of New York and Pennsylvania are today, and were settled in permanent fortified villages, where they lived a more complex and stable existence than the nomadic or purely hunter-gatherer tribes elsewhere. The secret of their power lay not so much in knowing how to till the soil as in the close affiliation of the five nations comprising the confederation. Their policies, the outcome of a true political process, were determined at councils where delegates from all the nations assembled. The unity of this alliance, called the League of Five Nations, gave it a power and strength that were felt far into the eighteenth century. White settlers feared the Iroquois, but other Indians feared them even more. La Salle had always enjoyed good relations with the chiefs of the Iroquois villages along the shores of Lake Ontario, but he harbored few illusions as to their character. "They are politically minded, wily, treacherous, vindictive, and cruel to their enemies, whom they burn on a slow fire with incredible torment," he wrote his friend Thouret in Paris. Between 1640 and 1660, they imposed a reign of terror on the colony of New France, and annihilated the Hurons, who were closely allied to the French. Their constant attacks ravaged the Jesuit missions around the Great Lakes and made martyrs of several missionaries. The Iroquois threat that hung over Montreal and even Quebec would have paralyzed the colony if Louis XIV had not sent an entire regiment to the rescue in 1665. With the help of a strong local militia, they succeeded in reestablishing peace. The Iroquois, now respectful of French military strength, no longer attacked the northern tribes under French protection. Instead they turned their attention to their immediate neighbors, and, in 1677, in spite of their small number, the 2,500 warriors of the League crushed a tribe in Virginia. The fear at present was that "to find a use for their weapons" they would turn on the tribes of the west, the Miami and the Illinois. La Salle's final advice to Tonty had been "to declare himself neither for one nor for the other, as it was not right to break the laws of hospitality and go to war with the Illinois, who had received them so well, nor to take sides against the Iroquois, which might touch off a war against Canada."[1]

As to where and in what condition Tonty might be, La Salle had received no word. Worried about his lieutenant and impatient to reach Michilimackinac where there might be news of him, he decided to take a shortcut overland while the main body of his men continued on to Niagara and the straits at the head of Lake Erie under La Forest's sure and efficient command. La Salle landed near present-day Toronto and took the short but very difficult route over the mountains to Lake Simcoe — clearly not the path for heavily loaded men with canoes — and on into Lake Huron. From there he sped straight to Michilimackinac where d'Autray was waiting for him, along with the other men who had been left at Niagara the previous spring. Rumors that the Iroquois were on the move circulated up and down the shores of Lake Michigan. They had been seen on the rivers south of Lake Erie headed toward the Illinois country. There was even the suggestion that they were trying to divide the Illinois from the Miami so as not to have to attack the two nations at once, as "the first were highly valiant" and the second, who were great runners, "very quick and apt to prepare surprises."[2] Once his men had all assembled, La Salle went down Lake Michigan to Fort Saint Joseph.

He left La Forest there with the men he would need to rebuild the fort, and headed toward the Kankakee with Nika, d'Autray, and five other Frenchmen along the trail they had traveled the previous winter. Then it had been cold and the area deserted of animals, whereas now, at the beginning of November, the prairie offered a peaceful view of all its riches. What a blissful experience it must have been, particularly for the new members of the party, to float down a quiet river while buffalo grazed, fat and contented, on the shore. The fear of hunger, always at the back of the travelers' minds, gradually receded. La Salle and Nika were the only ones who worried that the Illinois had apparently not organized their big buffalo drives that year or set any fires. It seemed strange that there were no hunters in the area. They kept a sharp eye on the trees along shore, where Tonty would certainly have carved messages if he had been obliged to flee eastward, but they saw nothing.

Judging that it was best to take advantage of the plentiful

game, La Salle decided to fill the canoes with food. They made camp and the men were treated to a hunt, New-World style. A dozen buffalo, a dozen deer, as well as scores of geese and swans soon lay heaped around camp. For three days they plucked and gutted and skinned the animals, whose flesh was then dried and smoked in the Indian way and carefully stowed in the canoes on a bed of dried rushes. Afterward, they resumed their gliding descent toward the great Indian village. The silence, punctuated by the too frequent howling of wolves, worked on the party's nerves, as did the emptiness of the woods, where there should have been Indians roaming. At last, at a bend in the river where only the year before had stood row after row of lodges, the men saw what filled even the most hardened among them with dread. A cry of horror went up from the lead canoe. "Nothing was left to show the former extent of the village but a few ends of burnt poles. On most of them, the heads of dead men had been stuck and eaten by crows."[3] In the fields and the surrounding area, there were half-devoured corpses, skeletons pulled from ransacked graves, strips of flesh ripped away by wolves, whose moans could be heard in the distance. Crows and vultures, temporarily disturbed, circled slowly over the Frenchmen's heads.

La Salle's concern on landing was for Tonty. Alone, he walked toward the carnage and made himself look closely at the disfigured faces, one after another, to see if there were any he recognized. The only clue was the kind of hair hanging from the fractured skulls. He concluded the hair was too coarse and too short to have belonged to Europeans. A few feet from the former perimeter of the village, however, he found six stakes set in the ground. They had been painted red, and on each was drawn the figure of a man in black with his eyes blindfolded. It could mean that the marauders had found the French a short way off and either massacred them or taken them prisoner.

Night was falling, and it was cold enough that night for the men to keep the fire going until morning. La Salle, too upset to sleep, pondered the situation. He decided to continue on with d'Autray, Nika, and also Hunaut and Yon — two men he had known well for a long time — and to leave the other three on an island with the trade goods. He advised them to store their provisions in wooden boxes lined with bark in case they were forced by the cold and snow to spend the winter there, and to hide the boxes in a hole dug in the side of a hill. Then, not knowing what they would find, La Salle and his companions went on toward Crèvecœur, whose name offered a sad premonition. They found the fort in ruins, but the boat they had built with so much effort hardly seemed damaged. A mysterious inscription was engraved on the planking: WE ARE ALL SAVAGES, ON THIS 15 A... 1680. They continued down the river, although everywhere in the surrounding countryside they saw evidence of the horrible cruelty the Iroquois had inflicted on the fleeing Illinois. Kettles filled with the half-eaten limbs of captives, and corpses of women and children, spitted and roasted, peopled their nightmares. La Salle stopped at every turn, landed, and examined the dead for the least trace of information, dreading to see some remnant of blond or fine hair. Finally, they reached the Big River, the Mississippi, about which he had so often dreamed.

There was no mistaking it. The river was not terribly wide at this point, but it definitely flowed south and the Illinois entered it at a sharp angle, which agreed with all the descriptions. The macabre signs of massacres and orgies were finally behind them, and the clear strong current at the confluence of the waters seemed to invite them on a voyage. Giving free rein to their enthusiasm, d'Autray, "a wise and courageous young man," Hunaut, and Yon proposed that they go down to the sea. But La Salle refused, though moved by their courage and "their affection" (after all, they had not lost heart at the sight of so many atrocities). Having finally arrived at the river he had devoted so much effort to reaching, this great visionary refused out of caution and a sense of honor. "It would be an act of rashness or despair," he told them, to undertake this voyage when they were so few and so poorly armed. More importantly, "he could not stop searching for the Sieur de Tonty until he discovered what had become of him."[4] They would make the voyage the following year "in greater safety." Before heading back, he left a general delivery message for Tonty according to the custom of the wilderness. There was a small tree growing from the rocks at the confluence of the two rivers — it was impossible to miss. La Salle nailed to it a tablet he had brought for that purpose, and drew his canoe and a calumet to show that he wanted peace, also attaching a letter for Tonty. He wanted his lieutenant to know that the French were going back up the Illinois and that they would leave a cache for him at Crèvecœur containing hatchets, knives, and "a few other things that he would need if he were with the savages." This system must have been tested earlier; La Salle was certain that if an Indian passed that way he would carry the letter to the Iroquois' prisoner. A Frenchman was always drawn with "short legs, a big beard, and carrying a gun."[5] For Tonty, he drew an iron hand.

It was now late in the season, and ice would be forming at any moment. Losing no time, the little team started back toward the village. They paddled day and night, traveling 250 miles in three and a half days, and rejoined the others of their party barely in time. A frost hit the area so hard that the river froze in a single night, something never before seen. The canoes were turned into sleds. The stores of food and trade goods were divided up, as La Salle wanted to cache a portion for Tonty or for his own return the following year. These housekeeping details, so important to survival in the woods, were interrupted one night when the sky was unusually clear by the extraordinary appearance of a comet. It was bright with a large tail, and swept its long vaporous trail across the night sky. Comets were said to bring bad luck, and this one terrified Norman peasants, courtiers at Versailles, and farmers in the Saint Lawrence valley; probably it frightened the Iroquois chiefs too. But La Salle was not superstitious: in the midst of the forest he remembered his schoolmasters' astronomy lessons and, wrapped in his long cloak, he observed the phenomenon with the most detached scientific curiosity. Using his astrolabe, he was able to measure the height of the celestial object on the horizon, and he made exact notes as to its characteristics and the time of its appearances.

On the day after Christmas, La Salle resumed the role of explorer and prepared to break camp. His plan was to reach Fort Saint Joseph and from there, since the expedition was in any case delayed, to go on to Fort Frontenac and Montreal to see to his affairs. He had lost none of his confidence in his ability to deal with the Indians, in spite of the events of recent weeks. Wanting to leave nothing undone that might help find Tonty, he set fire to the huts they were leaving behind. He hoped to attract any Indians in the area to ask them if they had seen a Frenchman with an iron hand somewhere in the wilderness; also to let them know of his own movements so that they would not follow his tracks, taking him for an enemy. It proved a useless precaution: the countryside was deserted.

They set off, but decided to follow the Illinois River, as they had found no clues to Tonty's movements while on the Kankakee two months before. This time, they made the right choice. While La Salle was investigating an abandoned hut, he found a small board that had been cut with a saw. It proved beyond a doubt that a Frenchman had been there. Judging from the evidence, La Salle guessed he had passed there two months before. The dates agreed. Relieved, he pushed on toward Fort Saint Joseph. A heavy, soft snow started to fall, making the going hard. It stayed suspended in the grasses so that snowshoes were useless, and it continued to accumulate for nineteen days. La Salle, who cleared the trail for his men summer and winter, sank up to his waist despite his long legs; he could make a path for himself only by pushing the snow aside with his body. At nightfall, they stamped down a few square feet of the snow in order to lie down. On a lucky day they might find wood for a fire, but they never found the bark that would have allowed them to make shelters. To protect themselves from the strong winds that blew day and night, they slept like dogs in holes dug into the snow. They arrived at Fort Saint Joseph at the end of January 1681, their faces cracked by frost and partly blackened, their lips raw and bleeding. La Salle was not in the habit of complaining, but he admitted that he had never been so cold in all his life.

Seeing the fort restored helped bolster their spirits, particularly as La Salle more often saw his forts in ruin than in working order. La Forest had repaired the buildings and cleared a large area around the fort; the carpenter was well along in the construction of a boat for sailing on the Great Lakes. The events of the last months had convinced La Salle that it was senseless to establish forts and trading posts along the Illinois or Mississippi as long as the Iroquois were hostile. Their cruel campaign against the Illinois had alienated French sympathies from them, and a shake-up in the pattern of alliances was due. It was impossible to colonize the region, even in the superficial way the French planned, without promising to provide the nations that welcomed them protection against such savage attacks. La Salle then conceived the idea of bringing together the western tribes in a defensive league against the Iroquois, forming an association that would be partly feudal and partly commercial in nature, and which he would direct from the Illinois valley. He began immediately putting his project into effect, turning to the Miamis who occupied the area just inland from Fort Saint Joseph.

A few facts about the Indian world have to be kept in mind in order to make sense of La Salle's actions. The first is the small number of native people. The largest nations could muster more than two thousand warriors, but most tribes comprised only a few hundred men and some had even fewer. A second factor is that the boundaries between the tribes were relatively fluid. The random element introduced by captives, chance meetings, and roving hunting parties allowed La Salle to make contact with a group if ever he wanted to, and the language barrier, so serious a problem during the first voyage, was never mentioned afterward. In La Salle's immediate entourage there were three Indians:

Nika, who was a Shawnee from the Ohio valley; Ouiouilamet, the son of a chief from a village near Boston, "a wise and cautious man" who had been with La Salle for two years; and a third, a faithful follower since the days of the *Griffon* shipyard, where he had kept the men supplied with bear and deer meat. These young men gathered information for La Salle, negotiated on his behalf, and formed a kind of living proof of his good faith. Finally, men and news traveled farther and more rapidly than one would imagine. Seventeenth-century Europe was cloistered and static — completely different. French peasants were ignorant and oblivious to events outside their villages. They were a sedentary people without the benefit of the telephone. But in the nomadic American wilderness, events had repercussions that extended thousands of miles. After the English won a bloody victory in New England, defeating the Abenaki and Mohican tribes led by an Indian chief known as King Philip, Indians fled to the southern part of Lake Michigan, at the very doors of Fort Saint Joseph, a thousand miles away as the crow flies. La Salle would draw advantage from these involuntary allies.

The defeated Indians, whose tribes had been annihilated by the English, were obliged to join the Illinois, Iroquois, or Miami peoples who together controlled the region. Ouiouilamet, speaking in La Salle's name, persuaded them to join the Miamis so as to receive protection from the French. With the revival of the Iroquois threat, other more distant nations also sent emissaries to Fort Saint Joseph to declare their partisanship with the French. La Salle, glad to be valued as an ally, accepted alliances but was careful to specify the limits and conditions of his backing. To a Shawnee chief, for instance, who commanded one hundred and fifty warriors in the Ohio valley, La Salle sent the message "that his country was too distant and inaccessible to agree to his request, but that if the chief cared to help him find the mouth of the Mississippi, he could protect him from the Iroquois and his other enemies. The chief agreed to the proposal and sent word he would arrive at the end of autumn for the great departure."[6]

Encouraged by the success of his diplomatic efforts, La Salle decided to return to the Illinois country, where he expected to find the survivors of the Iroquois attack. He wanted to bring them news of his plans and ensure their participation in his alliance. On March 1, he left the fort followed by Nika and Hunaut. The weather was fine and dry, ideal for snowshoeing, and the party made rapid progress over the frozen snow. La Salle refused to wear Indian sunglasses, an unwieldy contraption made of slitted bits of wood, and the strong reflection off the snow "in the open countryside" provoked a bout of "snow sickness," the same painful blinding he had experienced many times before. He was forced to stop while Nika and Hunaut went looking for pine needles with which to soothe the pain. They returned several hours later with unaccustomed shouting and laughter. Their joyful news, coming at a time when La Salle had stopped expecting word of Tonty, was that they had met Indians who told them that Tonty was alive and living with the Pottawatamies, the tribe on Lake Michigan whose chief had been so charmed by Frontenac. Furthermore, Hennepin, Acault, and the man from Picardy had been seen in Green Bay.

Relieved of the worry that had gripped him for three months, La Salle had the feeling that the whole world was smiling on him. He quickly regained his sight. The snow and ice had melted and his men had built a canoe to descend the unblocked river. They arrived at the ruined Illinois village several days later. A dozen of the Illinois, having returned to the wreckage, recognized La Salle and approached him eagerly and told him the story of their defeat and Tonty's bravery. Taking our cue from them, let us go back a bit and reconstruct with La Salle Tonty's epic.

It was in March 1680 that Tonty returned from an expedition to find Fort Crèvecœur destroyed in the wake of a mutiny. The men had run away leaving the inscription that so intrigued La Salle:

WE ARE ALL SAVAGES. Stripped of everything but the forge and their weapons, Tonty's party, consisting of Tonty himself, three young men, two Recollet friars, old man La Ribourde, and Zénobe Membré, had no recourse but to ask the Illinois for protection and to "feed from their kettle."[7] Conditions were bad. Tonty spoke no Indian language, and besides, a show of weakness was sure to elicit brutality from the natives. The priests somehow managed to understand that La Salle had been killed. By September, Tonty's party had decided to go back to the Great Lakes. Their departure was ill-timed. On the very morning of the day they planned to leave, some young Illinois reported seeing an Iroquois war party advancing on them. It was a large army of 600 men, and what was worse news for Tonty, a Jesuit was leading them. In actuality, it was an Indian dressed in a black hat and a long cloak. But the news, though false, added to the fact the French were leaving, confirmed the Illinois' suspicions: Tonty and his men were traitors. Terrified and enraged, the Indians converged on Tonty with the intention of massacring him. Although Tonty had met an Indian for the first time only the year before and spoke no Illinois, he understood perfectly from the furious looks on their faces, the sound of their frenzied voices, and the rain of blows he had to fend off that his life hung by a thread. According to Father Zénobe, "he was full of strength and intelligence." He managed in fact to make the Illinois chief understand that he would fight at his side. "To make you see that I am not a friend of the Iroquois," he wrote, reconstructing the dialogue in his narrative, "I will die tomorrow with you, and I will fight against them with all the young men that I have here."[8] A great feast followed, and soon the enemy camps were advancing toward each other. Tonty showed admirable cool. Not rattled by the wild clamoring and yelling and contortions from both sides, Tonty accepted the Illinois chief's proposal that he act as go-between in "offering a wampum necklace" to the attacker. The chief had little faith in his band's chances of surviving an armed encounter. Tonty would have balked at the mission had he been any less noble in character for, he admitted, "I knew no Iroquois. Nonetheless, in the hope of finding a captive among them who might understand me, I took a necklace of porcelain beads and went to them."[9] Things started badly. An overzealous Indian plunged a knife "into his left breast," while another seized him by the hair with such rage that Tonty half hoped they would fracture his skull so that he might avoid burning. But the chiefs, anxious not to encourage aggression against a Frenchman, brought their warriors under control. They threw down the necklace and told Tonty to have the Illinois ask for peace themselves. The negotiations lasted several days. Tonty was not present when they ended, however. One morning, the Iroquois chief took him by the arm and said "Go away" in a tone that made the French realize that "there would be no more mercy" for them. They left by canoe the next day, the chief having first asked for "a letter for the Comte de Frontenac, by which he might know that they had not killed us." La Salle did not need to hear more. Back in December, at the Illinois village, he had seen what the Iroquois could do. But now it was spring again and the Iroquois were gone; the Illinois, though greatly weakened, had returned to their villages to resume life.

La Salle then explained his plan for an alliance with other tribes. He expressed his disgust with the Iroquois and described the benefits the Illinois would receive by coming under French protection again. He won his listeners over by his eloquence, and they assured him they would get the approval of their elders. Without waiting, La Salle headed back the way he had come to Fort Saint Joseph. Once there, his first care was to send a canoe up the western shore of Lake Michigan to collect Tonty from the Pottawattamies and instruct him to wait at Michilimackinac. He planned to stay on at Fort Saint Joseph long enough to see the wheat planted, along with corn, peas, cabbage, and beans. He wanted, as he said, "to bring increase to the desert."[10] He also wanted to make certain of his newfound allies' friendship by going up the river a dozen miles to a Miami village where he had been invited by the Indians.

Immediately on his arrival, he had a chance to demonstrate the extent of his authority, and the incident enhanced his reputation more than weeks of powwowing. Living in the village were three Iroquois warriors who behaved insolently and, more seriously, spoke of the French with contempt. La Salle walked toward them coolly and, talking loud and clear, gave them to understand his dissatisfaction in such terms that they took off into the woods without stopping to collect their possessions — beaver pelts, as it turned out. The effect on the Miamis was phenomenal. It also had an effect on the peoples from Rhode Island, New York, and Virginia who had come to swell the initial core of refugees from New England and now gladly accepted the protection of the Great King, which La Salle had offered separately to each tribe. He then sent to the fort for the presents he needed to give his words weight, and asked the Miami to convene a great council.

One has to picture this native of Normandy, the former schoolboy from a Jesuit college (where he had received the most refined, subtle, and abstract education), this man who had seen his first Indian at the age of twenty-two, as he took his place in the lodge of the Miami chieftain. The bark partitions had been removed so that all could hear him. Standing very straight, surrounded by ten Frenchmen, the New England natives, and thirty Loups, he prepared to show why he was rightly known as the greatest orator in North America. He needed no interpreter, and could speak in the Indian style, using its images and metaphors, without losing the Cartesian thread of his own thought. He first presented the Miami a series of seven gifts to honor the dead; among them fifty hatchets to erect "a magnificent tomb for their deceased relatives," and thirty sword blades to make a steel palisade in defense of the tomb. Then, in a solemn declaration, he announced his intention not only to honor the dead but to bring the greatest among them, Ouabicolcata, back to life. La Salle described this resurrection in the most natural terms, as though it were not totally inconceivable to him as a good Christian.

"Do not believe," he said, "that Ouabicolcata is dead. His spirit and his soul are in my body; I bring his name back to life. He is no longer dead, he lives and his family shall lack for nothing."[11] Acting in the guise of the resurrected man, he offered three large kettles to show his goodwill, as it was reasonable for the late deceased to celebrate his return to life with a feast. In a further gesture of generosity he distributed twenty greatcoats, twenty shirts, twenty blankets, and a case filled with knives, nails, and needles, all brought from the other world. The audience noisily sounded its approval. By gaining the natives' confidence, using their own language — and not, like the missionaries, trying to teach them ideas totally foreign to them — La Salle managed to win them over. He wanted the Miamis and the Illinois to be united in friendship in order to provide the French a solid base of support in the region. The only way of persuading them was to show them the power of the French, and nobody could do this better than their newly revived hero, Ouabicolcata, speaking from the mouth of the man who incarnated him and — to be on the safe side — now offered them the last and largest of his gifts, a set of six guns:

> I am now French and ask for justice only from the master of the French. He who is my master, and the master of all this country, is a mighty chief, feared by the whole world. He is powerful and he wishes his words to be obeyed. He is called the King of France, the mightiest among the chiefs beyond the great water. His goodness extends even to our dead. His subjects come among you to bring the dead to life. He wishes to protect his subjects, but he also wishes you to obey their laws and to make no war without leave from the one who represents him in Quebec. Therefore live in peace with your neighbors, and above all with the Illinois. You have had causes of quarrel with them; their losses have sufficiently avenged you. They ask to make peace with you. Be content with the glory of having obliged them to ask for it. Be of my mind, and use these guns that I have given you only to hunt and to defend yourselves.[12]

The effect of his speech surpassed even La Salle's hopes. The Miamis held dances and feasts for him and covered him with wampum necklaces. He could now take comfort in knowing that the Indians would support his next expedition, and he prepared to face his usual problems — holding his creditors at bay, procuring the merchandise he needed, assembling carpenters, sawyers, and loyal soldiers. This would require him to make the long return trip to Fort Frontenac and Montreal. He loaded his canoes and headed up Lake Michigan, happily finding Tonty at Michilimackinac. Tonty confirmed the story that the Illinois had told and narrated the last part of his trials. On the abrupt orders of the Iroquois, he had left the village and started toward Lake Michigan, but he was so sure La Salle had been murdered that he left no indication of the path he had taken. At a rest halt the old priest, La Ribourde, went off a short distance to say Mass "to distract himself" and never came back. They searched for him for two days without result. He was killed by Kickapoo Indians, and his scalp turned up later in Green Bay. The five survivors reached Lake Michigan on All Saints' Day in 1680, but they emerged on the Chicago side. La Salle was opposite them at Fort Saint Joseph, and they missed each other. Tonty and his party started up the west shore of the lake, where their inexperience almost cost them their lives. Unable to hunt, they were reduced to chewing on leather from the coat of poor Ribourde and went around hopelessly in circles. They were preparing to die "in the warmth of a hut" when some natives saw their fire and came to their rescue. That winter was spent in a Pottawatami village, and in the spring they learned from a coureur de bois that not only was La Salle alive but that he had made several voyages on land and around the lake looking for them.

It is easy to guess that La Salle was not demonstrative. "I am wanting in expansiveness and show of feeling toward those I am with because of natural timidity, and because of this defect I have chosen a life more in step with my solitary disposition."[13] But his joy at seeing Tonty was evident, and the two friends were soon paddling together toward Fort Frontenac.

❖ 10 ❖

The Mississippi River

1681–1682

THE CONTEMPORARY TRAVELER TIRES following in La Salle's foot-steps. Walking from Chicago to Montreal once is still within rea-son, but to repeat the journey every year, as La Salle had been doing since 1679, is inconceivable. Certainly, he had grown famil-iar with the terrain and knew the rivers and trails, but the effort required was still enormous. Doubting the need for these re-peated trips, one of La Salle's biographers has compared the ex-plorer to a plumber who keeps having to run back to his shop to fetch a tool he has forgotten — only in this case the shop is over a thousand miles from the worksite.[1]

Actually, La Salle had two reasons for wanting to stay in contact with the people and government of the colony, despite the great difficulty of doing so. The first was his debts. Experience had shown him that being absent for a prolonged period made him highly vulnerable. At the slightest crisis of confidence, his credi-tors would seize his property and drive him to the brink of ruin. He was well aware that their support was conditional, and that his partnerships were growing more tenuous as he advanced in his enterprise. The merchants were delighted to have access to the

Great Lakes market, but at the prospect that goods might some day be exported down the Mississippi, they bridled — in particular, Le Ber and La Chesnaye, two of the most powerful among them. These men had bought from the king the right to transport furs through Canada and they viewed any attempt to open another door for trade with suspicion. They played a perverse role, providing support for La Salle, but at the same time reserving the right to withdraw it at will. Furthermore, there was no one in Montreal to watch over La Salle's interests, and what made his position all the more precarious was that neither the provincial administrator nor the Jesuits were protecting him. On the contrary.

The second motive for his repeated journeys was his relationship with the governor. Frontenac had supported La Salle unstintingly since his arrival in Quebec. He grasped the full political and commercial import of La Salle's enterprise, but he had profited so greatly from their partnership that he was obliged to remain in the shadows. He was watched. His commercial activities, his annual trips on Lake Ontario, his stays at Fort Frontenac, all of which brought him obvious and unlawful gains, were reported down to the last detail by the new provincial administrator, Duchesneau, who hated Frontenac. The Jesuits also commented harshly to the minister on Frontenac's activities. La Salle could never have made the progress he did in opposing the Iroquois and cementing an alliance of the western tribes if he had not been certain of the governor's rock-solid support. But face-to-face meetings were essential. The question of whether or not to return never arose: La Salle had to go back and explain his enterprise in precise detail.

The setbacks of the year before had made him abandon the idea of building a decked ship. He had learned at his own expense how costly such a project could be. Specialized artisans had to be transported to a worksite in the middle of the wilderness, where they stood up poorly to the inevitable challenges. And the supply line to bring in the necessary hardware was very unreliable. Rather than throwing away large sums of money unnecessarily, La Salle now wanted to reach the mouth of the Mississippi as quickly as possible. Building and manning forts would only slow him down. He had to fulfill his mission of discovery within the time allotted. The concession granted him by the king was for five years, starting May 12, 1678. He had no time to lose.

He received every possible assurance of Frontenac's continued support in the course of a long conversation with Barrois, the governor's secretary. La Salle had known and respected Barrois since the two crossed the Atlantic together in 1678. La Salle then drew up a will in favor of his cousin François du Plet, whose loans had allowed him to keep his property at Fort Frontenac. Mademoiselle d'Allonne renewed her credit to him, and, in September 1681, La Salle left again with about thirty men.

He chose not to go by the easier route through Lake Erie, because the Iroquois were restive and, being very numerous along the southern shore, were likely to set ambushes. He had his entire party take the difficult Toronto portage to Lake Huron. The Indians accompanying them came down with fevers, and La Salle took advantage of the forced halts to write a long letter to his friend Thouret, narrating everything that had happened since 1680. He ended it as follows: "I have a hundred other things to write you, but you would not believe how hard this is to do among the Indians. To get them to make the portage, I have to speak to them continually and submit to their constant pestering, or they will do nothing I ask. This page has taken more than twenty sittings to write. I hope to write you more at leisure next year and tell you the outcome of this business, which I hope will turn out well, as I have Monsieur de Tonty with me, who is very willing, and thirty good Frenchmen, plus more than a hundred Shawnee and New England Indians who are all able to use guns."[2] He was alluding to the new allies waiting for him at the other end of Lake Michigan, who would be more useful, he hoped, than the Illinois, "whom," he claimed, "the bounty of their country has made lazier than any other Indians in America."[3]

The important new development in the expedition of 1681–1682 was, in fact, the recruitment of Indians. The Canadians all knew that the Indians could not be induced to perform regular work in the colony. Men who let themselves die when forced to live like Europeans could never be made workers. The Jesuits and the Ursuline nuns reported cases of Indian children who wasted away and died when they were kept shut up in a classroom. "Young Indian girls," wrote Mother Marie de l'Incarnation, "cannot be constrained, for when they are, they grow melancholy. We find [them] docile and intelligent, but when we least expect it they climb over the fence — like squirrels — and run away into the woods."[4] Even in the woods, the Europeans could rarely count on the Indians' perseverance. La Salle alone was always able to talk them into finishing a task once they had started it — though only by going to great lengths and always thanks to the good offices of his faithful Nika. He had also learned to his cost that Europeans were just as unreliable in the woods. He was quite sure, however, that he could persuade the Indians to participate in a long-term effort. "He had a great talent [for making the Indians understand him]," wrote the Abbé Bernou. "He knew all their ways and obtained everything that he wanted from them through his skill, his eloquence, and because he was greatly revered by them."[5] When he arrived at Fort Saint Joseph a little before Christmas, he had already lost five Frenchmen, one of them an interpreter: "[They] had taken flight and hidden in a river, because they feared the hardships of the voyage, as painted to them by La Salle's enemies."[6] One likes to think that he was not surprised.

La Salle now organized the great departure. Tonty was sent ahead with several men as a scouting party to hunt and ready the provisions for the Chicago portage. La Salle stayed on at the fort for a few extra days to hold final discussions with the Indians. All the tribal chieftains who had been won over the previous spring kept their word and sent their men, often accompanied by their wives and children. La Salle strolled among the wigwams, accepting invitations from the chiefs to meals, smoking a long pipe, squatting at their sides, and all the while choosing the men who would accompany him. These Indians, whose blood-curdling yells had wakened the villagers of New England with a start, and who, with bloody scalps dangling from their belts, had danced around their terrified victims, now sat quietly by La Salle, holding forth on his project and negotiating their participation in it. An agreement was easily reached: each man would receive the value of a hundred beavers and contribute half the meat that he got from hunting. They wanted their wives to accompany them to prepare food they liked, and La Salle readily agreed. He knew how useful Indian women could be — they were hardworking, able to carry large loads, skilled at cleaning game, and tireless at the task of gathering food.

The party that set off was practically a floating village, half-French and half-native. On one side were the Indians — painted warriors and squaws, their babies strapped with strips of skin to a small wooden plank, which the women could hang in a tree to have their hands free. On the French side were a notary, a gunsmith, a surgeon, all busy packing the tools of their trade. The two groups eyed each other curiously. Ludicrous questions were asked, which the Recollet Zénobe Membré and La Salle answered patiently before at last giving the signal for departure. On December 28, 1681, the party joined up with Tonty. Winter was at its coldest. The Illinois River was frozen over. The canoes had to be replaced by sleds, which were built on the spot. The men put on harnesses and pulled them like draft animals. La Salle — who was admittedly more energetic than most — claimed that in one day a man could transport 150 pounds a distance of eight or ten leagues (about twenty-five miles) *without tiring*.[7] They found open water on the river at about the height of Fort Crèvecœur, and swapped conveyances again, leaving the sleds behind and taking to canoes. The travelers quickly reached the confluence of the Mississippi and there they had to stop. The great river, coming in from the north, was still solid with ice. The men were heavily laden with provisions and did not take the trouble to hunt in the woods; they saw eagles circling over the water in large numbers. Fish, caught in plain sight between two layers of ice, attracted the birds of prey, which dove at them fiercely but without being able to break through. One morning before sunrise, an underground rumbling was heard. It was the ice shifting in the depths of the riverbed. With the noise of a thunderclap, a first crack ran across the frozen surface, splitting it like lightning in a giant zigzag. A chain reaction followed, and multiple cracks fanned out across the ice, which broke into large blocks. A sunny day melted them, and all of a sudden the river was free. The canoes lined up in single file and, wafted on the gentle current of the Illinois, floated smoothly into the rapid waters of the Mississippi.

Five accounts of this voyage survive, written by La Salle, Father Zénobe, Tonty, a certain Nicolas de La Salle who was not related to Robert, and the notary, Jacques de La Métairie. It is as though the Saint Lawrence had dulled their capacity for surprise and enthusiasm toward any other river: the "Father of Waters" drew not a single exclamation of astonishment from them. With veteran detachment, they take a few words or lines to note the clear water, the high cliffs on the left bank of the river, the vast prairie extending on their right. Nothing more. The pace was swift, and they quickly covered the fifteen miles or so separating them from the mouth of the Missouri.

The Missouri is a swift and turbulent river whose silt-laden waters run violently into the Mississippi. The Illinois enters on the bias, while the Missouri strikes the Mississippi practically at right angles. With no other warning than a low rumble that could have been rapids, the travelers were caught in a muddy torrent parting the transparent waters of the Mississippi. Whole islands floated alongside them, vast chunks torn from the banks and swept down by the river's fury, some with trees still standing on them or leaning over half-uprooted. The canoes spun in the debris of trees and branches, and had it not been for the know-how of men trained on the rapids of Canadian rivers, they would all have spilled into the swirling water. Where the two rivers join, the impact is violent and has always been feared. It takes the rivers ten miles of foaming and turbulent contractions to mix their currents — a modern traveler describes the water there as "all muscle, clenching and unclenching."[8] In our day, boats travel by canal around this dangerous segment, which is at the level of Saint Louis. The only thing that La Salle mentions is that the water of the river, which he calls the Colbert, became so muddy that it made you think twice about drinking from it. He had seen worse.

They traveled swiftly downriver, the current carrying them ever more impetuously as dozens of tributaries fed into it. Farther along, the current would slow and allow the river to meander, looping around itself like a lazily coiled snake, undulating endlessly. The Indian canoe once again performed wonderfully, as it was impervious to one of the river's most insidious dangers — the sandbanks that shift from one bank to the other in reaction to deep currents, setting up countercurrents and drop-offs that are dangerous for larger boats. The small size and maneuverability of the canoes allowed the party to travel in close to the bank and avoid the whirlpools that swallowed tree trunks as though they were matchsticks.

For the first time in his career as an explorer, La Salle's anxiety dissipated. Physical obstacles had never frightened him and besides, he did not find the dangers of the Mississippi particularly impressive. He savored the peace that reigned over his riverborne village. And he liked the company of Tonty, Boisrondet, d'Autray, and Father Zénobe, who were curious and enthusiastic. The men were well fed and, cheered by the sun and the mild temperatures after a winter on the Illinois, paddled, sang, and voiced no complaints. The Indians kept their end of the bargain as well, an easy task given the abundance of game. Occasionally, the canoes would be forced to stop by buffalo drinking in the river. The herds were so densely packed that the travelers could not clear a path for themselves between the animals. When the herds moved, like a vast army, it could take several days for them to file past. No wonder one traveler who crossed the American prairies saw aggregations of buffalo numbering two or three million animals.[9] The hammering of their hooves could be heard several miles away. Voyagers have always been intrigued by the strange appearance of these slow and placid beasts. "Between the Missouri and the Mississippi, they reach the size of an average elephant. They have the mane of a lion, the hump of a camel, the hide and hindquarters of a rhinoceros or hippopotamus, and the horns and legs of a bull,"[10] wrote Chateaubriand.

The French did not venture to take part in hunting buffalo. Though normally peaceful, the animals could be dangerous when wounded and charge fiercely. The Indians had developed a special technique. It called for the hunter to turn himself into a buffalo: he rubbed his body with buffalo fat, wrapped himself in a buffalo robe, and walked crouching toward the herd from downwind. Once he had mingled with the animals, he shot his prey with an arrow. When a sufficient number had been killed, he stepped back and threw stones to scare off the rest of the herd, which made the ground literally tremble in its flight. The men hauled the carcasses back to camp where the women set to work. Bison droppings give off such a hot flame that the Indians needed no wood to roast the hump and the tongue, the two most delicate parts of the animal.[11] It was a rare occurrence, and proof of the excellent atmosphere in camp, that the Frenchmen began to take pleasure in the squaws' cooking. From the swamps the women gathered large roots, called macopin, which tasted something like a sweet onion. La Salle has left an exact recipe: "The Indians make a hole in the ground and into it put a layer of stones that are red from the fire, then a layer of leaves, then one of macopins, another of reddened stones, and so on to the top, which they cover with earth and let the roots sweat inside. It is quite a good dish, as long as the roots are well cooked."[12] In three days, the flotilla reached the confluence of the Ohio, the river on which La Salle had undergone so much suffering five years before. Fed by melting snow, "the Ohio, more transparent than crystal, calmer than air,"[13] forms a striking contrast with the muddy Mississippi, about which a later generation of farmers would complain that it was too thick to drink and too thin to plow. The two rivers oppose each other with equal force and their currents slow down, running parallel, as though sleeping side by side before they join.

It is no coincidence that the city built on this site in 1818 was named Cairo. South of the confluence, the landscape changes and the Mississippi wanders in a bed so large that it occupies the whole of it only when it floods the surrounding countryside. (In 1927, approximately 30,000 square miles of land between Cairo and New Orleans were under water — a surface area larger than Belgium and the Netherlands together.) Like the Nile, the Mississippi spreads alluvial deposits, sometimes accumulating to depths of thirty feet, over a landscape to which it seems to have given birth. All of the region from Cairo to Memphis, 150 miles south, is known as Little Egypt. It was the beginning of spring and the water was starting to rise. Soon only the tops of submerged willows, arrayed in two rows, would mark the summer confines of the river. With the flooding and the thick growth of rushes rising ten feet high along the river bank, hunting became difficult. And navigating was trickier too, though the explorers never complained of it. The river changed at every moment. Sometimes the canoes scraped bottom, and sometimes the water was deeper than they could sound. The sandy banks crumbled, dispersing quantities of debris — stones, roots, and branches — that snagged and formed bars and temporary islands. The oxbows added to the confusion. The river turned on itself, sometimes flowing west, sometimes east, sometimes even bending to the north, and only going directly south when the current took a shortcut and sliced across the curve of an oxbow. In the shapeless valley through which the travelers wandered, only the sycamores, with trunks so white they shone like beacons after nightfall, served as landmarks.

At about the height of Memphis, La Salle ordered a halt. Precautions had to be taken on landing because they found the banks snake infested. The snakes came in all different colors: some were black with yellow rings, some entirely green, others mottled or even transparent. The whistling snake, whose green skin was flecked with black, the numerous rattlesnakes, and the spiny snake, whose bite was said to be fatal, frightened the French and the Indians alike. Buffalo could be seen behind the canebrake, and the nearby ponds abounded in pelicans and blue herons. Making one's way in this blurred and amphibious world was not easy. La Salle observed that it would have been impossible to advance on horseback, with the rushes growing so thickly that it took two hands to push one's way through.[14] Acknowledging the difficulty of not getting lost in this water-logged landscape, where a series of lakes, ponds, and sloughs seemed to double and triple the twisting course of the Mississippi, he advised his men not to go anywhere without a compass, and was particularly emphatic with the armorer, Pierre Prud'homme, who had never hunted before but wanted to try it. The Indians and the French set off, each in his own direction, and all came back a short time later weighed down with game, beans, and roots. All except for Prud'homme.

They looked for him all night, and by daylight found Indian tracks. The Indians were taking care not to show themselves, which worried La Salle. Whether Prud'homme had been captured or eaten was not clear, nor how they would find him in this tangle of reeds. La Salle was too loyal to abandon him, and too enterprising to do nothing. He put their forced halt to use by building a fort and making contact with the neighboring Indians. After ten days, he had given up hope of finding the gunsmith and decided to continue his route, when suddenly, at a bend in the river, they discovered Prud'homme astraddle a tree trunk he was using as a raft. His face was haggard, he was emaciated and slightly delirious. While lost he had found nothing to eat except a few rotten roots. In consolation, La Salle christened the new fort Prud'homme and left him there, along with several other men, to recover his strength.

Once south of Memphis, it is practically summer by the month of March, and the men, who were used to endless winters, storms in April, and snow at Easter, were now discovering the softness of

warm, hazy mornings, and the downy growth of reviving vegetation. The trees were draped with an aerial mossy plant, as light as
air, which they called "Spaniard's beard." It veiled branches behind a greenish shadow and gave the trees a fairy-tale aspect.
Ebony trees loaded with bright orange fruit stood out against the
green of smaller oaks. An infinite variety of flowers broke the
dry, cracked surface of the mud on the riverbank. The sun was
growing stronger and stronger, enveloping everything in trem-
bling light. The daily cloudburst was both a trial and a relief. The
rain fell from the slate gray sky in sheets. You could see nothing,
but at least breathing was easier and the insects stopped their torture while the downpour lasted.

They were surprised one night by roars that seemed to come
from the depths of the river. And sure enough, the next morning
they saw their first alligators. These large animals, three or four
yards long with a bluish cast, were peacefully digesting their prey
from the previous night. The monsters that had been described
to them in the Illinois villages could be murkily made out in the
mud of the river. Catfish, bizarre and incredibly ugly with their
flat mouths and buggy eyes, grew to more than six feet in length
and could upset a canoe with a slap of their tails. Another fish
was even more menacing. Its skin was like armor and its mouth
filled with dozens of triangular teeth as sharp as scalpels. This
was the gar, a highly aggressive fish, which the men treated with
respect when they found them surfacing behind the boats, as
they believed them capable of killing and eating a man. Farther
on, the travelers came to a place where the Indians had caught
gar, killed them, and stuck them head first in the mud at the
edge of the river, as though to punish them for their viciousness
by leaving them to rot. They also learned to watch for large
turtles that could shear off a finger, or even a wrist, with a snap of
their jaws. But all these animals, though unexpected and somewhat worrisome, were another manifestation of the lush natural
world suddenly presented to them. The mood of the men remained cheerful, which pleased La Salle, who was unaccustomed

to harmony in the ranks. Then one day when the fog lay thick, the silence was broken on the right by the sound of a drum and the piercing screams that accompanied Indian war dances.

La Salle gave orders to pass to the opposite shore, chop down several trees, and cut rushes. In less than an hour, his men had built a primitive fort. The fog lifted and the Indians, astonished, watched the tall bearded men work at a speed unknown on these shores. One must remember that no whites had ventured into these lands within the memory of man. Marquette and Joliet had turned back some distance upriver, and since the death of the conquistador De Soto in 1542, no Spaniard had been back to explore. As the river was more than a mile wide, it was impossible to make oneself heard from one bank to the other, and the Indians therefore came across in a dugout canoe. When they were within hailing distance, Tonty spoke to them in Illinois, asking their name. A captive who understood the language answered "Arkansas" as he fired off an arrow to test the strangers. La Salle's men held their fire, proving their peaceful intentions, and La Salle strode forward with his calumet in hand. Once diplomatic relations had been established to the satisfaction of both parties, the French were invited to spend several days at a village near the entrance of what is still called the Arkansas River.

Being used to the dirt, noise, and disorder of native camps, they expected the worst. To their amazement, the Arkansas village was organized according to criteria that they could understand. Father Zénobe, as a clergyman, had suffered from the lack of privacy on the journey more keenly than the others and was quick to appreciate the unusual discretion of these Indians: "I cannot tell you the civility and kindness we have received from these barbarians. Seeing that we did not wish to sleep in their lodges, they gave us our freedom to do as we pleased. They swept the area where we wished to stay, brought us poles to make huts, supplied us with firewood. These savages are joyful, honest, and generous. In a word, we did not lose the value of a pin while we were with them. The young men, though the most spirited we have seen, are nevertheless so modest and restrained that not one of them would take the liberty to enter our hut, but all stood quietly at the door."[15] To measure the full import of this statement, one has to remember that the Jesuits always arranged for clocks to be sent to their missions, because they discovered that the only way to get rid of the natives who invaded their huts was to warn them that the magic object was about to ring, a signal imposing a strict obligation on them to withdraw.

After a feast that lasted three days, the French planted a cross on a post bearing the coat of arms of King Louis XIV. According to Father Zénobe, the Indians were "so pleased with it that they patted their bodies after rubbing them against the column."[16] Perhaps they would have been even more delighted to learn that they were now subjects of Louis XIV. La Salle held an official ceremony at which he offered them the protection "of the greatest prince in the world."[17] The notary got out his black hat and his goose-quill pen, and drew up a document in due and proper form. Three salvos of musket fire were offered in salute. The Recollet friar chanted "*O crux, ave, spes unica*" and the men shouted "*Vive le roi.*" Almost a century later, a little town was built on the same banks of the Arkansas, which its founders would call Napoleon. Thus by a strange irony of history, the birthplace of France's great empire in America is the site of a town commemorating the man who liquidated that empire by a famous sale in 1803.

But back to La Salle. The Arkansas supplied the expedition with two guides, and the French set off to explore the villages in the neighborhood. One day when Tonty and Father Zénobe were alone, they visited a village that was so strange they might almost have thought themselves back in Europe. Instead of wigwams or lodges there were real houses made of dried mud and straw, with dome-shaped roofs covered in a double layer of matting so skillfully worked that no rain passed through. "I have never been so surprised," wrote the friar. "And what is more," he pointed out admiringly:

The chieftains have much greater power and authority than among any of our Indians. They command and are obeyed. They have valets to wait on them at table. Food is brought to them from outside. Their drink is served to them in a cup that has been rinsed, and no one drinks from it except themselves. [The chief agreed to visit La Salle but sent ahead] his master of ceremonies with five or six servants who swept with their hands the path by which he was to come, prepared a place for him, and spread a carpet over it in the form of a reed mat, very delicately and artistically woven. This chief was dressed in a very beautiful white cloth. Two men preceded him ceremoniously carrying feather fans. No man has ever carried himself with such gravity as this chief during his visit.[18]

He warned La Salle that not all the tribes would be as mild as his own. La Salle refused to become discouraged. The river was so wide — always more than a half mile across and in some places more — and the rare villages set so far back from shore because of the risk of floods that the danger of hostile encounters was minimal. Once or twice, La Salle had a premonition of danger: he ordered the canoes to the middle of the river and let them float downstream without putting ashore. In fact, this enormous country appeared deserted — a perfect illustration of the New World, with its overflowing store of riches, opening itself peacefully to the Old. The travelers were passing through a soft and languid countryside with long beaches of ocher sand, and swamps screened by reeds, where oxbow lakes and inlets branched out into the tranquil landscape. Indians called them *bayuks*; they would become the bayous of Louisiana. In these calm waters, the trees intertwine and rise "to heights that strain the eye," the flowers form "a thousand caves, a thousand vaults, a thousand porticoes"; it is a place where "green snakes, blue herons, pink flamingoes, and bears, drunk on grapes and weaving in the shade of the elms, exude the enchantment of life"[19] and thousands of buffalo wander as far as the eye can see. "Sometimes a buffalo, weighted down with years, swims out breasting the current to lie down in the tall grasses of an island in the middle of [the Mississippi]. By his forehead, on which he carries two crescents, and by his ancient and silt-laden beard, you might mistake him for a river god, looking with satisfaction over the majesty of his waters, the wild abundance of his shores."[20]

La Salle's men, who were less poetic than Chateaubriand, found the natural world around them becoming more and more oppressive. The croaking of thousands of frogs and toads, the roaring of alligators in the night, along with the hissing of snakes, and the constant buzzing of mosquitoes combined to form an infernal concert. The men started to grumble. It was impossible to land and hunt — there was no land. The beautiful cypress trees, their Spanish beards waving in the breeze, riotously decked with yellow-headed, blue-bodied parrots and flame-colored cardinals, seemed to emerge from the river itself, as did large pin oaks, giant cousins of the Mediterranean cork oak, which stood with their trunks in the water. Between the trees were floating islands of water lilies, and beyond this riverine forest extended a sea of rushes, palm trees, and serrated stalks, punctuated by large bunches of iris where hummingbirds circled, their gray-green plumage a changing iridescence under the relentless sun. There were different species of eagles: nun eagles with a white collar, and black corvids "very similar to the crow, as much because of the carrion that they favor as because of their aspect."[21] Here and there, clusters of young trees indicated slightly higher ground where deer and bear found shelter. The only food at this stage was alligator, and the men felt that killing it was both dangerous and repellent. A piece of fish was dangled from a line; when the alligator approached it, lifting his head out of the water, a man would splinter his skull with an axe. The others would try to lift the animal into the canoe, but the thrashing of its tail, continuing long after its death, put the fragile craft at risk of capsizing. Dressing out the animal was long and awkward, and the men found the task disgusting. In contrast to southern gourmets, who now eagerly exchange recipes for alligator steak, La Salle's men hated the taste of it; nevertheless, it became their daily staple. The river flowed into a watery landscape. The grass took on the hairlike, waving, almost liquid aspect of aquatic vegetation. In the delta, the Mississippi no longer evokes the Nile flowing into the desert, but the powerful Amazon with its densely vegetated river edge, moist and mysterious.

On April 6, 1682, their energy revived. The air they breathed had a tang to it, a saltiness. Thinking the sea might be near, La Salle dipped his hand into the water. It was still fresh. And yet they could not be far from the gulf. Suddenly the river ahead of them divided into three branches. La Salle took the one on the right, Tonty the middle, and d'Autray the one on the left. A league farther on the sea opened up in front of them, huge and blue. Mission accomplished. The great artery connected the frozen lands of the north to the rich alluvial plains of the south, to the greater glory of the king of France. The three groups joined up again. They did not venture far into the waters of the gulf, but enough to make sure "that there is deep water at the entrance to the river." On his return, La Salle would tell Le Moyne, Frontenac's old interpreter, "that he had been out to sea three leagues without finding bottom with thirty fathoms of leadline."[22] The great river scoured the bottom of the gulf, and this observation would be engraved in La Salle's mind. The men would have liked to land their canoes on the beach, but the shore, where a thick growth of tall, close-set canes formed a stifling curtain, sank under their feet and landing proved impossible. La Salle returned to the spot where the Mississippi branches. The place is a tangle of canals, appropriately known today as Venice. The French and the Indians managed to crowd onto a slight rise. A tree was felled and squared off. La Salle's men stuck it into the ground, and (these men being products of the Age of Louis XIV) carved on it the arms of the king of France. Then they attached with nails an inscription: LOUIS THE GREAT, KING OF FRANCE AND OF NAVARRE, REIGNS HERE, APRIL 9, 1682. To be on the safe side, a plaque was cut from the bottom of a copper kettle, engraved with the exploits of ROBERTUS CAVELIER, CUM DOMINO TONTY, LEGATO R.P. ZENOBIO MEMBRE ET VIGINTI GALLIS, and buried at the foot of the cross. La Salle robed himself in the scarlet coat he kept for great occasions; the notary extracted his papers from his case, along with his seals and his black coat; then La Salle proclaimed in a loud voice:

> In the name of the most high, powerful, invincible, and victorious Prince, Louis the Great, by the grace of God King of France and Navarre, fourteenth of the name, I, this ninth day of April one thousand six hundred and eighty-two, do now take, in the name of His Majesty and of his successors to the crown, possession of this country of Louisiana, its seas, harbors, ports, bays, adjacent straits, and all the nations, peoples, provinces, cities, towns, villages, mines, minerals, fisheries, streams, and rivers.[23]

With these words, Louis XIV received all of the Mississippi basin, from the plains of Texas to the shores of the Atlantic. From north to south, his empire now extended from the the farthest lakes of upper Canada to the tropical shores of the Gulf of Mexico. Thanks to the courage, determination, and madness of a single man, it included savannas and forests, deserts and fertile plains; it was watered by millions of streams, and peopled by hundreds of tribes. We are so used to military conquests that it is difficult for us to realize that vast lands could be won in this way, and yet, undeniably, France had just acquired one half of a continent.

Louis XIV would only learn of it a year later. The news that his domain had increased phenomenally in size did not move him. "I am persuaded as you are that the Sieur de La Salle's discovery is quite useless," he wrote to Governor La Barre, Frontenac's replacement, on receiving the news.[24] In 1683, Louis was more preoccupied with his marriage to Madame de Maintenon, the construction in progress at Versailles, and the arrival of ambassadors from Algiers than with the American epic. War, the endless ongoing war with Spain, had flared up again in the Netherlands. Two months after La Salle, with his three officers and twenty men, had won a gigantic empire without firing a shot (the province would survive until 1803 despite France's official neglect and lack of interest), Louis XIV ordered a campaign that would be conducted with cruelty that became legendary. Twenty thousand infantrymen and a cavalry force of 1,500 invaded and ravaged Luxembourg. With its 1,600 square miles, Luxembourg would remain in the possession of France for a little over a century, like Louisiana.

❖ 11 ❖

Quarreling in Quebec
1682–1683

$\mathcal{L}$A SALLE WAS NOT THE ONLY FRENCHMAN traveling back and forth across North America for the greater glory of King Louis XIV. While he was working his way toward the continent's south shore, others were making forays to the north and west. The expedition led by Paul de Saint-Simon and Father Albanel had pushed north overland to Hudson Bay on a journey so arduous it won the admiration of the Indian tribes in the woodlands north of Quebec; Duluth had raised the king's standard in a large Sioux village on the northwest side of Lake Superior. On this almost empty continent, exploration was synonymous with possession, and France's territorial rights were recognized throughout Europe. It is hard to determine the value of ruling a vast empire inhabited by a few thousand people, with borders at several months' remove from its miniature capital. What is interesting and original about this empire is that it was based on trade and religion; the English colonies, by contrast, were based on actual use and occupation of the territory. Their frontier was signaled by cleared land, a distinct zone from which the former occupants, both human and animal, were expelled. The advance of the English colonists necessarily caused conflict, and the conflict would only end with the disappearance of the forest, the sacrifice of the animals, and the extermination of the Indians.[1] The French presence, despite Colbert's admonitions, had created a frontier somewhat like an invisible thread that simply linked Quebec to different outposts set down in the vast expanse of the continent. This thread, which followed the course of rivers and streams, did not mark a transition between European domination and the Indian way of life. Virgin forests, herds of buffalo and moose, wolf packs, bear, and Indian encampments were as likely to be found within the enormous perimeter annexed by the French as outside it. The natives were necessary, both to the missionaries, whose apostolic mission required them to recruit pagans to preach to, and to the traders, who relied on the Indians as intermediaries in tapping the country's wealth. La Salle and his countrymen had no idea that his formal taking of possession would set in motion a conquest that would strip the Indians of everything they had and radically alter the region's equilibrium.[2] A few forts placed strategically along the river and at its mouth were the extent of La Salle's ambition. The task of building them remained to be accomplished.

La Salle stayed on the edge of the Gulf of Mexico only long enough to execute a few sketch maps. A Venetian, Vicenzo Coronelli, was at that time producing for Louis XIV two enormous globes fifteen feet in diameter, and La Salle's friend Monsieur Tronson, a Recollet, had written from Paris to ask La Salle for as many maps and details as possible that might provide information on Canada.[3] By this date, an interest in decorative and ornamental work did not preclude a commitment to accuracy, especially where readings of longitude and latitude were concerned.[4] The explorers therefore tried to fix the geographic location of the mouth of the Mississippi. La Salle took sightings of the latitude with his astrolabe but was unable to calculate the longitude (obtained from the difference between the local time and an agreed upon meridian) for lack of instruments.[5]

In the course of five years of effort, he had overcome countless obstacles, but his achievement was only the prelude to further work. First, it was essential that news of the expedition's success reach Quebec before the last ship sailed in November, or the king would not learn of the tenfold increase in his empire until a full year later. Next, the question of money had to be dealt with. The Mississippi being navigable, as he had thought, La Salle could easily have brought back enough furs in one or two cargo boats to reimburse his creditors and pay his men's wages. His bark canoes, unfortunately, were already so loaded down that they could not even carry a few extra provisions and were useless for transporting hides. Finally, he had to make the best possible use of the time granted him by the letters patent of 1678 to engage in trade at the forts he had established. Unless he took immediate advantage of his concessions, he ran the risk of losing any financial benefit from the expedition. To rebuild Crèvecœur as soon as possible was the first order of business: it would serve to reassure the Illinois, who were still concerned that the Iroquois could return, and establish a handy trading post for gathering buffalo hides and beaver pelts. If the crew manning the fort managed to build a boat, furs could be exported down the Mississippi starting the very next year.

On April 10, 1682, the day following the little ceremony of annexation, the French took the return path, not bothering to examine the surrounding area or venture again into the gulf. They were impatient to leave this inhospitable spot where, because of the flooded ground, they could not build a fire to prepare the game and fish that they had caught. La Salle set out ahead of the rest intending to reach New France as quickly as possible, taking the Recollet father and two men. Tonty was responsible for bringing back the Indians and the bulk of the party. The canoes, light and maneuverable, drifted along on the countercurrents, and the river, which had flooded and spread out over the plain, offered little resistance. The Indians, though always ready to discharge arrows at one another from shore to shore, let the French pass, confirming an adage that is repeated to this day along the Mississippi: "It's not strangers we don't like, just people we don't know."[6] The unstoppable La Salle, however, was suddenly overcome with dizzy spells. His paddle grew too heavy and he had to put it down; he felt so weak he thought he would die. Father Zénobe and the others persuaded La Salle to let them carry him as far as Fort Prud'homme. They hung a message for Tonty from a sycamore tree, telling him to send on the surgeon as fast as possible. La Salle was bled, but his exhaustion was so great that he could not travel. The priest remained to care for him. Tonty, who was convinced that he would never see his friend again, continued upriver "in spite of his great grief."[7]

La Salle had developed a high fever (a mortal fever, he would later call it) and was unable to move for forty days. He was afterward so cast down and depressed that, by his own admission, it was "impossible [for him] to think of anything for the next four months."[8] Father Zénobe would lay him in the canoe and they would travel upstream little by little, as La Salle could stand the movement for only a few hours a day. But when he arrived back on the Illinois in the month of July, he took the trouble to stop several leagues above Crèvecœur to make a close examination of a rock he had spotted on previous trips. The bluff dominated the river from a height of 150 feet; the top was a flat platform large enough to build a fort on. The Rock, as the travelers called it, held an impregnable site.[9] It was an ideal emplacement for a fort, and, in a sign of optimism, La Salle decided to discard the name Crèvecœur and name it Fort Saint Louis, in honor of the king's patron saint and his own patron, Louis de Frontenac.

Finally, they reached Michilimackinac. It was already September. Father Zénobe learned on arrival that his superior planned for him to return to France. This delighted Father Zénobe, as it meant he would be the one to carry the news of the successful expedition to the court at Versailles; he rushed back to Quebec. La Salle and Tonty stayed on in Lake Michigan, disturbed by the news that Frontenac had just been recalled to France. Obsessed with his own expedition, La Salle had lost sight of the colony's internal problems, and now the abcess had burst. He could not tell what the consequences would be for him, but he feared the worst.

Unlike Colbert, Frontenac quickly understood that he was not governing just another province in the kingdom. Canada was different because of its distance from France, the incredible severity of its climate, the scant size of its population, the proximity of aboriginal peoples, and its access to vast unexplored territories. These were obvious facts, though hard to grasp from the perspective of Versailles. Another essential difference, even more difficult for men raised in the French social system to understand, was the uniqueness of the Canadian noble class: they were young, used to work, and they imposed little burden on the tenants of their land, who were more nearly renters than vassals; furthermore, Canada had no peasant class. An abundant supply of available land resulted in "the scarcity and high cost of workers."[10] Few men derived their subsistence solely from wage labor. To obtain land it was sufficient to ask for it. In France, La Salle would never have received a grant of land entirely free of obligation, and then managed to sell it back to his grantors two years later. Such an operation would have been unthinkable in the Old World. Canadians enjoyed a degree of freedom and justice unknown in France, partly because judges and administrators were appointed on their merits, and corruption in public office was uncommon.[11] Clearly, the people of Canada were to be handled differently than the natives of Normandy.

Frontenac had an unusually open mind for a man of his time and social milieu. A paradoxical mix of vanity and solicitude, he would happily have brought innovative methods to Canada and put the colonists in closer control of the government of their province. He suggested creating an assembly to represent all Canadians that would propose commercial and agricultural reforms. Colbert was shocked at the idea of a popular mandate: it was "good that each should speak for himself, and that none should speak for all,"[12] he said, energetically rejecting Frontenac's suggestion. What Colbert did not realize was that Canadians would do exactly as they pleased with or without representation. No amount of regulation, however clearly spelled out or however threatening, could make the colonists cluster in villages and stop going into the bush. The people could not express their wishes officially, but they were quick to vote with their feet whenever a law displeased them. Canadians "think of their households first and not of the orders they are given,"[13] Frontenac wrote to his minister, and he warned him against ordering a close inspection of the goods belonging to merchants and prominent colonists. Obliging them to make detailed declarations would be harmful "because of the resentment it might provoke, when they understood that it robbed them of the freedom which is the soul of commerce."[14]

His aptitude for understanding the colonists, in conjunction with his authority over the Indians, explain Frontenac's popularity in the colony. Count Frontenac was never more active, more efficient, or more constructive than in the first three years of his governorship. He traveled up and down the Saint Lawrence valley to judge for himself whether a fishing outpost could be developed: after being "besieged" by admirable quantities of salmon and whales, he reported that the fisheries could "take the place of veritable Indies."[15] He visited the iron mines on Lake Champlain and went so far as to taste the iron-rich waters. Above all, he listened to people with infinite patience. They complained that they had no salt on hand. If a ship carrying salt were to sink, as had happened the year he arrived, the colonists could not preserve adequate quantities of food: Frontenac brought it to the minister's attention. The physician at Quebec died: he requested another immediately. A veteran of the Carignan-Salières regiment was in need: Frontenac fired off a petition to the king. He devoted his first winters to developing an urban plan for Quebec; he drew a perimeter wall around the Upper Town to mark its limits, and plotted the squares and streets "so that in future when an individual builds, he will do it with symmetry and in such a way as to enhance the decoration and ornament of the town."[16] A populist with a paternalistic outlook, Frontenac did not neglect the Lower Town. He saw to paving the streets, a necessary improvement in a hilly city where melting snow and ice created virtual waterfalls. On the slopes of the Montagne, a particularly vulnerable area separating the two sections of town, "the water ran so hard that you could easily travel down it in a canoe."[17] He outlawed animal slaughter within the town limits and tried to control the number of pigs, dogs, and goats roaming freely. They generated an impressive quantity of manure, especially as it could not be carted off during the winter months when the streets were impassable. Frontenac organized street cleaning and the construction of private latrines; he had a plan drawn up for converting Market Square into a classic Royal Square, complete with a bronze bust of the king. The colonists often asked the governor to stand godfather to their children. Frontenac always accepted and gladly attended the baptism. An even better sign of the respect he inspired is the fact that many citizens asked him to arbitrate their disputes and settle the wrangling that constantly pitted one settler against another. His first period in office was therefore productive and untroubled. The bishop and the provincial administrator were both gone, leaving him free rein to govern as he thought best. The flaw in Frontenac's character was that he was unable to argue calmly. Any difference of opinion struck him as a declaration of war. Anger provoked him to absurd extremes, which invariably put him in the wrong. And unfortunately, anger took hold of him from the moment that Monsignor Laval and the new administrator Duchesneau arrived and never let him go.

There was a sharp clash of personalities and politics; and the crown's equivocating attempts to maintain a balance between the three men made the situation impossible. Bishop Laval, who first arrived in Canada in 1659 at the height of the missionary era, had enjoyed unusual authority during the early years of his tenure. The civil authorities at that time were weak and allowed him to acquire enormous power over the entire colony. He fought long and hard with governors d'Argenson and Mézy to keep his privileges when Louis XIV resumed control of the colony in 1663. The king judged the bishop's powers to be excessive. Monsignor Laval showed such bitterness that the superior of the Jesuit mission feared "the discussions [on the division of power] would lead to violence."[18] On his return in 1675 the prelate, who was barely younger than Frontenac, had not mellowed with the passage of years. At fifty, his austerity and power of conviction made him as formidable as ever. He was used to crushing his adversaries with a single glance, and he was surprised to find in Frontenac the sort of man who did not lower his eyes. The obvious authority the governor had over colonists and Indians alike exasperated him, as did the governor's conduct, which offered no target to the slander of his enemies. And as if the clash of these two strong personalities were not enough to stir up the colony, the irritating presence of Duchesneau added to the general exasperation. Duchesneau was of the same generation as Laval and Frontenac. Before sailing for Canada he had never been outside the province of Touraine, where he held the position of comptroller of finances. Fearful, hypocritical, inordinately submissive to the clergy, scrupulous to the point of stupidity as far as Frontenac was concerned, and incapable of undertaking great projects in the manner of Talon, he spent all his time spying on the governor and denouncing him. Frontenac despised him too much to grasp his effectiveness. Sometimes siding with the bishop and sometimes opposing him, according to Colbert's instructions, Duchesneau never brought peace but rather contributed to the unhealthy turmoil in the colony.

The bishop and the governor were at loggerheads on a number of issues, all of them of great importance, and Duchesneau would side with one or the other depending on the case. The question of selling brandy to the Indians was still a burning issue. The bishop had never accepted Louis XIV's decision to authorize trade in "the king of France's milk." Threatening excommunication, he tried every means he could to shut it down. Frontenac and the bishop also quarreled about the work of the Catholic missions. Why, the governor wanted to know, were the Indians in the missions not learning French? He himself had asked the tribes on the Ontario for eight children. They had arrived and he was now educating them with great care — there were four girls with the Ursuline sisters and four boys under his own supervision. Trading in furs raised a more subtle problem. Each was trading on his own behalf, Frontenac as well as Duchesneau, and even the bishop traded through the missionaries. Each of the three denounced the others to Colbert.

The governor was also annoyed at the excessive meddling of the clergy in the daily life of the Québécois. In France, and particularly in the circles that Frontenac moved in, the clergy had never exercised such a strong and rigid influence. In Canada, he reported to Colbert, the priests "all have such a great desire to know what is going on within families that they hire spies in town to report on all that happens inside people's houses. They are so curious when hearing confession that they put one's conscience in the greatest quandary: not only do they wish to know the sins one has committed — they also want names, accomplices, and a thousand other circumstances that are not germaine to confession."[19] An officer called La Hontan complained bitterly that a Jesuit had stolen into his room and torn up his edition of Petronius. Frontenac, soon after arrival, furnished his house and organized receptions that were highly appreciated by the rare ladies of Quebec society. To his astonishment as a courtier and a recent intimate at Madame de Montespan's suppers, he was told that the bishop condemned the elaborate dress of his female guests for their revealing necklines, although given Canada's climate these were quite modest.

The quarrels flared up in part because Colbert acted indecisively, but also because his political leadership was inadequate. Colbert was entirely opposed to the claims made by the bishop, who "assumed an authority far exceeding what is allowed a bishop in the Christian realm, and particularly in the kingdom [of France]."[20] He did not dare confront him directly, however. Similarly, he confirmed Frontenac's precedence over Duchesneau, yet he encouraged the latter's denunciations. Neither the king nor his minister had pondered the problem of applying to Canada a system that divided authority between a governor and a provincial administrator. It worked well in the provinces of

France, where the governor's part had become largely ceremonial. In Canada it was stalling the machinery of state. The governor's mandate to run the colony's military affairs required real and unchallenged authority. There literally was not room in the tiny capital for two representatives of civil authority and an emissary of the Church who believed himself an absolute sovereign. Each of the three men lived in his own "palace" in the Upper Town, separated from the others by twenty yards. They saw each other constantly, watched each other, and kept track of what visitors went in or out the other's door. With continual contact, mutual jealousy festered. The quarrel between Frontenac and Duchesneau illustrates this situation brilliantly, but it should not be forgotten that their predecessors, Courcelles and Talon, argued over every issue as well. At any rate, the colony was divided into two factions. One was headed by the governor and consisted of all those who lived on seigneuries and found Frontenac's military skills and authority over the Indians reassuring; those who lived by hunting and trapping; the Recollets; and ordinary people who valued his protection and concern for their well-being. The other faction was led by the bishop and included the Jesuits, with their enormous influence, and the merchants, who, owing to the intrigues of the provincial administrator, were afraid that Quebec would lose its monopoly over the fur trade. By 1682 Monsignor Laval, Frontenac, and Duchesneau were no longer on speaking terms. Instead, they sent vituperative and incendiary letters to Versailles denouncing one another. Their rivalry surfaced in the daily life of the colony as quarrels over etiquette: where to position a prayer stool, how to present the incense, and in what order to take part in a procession. Colbert did not waver in giving precedence to civil authority, but the antagonism between the governor and the provincial administrator brought the wheels of government to a halt. Angered by the constant recrimination of the two parties, and irritated by Frontenac's latest escapade, in which he held Duchesneau's son prisoner for having sung impertinent couplets, the minister decided to recall them both. The situation was becoming ridiculous and was therefore no longer tenable.

Frontenac's departure was catastrophic for La Salle. He was losing the support of a man who, putting aside his desire for personal enrichment, shared La Salle's ambitious dream of a French empire. Frontenac also exuded the energy and magnetism needed to keep the Iroquois in line at a time when they were showing signs of restlessness. His replacement was an old man — weak, incompetent, and nearsighted, both figuratively and in fact. The new governor, Lefèvre de La Barre, a former provincial administrator who later became governor of Cayenne, was so far from being a military man that he insisted on being addressed as General rather than Mr. Governor, as though it would hide his shortfalls. He quickly revealed that he was opposed to any enlargement of the colony and would therefore be a precious ally for La Chesnaye, the chief spokesman for the Montreal monopoly. "I do not put great stock in [La Salle's] discovery; furthermore, the spirit of discovery is foreign to me. What is reported of La Salle's discovery seems to me of little use and is larded with lies," he wrote the minister before he had even met or spoken to La Salle. Whether because La Salle did not accurately measure the hostility he would confront, or he felt too weak to undertake the journey, or else he thought it more important to build a fort on the Illinois, at any rate he did not go and explain himself to the new governor or try to convert him to his point of view. Instead he stayed in Illinois country with Tonty.

The task of erecting a fort had become routine for these adventurers. Clearing several acres of forest in the dead of winter, climbing a sheer height of two hundred yards with loads of logs and planks, building fortifications and houses on an exposed bluff under the battering of the December winds, and organizing an appropriate means of supply — these activities do not rate a single mention in their letters or accounts. They simply did the work. La Salle and Tonty did it so well that they attracted a considerable number of Indians, glad to accept protection from a man they called their father.[21] The Iroquois threat seemed to be growing. By the month of April a large native village of bark lodges had sprung up near the fort. Shawnee, Illinois, and Miami Indians lived there peaceably, and gathered to hold their feasts and councils. From the top of his rock, La Salle could see the women busy tanning hides while the hunter-warriors rested in the sun and played with their children. The natives' laziness still astounded him, but he congratulated himself that his standing among them was such that the chiefs turned to him for their safety. Yet to defend the Indians he would need arms and ammunition. When he requested as much from La Barre, the governor did not favor him with an answer. La Salle's rivals, who were determined to destroy him, pressured La Barre not to send help. The danger was that the Iroquois might believe they were free to resume their hostilities against Canada's Indian allies. Undiscouraged, La Salle wrote the governor again. In spite of sojourning in the impenetrable woods and keeping company with natives, La Salle had not forgotten how meticulously his country conducted its administration. To support his request, he enclosed copies of his letters patent and informed La Barre that he would grant a concession to any Frenchman who asked for one, as was his right.[22] He wanted the assurance that when his colonists went to Montreal "in quest of basic necessities" they could obtain travel permits and be allowed to return to the fort without being treated as outlaw coureurs de bois. This precaution illustrates the virulence of French rivalries and the harmful consequence of there being no single, uncontested authority within the colony. Providing La Barre with direct evidence of the king's grant was not a bad way of convincing him that La Salle's men were authorized to trade in buffalo hides. Sure of being in the right, La Salle ended his letter with a virtual challenge: "If you should wish [my colonists] to cease traveling to Montreal to supply their needs, for the reason that they are unable to return to me here, kindly do me the honor of making your wishes known. Thus, if I lack for men and provisions after following your orders, I may know that it is the king's will and thereby defend myself against my partners, whose interests will not keep me from observing that I am, Sir, ever your most humble and obedient servant."²³ He had lost neither the art of handling polite formulas nor the ability to express himself clearly. La Barre, however, did not dare to take sides against La Salle, nor did he dare support him. He chose once again not to answer. La Salle returned to the attack in still more colorful terms: "It is in vain, Sir, that we risk our lives here and that I exhaust myself to fulfill His Majesty's intentions, if all my measures are frustrated in the settlements below, and if those who go down to bring munitions, without which we cannot defend ourselves, are detained on trumped up charges. The king's patent to build forts is useless if I am prevented from getting supplies of arms, gunpowder, and lead."²⁴

In refusing his open and energetic support, which would have allowed La Salle to strengthen his Indian alliances, La Barre was doing far more than supporting one Canadian faction against another. He was playing into the hands of the English. The implications of the French advance across the continent were perfectly clear to them. The English were unable to set off in search of new tribes, as their only access route to the interior was still the Hudson valley, which led directly into Canadian territory. However, they used the Iroquois as intermediaries, and the Iroquois had proven that they were not afraid of attacking Canada's Indian allies. They had done it twenty years earlier when they massacred the Hurons, and they were capable of doing it again The Illinois, Miamis, Shawnees, and other tribes even farther afield were rightly afraid of them.

La Salle wasted no time trying to decipher La Barre's state of mind or negotiating with this obtuse and stubborn adversary. Having learned that the governor had ordered Fort Frontenac seized, he was certain that nothing would come of discussing matters in Quebec and resolved to return immediately to France. Colbert had just died, and La Salle wanted an interview with his son, Jean-Baptiste, Marquis de Seignelay, who had become minister in his father's place. He hoped to be received by the king also and win him to his views. He left the fort on the Illinois in the autumn of 1683 to catch the November ship. Along the way he met a young man, the Chevalier de Baugy, whom La Barre had sent to assume command of Fort Saint Louis and order La Salle to return to Quebec. La Salle, shrugging his shoulders, gave Baugy a message for Tonty asking him to make the visitor welcome. It was in fact an advantage for the two to get along, as they would have to stave off an Iroquois attack a few months later. The Iroquois besieged the fort for six days but were driven back. In the meantime, just a year after Frontenac's departure, La Salle was sailing back to France.

❖ 12 ❖

A New Departure
1684

A SECRETIVE AND IMPASSIVE MAN, unable to put his feelings on display, La Salle was too proud to show his bitterness or disenchantment. He had suffered his share of disappointments since arriving in New France, but in the autumn of 1684 there was a new factor to provoke his disgust — the general refusal to recognize his achievement. He had kept his part of the bargain, at the cost of prodigious effort and by going to the brink of death. He had pushed the frontier back several thousand miles, and his foray into the unknown had opened new commercial possibilities for New France. Instead of heralding him, the governor had unfairly seized his two forts. He had also charged that La Salle's rashness was threatening to incite the Iroquois to renewed hostility and had vowed to use all available means to keep La Salle from making a profit from his discoveries. La Salle was filled with a cold rage. He was determined to plead his cause to the minister and, if possible, to the king.

The fact that Frontenac was in Paris, though in a state of semidisgrace, could be of some help to La Salle, if only to bring him up to date. A provincial was inevitably a figure of fun at Versailles: he wore a doublet and breeches, and had lace ornaments at the knee, when you were supposed to wear a powdered wig, a tightly fitting suit, and one-piece hose. He did not know that tulips were preferable to carnations, but at least he could say if the country were at peace or at war, Colbert alive or in his grave, and whether the Rhone in overflowing its banks had again this year flooded a great many fields. A Canadian was spared a bumpkin's ridicule because he had unusual stories to offer the ladies — it is not hard to imagine what effect La Salle and his long-haired slave had on jaded souls. But for La Salle to act effectively, he would have to digest a year's worth of news in a few days and, as he had been away a long time, ponder the extent of the changes brought about by Louis XIV.

After a short crossing to La Rochelle, La Salle made a stop at Rochefort and a visit to Rouen. It was here that he realized how much his credit had suffered. No one, in spite of the success of his expedition, was willing to take part in financing his new projects. He went on to Paris, found his old lodgings at the Rue de la Truanderie, and set to work. Colbert was dead, but his son, Seignelay, knew the Canadian dossiers well and was favorably disposed to La Salle. He received La Salle and La Forest together. The two men presented their case clearly and with proof to support it. They had no trouble convincing the minister that neither Fort Frontenac nor Fort Saint Louis had been abandoned; consequently, La Barre's seizure of them was inexcusable, and justice required a reinstatement of La Salle's rights. Seignelay, "a bold minister who knew better than anyone how to harm or to help,"[1] quickly set things to rights. With a short and sharply-worded letter to La Barre he canceled the measures taken against La Salle. La Forest boarded a ship for Canada to resume command of Fort Frontenac, and Tonty was reinstated at Saint Louis in place of Baugy. To underscore where the blame lay, Seignelay had La Barre recalled in 1685 and posted the Marquis de Denonville to take his place. La Salle had received satisfaction, but his hopes were only partly realized. The next step would in all likelihood be more difficult to achieve.

La Salle wanted the right and the necessary means to make the Mississippi valley a productive resource. The simplest choice for him would be to strengthen Fort Saint Louis and make it a second capital on the Illinois, an inland Quebec forming a solid core for the new territories. From there, he could go down the Mississippi in large boats and organize at the mouth of the river a port sizable enough to start a new trading network. It is a good bet that once matters were in hand, La Salle would have resumed his explorations westward. He was not a man to sail in known waters, however profitable the trip. Even before setting foot in France, however, he knew that his proposals had no chance of appealing to the king. To create a second metropolis and a line of forts along the enormous river, plus a port in Louisiana, would require men, soldiers, and money. In the past Colbert had stated that he saw no need for it, and nothing indicated that there had been a shift in policy. La Salle did not act hastily. As he had done several years before, he consulted with the Abbés Bernou and Renaudot, the latter having nothing clerical about him except his title.

These two men had the unusual occupation of being petition writers, in the broadest sense of the term. They gave the petitioner advice, helped him to present his case, and when the petition was successful they accepted an interest in the profits. The first of these men, Abbé Bernou, was fascinated by maps and geography, and was in complete sympathy with La Salle. He had the advantage of being a client of the Maréchal d'Estrées, a cousin to the Duc de Vendôme and an equally brilliant general, who was much in favor for just having won great victories over the Dutch. The second, Eusèbe Renaudot, was a character whose talent and originality were a family trait. His grandfather, Théophraste Renaudot, was a doctor, a chemist, and a journalist, who started a weekly newspaper, *La Gazette*,[2] the novel feature of which was that the news of Paris appeared last, while events from other, more distant parts of the kingdom were given greater prominence. Another innovation was a page devoted to advertisements. Renaudot had conceived the idea of printing a list of the medicines he had available on the back page of his paper. He thus invented advertising and brought together all his various professions. He was also the first to open an address bureau, where one could go to obtain the address of any person living in the capital, whether celebrated or ordinary. Soon a placement office was added to the address bureau, and one went there to find domestic servants of all sorts.[3] His son, the personal physician of Louis XIV's daughter-in-law, Anne of Bavaria, continued to publish the collection of addresses, as did his son after him, and the reporters on their newspaper were therefore kept informed of everything of any importance that happened in Paris. Doctor Renaudot, what is more, applied himself energetically to the study of Oriental languages, drafted reports on the situation in Rome, England, and Spain, which were read in the king's council, and became part of the Cardinal de Noailles's circle. His close links to François de Callières, one of Louis XIV's private secretaries and the cousin of a former governor of Montreal, were of the highest potential value to La Salle.

Bernou and Renaudot presented La Salle to all the brightest company in the capital. Their protégé spoke wonderfully; he never contradicted himself. He was alien to vanity, and besides had no need to trumpet his merits. The least of his adventures made his audience gasp. But times had changed and the New World was no longer in fashion now that France had triumphed over all of Europe. The Sun King's subjects took exquisite pleasure in savoring France's military and artistic preeminence, and the frisson to be had from hearing the hardships of that great eccentric La Salle lasted only a moment. If the preceding reign had been a time of religious fervor, now, by contrast, courtiers were less preoccupied with the souls of American savages than with the costumes they would wear to the ball at Versailles.

Neither Bernou nor Renaudot accepted discouragement. If buffalo robes and native Americans could not draw attention to La Salle, they would find a way of recasting the enterprise to fit the current political discourse. In 1684, Louis XIV, "at the apogee of power, the arbiter and peacemaker [of Europe], king of a happy nation, and the model for all other nations at that time," had one and only one source of irritation: Spain. The Spanish had accepted the Peace of Nijmegen grudgingly, and countered their submissiveness in Europe with vigorous activity in the New World. Spain had barred French ships and merchants from access to its ports in America. Louis XIV had proclaimed the oceans to be free, yet French vessels had been seized and their crews imprisoned. In the meantime Seignelay, who had overseen the rebuilding of the French navy, longed to put his new weapon to use. Establishing a port in the Gulf of Mexico as a permanent threat to Spain and as the natural starting point for any future conquests was a grandiose project, just the sort to appeal to Louis XIV. Renaudot understood that to make La Salle's fortune (and accordingly his own), it was simply a question of redirecting focus from the Indians to the Spaniards. The idea had been suggested to him by a certain Count Peñalossa. This man was a Spanish creole born in Peru, who had been governor of Mexico until the Inquisition took too close an interest in him and he was forced to seek refuge in Europe. Now living in France, he would describe in glittering detail to anyone willing to listen the fabulous riches of the silver mines of New Biscay. A thousand buccaneers from Santo Domingo, if ably led, would be enough to seize them. Penalossa was too baroque a character to make headway with the king's entourage; but the two abbés, neither of whom had made a vow of poverty, considered the adventure worth trying. From this perspective, La Salle's arrival could not have been more timely, and his mentors quickly analyzed the situation for his benefit.

For the petition to succeed, the issue had to be presented the other way around, and the north–south, Quebec-to-Louisiana axis shifted southwestward to the Gulf of Mexico, that is, in the approximate geography of the day, to northern Mexico. The proposal would be to establish a settlement on the gulf from which "considerable conquests [could be made] on land and on sea for the greater glory of the King; or if execution of these conquests were deferred because of the peace, they would be poised for certain victory whenever it should please the King to order it."[4] La Salle, a man of disinterested curiosity, an explorer haunted by the line of the horizon, an adoptive Canadian who had bonded with "his" Indians and knew about trapping and the workings of the fur trade, now faced a project entirely different from the one he had in mind. From a commercial and possibly religious venture, it had become a preamble to conquest. But La Salle was not a military man. While perfectly capable of firing a gun when attacked, or to keep the Iroquois or another Indian tribe at bay, he had never taken part in a full-dress battle against the English or the Dutch. Exploration, trade, and settlement were his provinces. He was now being offered command of an expeditionary force that would operate in an area he had only barely glimpsed. A reasonable man would have hesitated to launch himself on such a risky adventure and bring a large party with him. But the prospect of returning to America with the support of his king, solvent once again, must have gone to his head — particularly after the demeaning treatment he had received from La Barre. Perhaps the hardships, near-fatal fever, and frenzied pace of the last years had clouded his mind. Bernou and Renaudot, imagining America's great riches, certainly played up the benefits of the adventure and drew a shimmering picture of the possibilities. At any rate La Salle, who until then had always been meticulous in his preparations despite his rare imagination, now lost his footing and threw himself into a dubious enterprise. He refused, however, to enter into partnership with Peñalossa, and by exercising his fascination over Seignelay he managed to avoid it.

La Salle advanced his plan in a long memoir to the minister. It is an odd mix of fantasy and reality. First he proposed "to return by the mouth of the river in the gulf of the Mississippi to the lands he had discovered" and build a fort there.[5] He supported this measure by pointing out that "the King's right to the country. . . must be safeguarded now that it is formally in his possession."[6] He then went on to describe the geographic and strategic benefits: the fertility of the soil and the mildness of the climate would make it possible to produce locally "all the comforts of life." The river being narrow at this point, it would be very easy to defend from attack, particularly as "the coast and the riverbanks are flooded for more than twenty leagues above its mouth, making it inaccessible by land,"[7] and "unapproachable for more than twenty leagues around because of woods, marshes, canebrakes, and quaking bogs where it is impossible to walk, a fact which may explain why the Spaniards neglected to explore this river, if they ever knew of it."[8] Up to this point, there is nothing that is not strictly true, including the prescient remark about the difficulty of making a landing on the gulf. Then he turned to military considerations. A fortified site on the gulf opened great possibilities: "the seizure of provinces that are very rich in silver mines, near the Colbert River, far from help, and defended by a small number of people who are too indolent and effeminate to endure the rigors of such a war." He suggested conquering the province of New Biscay, the northernmost province of Mexico where Texas is today, and he supplied an ingenious argument for the attack: "The silver mines would be of much greater profit to the French. They can transport the metal easily thanks to the nearby river,[9] whereas the Spaniards must cart the silver overland to Mexico, either from ignorance or fear of the savages, and so that the viceroys may profit. The cost of cartage is as unnecessary as it is inevitable given the distances."[10] Pursuing his resolutely optimistic vision, he proposed that the conquest should be undertaken by an army of Indians. The natives, he explained, "are irritated by the Spaniards' tyranny, and wage a bloody war on them though until now they have had no firearms. They will do much more harm when they see themselves backed by the French, whose milder and more humane government will be the main inducement to remaining at peace with them."[11] He went as far as to claim that he could put an army of 15,000 natives in the field,[12] supported by 4,000 Indians brought down the Mississippi by Tonty from his fort on the Illinois. The idea was absurd, and La Salle knew it. He had spent whole days choosing Indians one by one to accompany him down the Mississippi — and he had congratulated himself on finding thirty Indians who would stay loyal. Perhaps he was convinced the attack against the Spaniards would never take place and that his bad faith declarations were therefore immaterial. The important thing for him was to be given the right to establish a settlement in Louisiana. It was at any rate on the strength of this memorandum (and the success of Renaudot's maneuvering) that he obtained an audience with the king. To be invited to express one's views and wishes to the king was a signal honor. Nothing was rarer than to be granted an audience in his study, "even when on duly commissioned business of the king's. An audience was never granted, for example, to a diplomat going or returning from a foreign mission, nor to any general officer, except in a few very special cases,"[13] Saint-Simon observes. A great deal was to be gained from these audiences, as La Salle would learn, because "the king listened patiently, kindly, with a desire to be enlightened and instructed, [and] never interrupted except to that end."[14] No word came of Louis XIV's reaction, and it being the rule at court to trumpet one's success, the silence made La Salle's friends fear the worst. In fact La Salle got more than he had asked for; Louis XIV had caught the American fever. On April 14, he declared that "having commissioned some enterprises in North America, [we choose] La Salle to command all the Frenchmen and Indians he may need to execute the orders we have given him and we commission said nobleman to command, under our authority, in all the lands of North America that may hereafter be submitted to our rule, from Fort Saint Louis on the Illinois river to New Biscay."[15]

To accomplish this vast program, La Salle was given four ships: a thirty-six-gun warship, the *Joly*;[16] a small frigate of six guns, the *Belle* (given to La Salle outright); a store ship of 300 tons, the *Aimable*, to transport the settlement's provisions; and a thirty-ton ketch to carry the wine, meat, and vegetables as far as Santo Domingo. There, they would take on fresh water and thirty buccaneers as reinforcements for their small army. The party consisted of about three hundred and twenty people. A disparate group, it included a hundred or so soldiers from La Rochelle and Rochefort, all untried men, whom the minister himself believed to be "no more than children and men of little use."[17] There were also thirty volunteer officers; a few dozen workmen, masons, carpenters, edge-tool makers; a few families with four or five young children in tow, ready to launch into the colonizing venture;[18] the inevitable orphaned girls who were looking for a husband and a better life; an engineer; eight merchants; and three Recollet friars. Father Zénobe, La Salle's companion on the return trip up the Mississippi, had asked to rejoin him on his travels. And there was finally a small group of family consisting of La Salle's brother, Abbé Cavelier (apparently on friendly terms again), two nephews, and Henri Joutel, an old acquaintance from Rouen whose father had been a gardener for the La Salle family. Joutel had just returned home after sixteen years in the army, when he was swept up by the excitement in Rouen over the new adventure; he dropped his plans of retirement in order to volunteer his services and served as the expedition's chronicler.[19]

La Salle, when he traveled alone with Nika, was amazingly efficient; and the loyalty shown him by Abbé Gallinée, Father Zénobe, La Forest, Tonty, and many other companions proves that he was capable of inspiring admiration and respect. But his cold, taciturn personality made him unfit, as we've seen before, to lead a large and diverse group of strangers. The problem was compounded by the fact that he was confused in his own mind about the expedition's goals and hard put to make them clear to others. Also, the command of the expedition was divided. Seignelay, having newly renovated the royal navy, was unwilling to lose any ships and refused to appoint La Salle sole master on board during the crossing. Sea command was given to Captain Beaujeu, with some restrictions. "He was to comply with the Sieur de La Salle in all matters of command. His Majesty desires said Beaujeu to command on the ship with regards to maneuvers, but where the route is concerned His Majesty intends that he perform all that the Sieur de La Salle may desire."[20]

When Beaujeu read these orders, he almost had a fit. That he, the son of a personal valet to Queen Marie de Médicis, with more than thirty years' service in the navy, thirteen of them as a ship's captain, should be required "to submit to the orders of the Sieur de La Salle, a good man, but one who, after all, has never made war on any but savages, who has no rank,[21] and no clue how to act, having always lived with ignorant schoolboys and Indians,"[22] was enough to make him choke with rage. La Salle was behaving bizarrely. Suspicious to the point of persecution mania, he could only poison the situation further.

For the first time in his life, he was riddled with doubt. The king might have been convinced, but he, La Salle, was suffering from anxiety. His knowledge of the area where he was to land was sketchy, and he had no illusions about the problems that a colonizing venture would face. The odds against establishing a settlement in a place where, two years before, neither his men nor his Indians had been able to light a fire to cook their meat after a hunt were phenomenal, especially as they were relying on Frenchmen who had never experienced the hardships of an uncivilized country. And he was well aware that plans of conquest were at the very best doubtful. La Salle was so uncertain that he considered returning to the mouth of the Mississippi via Canada. It would be impossible to explain this change of plan without drawing attention to the weak points in the version that the king had accepted. La Salle knew this and held back from proposing the change, instead fretting in silence. His uncertainty was plainly visible to Beaujeu, who was surprised that La Salle had not even informed him of their route or final destination. "The man is so suspicious," the captain wrote, "and so fearful one might penetrate his secrets, that I hardly dare to ask him anything. He was incensed one day that I should say it might be wise to consider where to find a pilot with experience in those parts. To date, he has refused to speak clearly on this."[23] Obviously, under the circumstances, the order for departure was not given. It grew so late in the season that Beaujeu was concerned about cyclones in the South Atlantic and stated a preference for the northern route with a layover in Canada. La Salle seems to have come to his senses then. He asked Beaujeu to choose a pilot who, besides knowing the coast of Santo Domingo and the Gulf of Mexico, was familiar with the Saint Lawrence.[24] Three days later, however, he had shut himself in silence once again. "I do not like his suspicions," the poor captain wrote. "I think him a good, honest Norman, but Normans are out of fashion. Today it is one thing, tomorrow another. This morning he came to see me and told me he had changed his mind, and meant to give a new turn to the business, and go in a different direction."[25] And finally: "Almost everyone believes he is unbalanced. I have spoken to people who have known him for twenty years. They all say that he was always rather visionary."[26] The trip's final destination was crucial, and a number of other decisions hinged on it. Should they take on biscuit or flour? wine or brandy? The length of the voyage would determine the issue — flour clearly took less room than biscuit, and could be stored in sacks between decks. Then there was the question that recurred endlessly in that century: with whom should one dine? "We had another quarrel," the captain reported. "He asked me where his men, which is to say his officers, should take their meals. I answered they might eat wherever he pleased; for having no orders, I was not concerned with it. He answered that they would not mess on bacon, while the rest ate fowls and mutton. I said that if he would send fowls and mutton on board, his people might eat them; but as for bacon, I had often eaten it myself."[27] The two men wore each other down with arguing. When La Salle asked Beaujeu to commit himself by signing a long list of contractual articles, the captain gave in to the request while expressing his surprise to Seignelay: "I don't like sailing and conducting war according to an itemized contract, but I have conceded on every point to get along with him. I called for a judgment from the provincial administrator, who kindly took the trouble to alter his memorandum and make another, which I signed to please Monsieur de La Salle and remove any excuse or cause for complaint. By this you can judge Monsieur de La Salle's character better than by all that I could say. It is plain that I am not putting difficulties in his way but that he is making difficulties for himself."[28]

On July 18, 1684, La Salle wrote a farewell letter to his mother in which he gave her good news "of little Colin," the youngest of his nephews, and promised to embrace her in a year "with all the pleasure of a very grateful child in having so good a mother" as she had always been.[29] Six days later the ships set sail.

❧ 13 ❧

Tristes Tropiques
1684–1685

I WONDER WHETHER, LIKE CLAUDE LEVI-STRAUSS, La Salle didn't hate traveling and whether, like him, he didn't deplore the "loss of weeks and months spent on the road, and that it took so much effort and useless expense" to reach one's goal.[1] He declined to look around him. The journey itself was not of interest. His first letters from 1685, although written on shipboard, are filled with tales of ruffled feelings and suspicions that one might expect him to have left behind on shore. No mention is made of the spectacular surprises of the southern Atlantic crossing. It is easy to see La Salle, a tall, gloomy man, pacing the decks of the *Joly*, obsessively rehearsing his grudges, plagued by hopes and anxieties, too tormented to notice the splendid sunsets as other travelers did, or to be amazed at the shoals of flying fish that, propelled by a thump of the tail, their fins spread wide, spurted out of the water like sparks around the boat. In Canada the cold did not seem to affect him; in these tropical waters the heavy, humid, and unbearable heat aboard the overcrowded ship rates not a single mention. Christopher Columbus, who affected no such stoicism, claims that as his crew approached landfall they believed they would burn up in the rays of the sun.

The presence of Beaujeu must also have been a constant irritation. A long sea voyage is trying in the best of circumstances. The inevitable shipboard incidents, magnified by the fact that the two antagonists communicated only through their lieutenants, several times threatened to put an end to the enterprise. When the *Joly*'s mast broke forty leagues from La Rochelle, La Salle was convinced "that this accident was not the result of bad luck."[2] In other words, he was accusing the captain of sabotage, and his suspicions were only dispelled by the captain's industriousness in replacing the broken mast. Three weeks later, Beaujeu was worried about running out of water. As he was carrying 250 people in a boat designed for 125, and consequently had been forced to cut back on stores, he requested to put into port at Madeira "to take on a few refreshments."[3] La Salle, however, suspected him of wanting to anchor only to engage in trade. As he was also concerned that they might lose their favorable winds during the stopover, he refused his permission, to the great anger of the travelers and crew. During the crossing of the Tropic of Cancer, there was nearly a mutiny. The seamen were in great good spirits preparing to initiate all who had not yet "crossed the line." La Salle knew the custom well from having observed it — from as far away as possible — when approaching the icy latitudes of the North Atlantic. He knew that the men received big gratuities on this occasion and accepted flasks of brandy from passengers who wanted to avoid the traditional dunking. He nonetheless insisted that his party take no part in the ceremony. Joutel, seeing the crew's fury, wrote that "the seamen would certainly have been glad to kill us all."[4] Luckily, the crossing was short and favorable (one of the women on board, Madame Talon, gave birth to a boy, Robert, whom La Salle accepted as a godson), and they reached Santo Domingo before the men came to blows. More than fifty of them, in any case, were lying sick with fever in the bottom of the hold, oppressed by heat, thirst, and the terrible crowding that heaped them one on top of another, to be splashed by cats and weasels jumping into puddles as they chased mice and rats through the nauseating darkness.

The sick were taken ashore, but as no lodging could be found they were installed at some distance from port on a small island where, ominously enough, the Protestant cemetery was located. Passengers who had money started looking for houses to rent while waiting for the other boats to join them and for the captain to finish reprovisioning for the second portion of their voyage. Here again, even more than on the ocean crossing, one is disappointed with the dry and uninformative accounts. The stopover at Santo Domingo, on the threshold of an unknown world, must all the same have given them something to think about. The island had been discovered almost two hundred years before (Santo Domingo and Haiti are Columbus's Hispaniola), and though the population had once numbered more than 100,000 inhabitants, the island now offered a sorry spectacle. The Europeans lived in disorder and idleness, while the native societies had fallen apart on contact with the white man. "The air is bad," Joutel wrote, "the fruit no better, and a great number of women even worse than the fruit."[5] In fact a number of the soldiers and several of the officers took away a searingly painful reminder of their stopover. What a contrast with New France, also at the edge of an unknown world, but offering a solid and organized point of departure from which to draw strength and obtain provisions before launching a voyage.

In the Antilles, it was impossible to buy supplies. Whereas in Canada, fish were caught by the shovelful and turtledoves knocked down from trees with sticks, in Santo Domingo the price of goods was phenomenally high: a hen cost forty sous, or nearly five times what it cost in France.[6] Yet the ships had to be restocked — especially as the ketch, which carried the lard, flour, kettles, ammunition, and ship parts, had been captured by the Spanish. La Salle had to borrow from two merchants who accompanied him, the Duhaut brothers, who found buyers for the fabric, lacework, dress, "and other items of the kind that would be useless in the wilderness where they were headed."[7] What was more worrisome was the general ignorance about the geography of the Gulf of Mexico. A century before, Philip II of Spain had announced that he would execute any foreigner found in the gulf, and the threat had effectively prevented any exploration of its waters. No maps were available and the landmarks were unknown. No one could tell the travelers what to look for except that the currents would carry the boats eastward out of the gulf. Whether because of anxiety or weakness, La Salle fell ill at this juncture with such a violent burning fever that "his imagination presented him things at once terrible and wonderful."[8]

La Salle's suspicions, when he regained consciousness, were stronger than ever, as though fed by his fever. Convinced that he could count on neither Beaujeu nor Aigron, the captain of the *Aimable*, La Salle decided that he and a few trustworthy men would transfer to the *Aimable* "with their cases, their trunks, and their beds" to prevent the crew from making an attempt to desert. To accompany him, he chose his brother, Abbé Cavelier, as well as Nika (whom the other passengers always called "Monsieur de La Salle's Indian"), Father Zénobe, Joutel, and his young nephews. Beaujeu would therefore remain on the *Joly*, the fastest of the ships, but with orders to stay in the rear of the convoy: La Salle was afraid the captain would otherwise go on ahead and leave them. In these circumstances, needless to say, defections were numerous, and the situation was aggravated by the local inhabitants, who enjoyed discouraging the men by telling them that they were headed for "an arid, desert country without any sign of game."[9] Joutel reports that everyone had a different reason for not returning on board. La Salle ordered all his men back to the ship, to remove temptation, and announced an early date of departure. The captains of the three boats gathered for a conference with a privateer, who claimed to know the coast. All three agreed that they would head for Cuba, round the western point of the island, and enter the gulf from there. Beaujeu at this point asked La Salle for a certificate of good faith performance to protect him from any subsequent accusations. La Salle supplied it readily, and a few days later one hundred soldiers set sail, along with eight merchants, nine volunteers, forty-four hired men and valets, eight women, seven children, a cow, a nanny goat and a billy goat, and a few piglets.

If La Salle set off with such a doubtful, ill-provisioned, and demoralized crew, it is because he wanted to believe that he was traveling toward a known land rather than into unexplored territory. He must have realized that his sightings were inaccurate, but thought that the brown waters discharged by the Mississippi would surely be visible. He foresaw no difficulties. If the mouth of the Seine did not go unnoticed, was it possible not to spot the Mississippi from a distance? On December 30, 1684, after twelve days at sea (not counting a short stop at Cuba, where they ate crocodile and an animal that looked like a rat but was the size of a cat), La Salle ordered soundings to be taken. They felt bottom, indicating they had reached the coast. According to their calculations, they were in Appalachee Bay on the northwest end of the Florida peninsula. Contributing to their confusion, their charts placed Petit Goave, their point of departure, three degrees west of its actual location, which translates into an error of some 150 miles. At any rate, they set sail toward the west. In fact, they had reached their destination on the first try, the currents not being as strong as they had allowed for. They made landfall just west of the delta they were seeking, but did not and could not know this. Dozens of rivers entered the gulf, meandering around clusters of trees and flat islands that barely emerged from the murky water. The coast, with its wavering shoreline shrouded in mist, presented no recognizable landmarks.

A coast implies some demarcation between sea and shore. To most minds, the coast is a line around the land. It is visible; there is a passage from one element to another, from land to sea, solid to liquid. But the approaches to Louisiana don't lend themselves with such a simplification. Arriving by water — if the fog by some miracle has not masked the area — the seafarer sees not a line but long strips of land, low islands overlapping one another, behind which there is no visible land, the shoreline so submerged it seems a vast watery spread spattered with islands. This explains why it is hard to make out the mouth of even a large river in this liquid landscape. But not finding the Mississippi Delta has always seemed so incredible to me that I wanted to retrace La Salle's movements myself. It is not easy to travel by boat along the coast in our day because the gulf is so full of offshore oil rigs; tourists aren't encouraged to pick their way among the tankers and outboards. The roads all end a long way inland, and to drive in the coastal area you would need an amphibious vehicle. An airplane, on the other hand, offers an unparalleled view.

A small twin-engine plane takes forty minutes to follow the river from New Orleans to the gulf. From above, the Mississippi at New Orleans looks more like an avenue than a river: its asphalt brown waters, confined between high dikes, carry long lines of barges. At Venice, the very spot where La Salle and his companions erected a cross in 1683, the river runs freely again. The dikes on either side disappear, the road along the shore ends, and the Mississippi bursts into three main branches. These in turn divide and ramify so that, from the sky, the estuary looks not like a mouth but like a liquid fan, a carpet of water sprinkled with fragments of land. The pilot flies out over the gulf to give a wider view of the shoreline on the way back. Even from this height, so much higher above the water than the deck of a boat, the eye grows tired trying to tell apart the different channels, islands, and bays. After only a few minutes in this shifting, fluid landscape it is easy to lose one's bearings and not recognize what one has just seen. La Salle, moreover, had seen the country backwards first, from the land side going toward the sea. This made finding his way in from the sea all the more difficult.

What you cannot tell from a plane is how fiercely the coast repels. La Salle discovered this on New Year's day 1685 when he landed with Minet, the engineer, to study the terrain. Behind the narrow islands was a marshy plain, into which they sank as though it were quicksand. In Louisiana, people distinguish between inland swamps, where a few trees manage to survive, usually cypresses, and coastal marshes, where the trees have been drowned. But you sink up to the knee in both places, and receive the same cuts from hostile vegetation — big bunches of high grass, called saw grass, with blades like knives that keep an intruder out as effectively as barbed wire. La Salle did not push his investigation far, especially as the country was distressingly the same in all directions. No hill, no rise in the ground gave any vantage from which to look beyond the sheet of brackish and undrinkable water. The two men soon climbed back into their canoe to return to the ships. Without hesitation, they set a westward course and the three boats advanced along a parallel route: the *Joly* outside the reefs in deep water; the *Aimable* closer to land, trying to stay in less than eight fathoms of water; and the little *Belle* hugging the shore as closely as possible. La Salle, remembering the deep bottom at the mouth of the Mississippi, was convinced that he would know they had reached the river's entrance from his depth readings. He stopped looking at the features of the coast, which was uniformly flat, and gave the pilots orders to sound the bottom day and night.

A second landing, in a bay known today as Atchela Bay, was aborted because of fog, shoals, and a strong surf. An Indian party appeared on shore, and to show their peaceful intentions, the warriors stuck their arrows in the ground. The French signaled for them to approach the boat, but "the waves overpowered them so"[10] that the Indians were unable to swim out. Nine of them then pushed a large dead tree into the water and, holding onto the trunk with one hand and paddling with the other, managed to reach the launch. They were brought aboard the *Aimable*, numb with cold and violently seasick, where La Salle gave them a pipe and a few swallows of wine. Once they had warmed up, he tried to find out from them just where he was, but neither he nor Nika could understand their language. The one benefit from this exchange was that La Salle earned the admiration of his companions for speaking several Indian dialects.

The coast was flat, sandy, and monotonous, and a water-covered plain extended far inland. The travelers could see nothing on it, except when Nika showed them deer or buffalo in the distance — "these people," Joutel noted, "have much better eyesight than we do." The animals, grazing in the marshes, would flee at a gallop when the wind carried to them the scent or the sound of humans. La Salle was worried about the distance they had traveled and tried to land from time to time, but always found the surf too strong. On January 17, with drinking water running low, a resolute attempt was made. The dangers and difficulties overcome, an advance party managed to land on a point between Matagorda Bay and Corpus Christi, at the very southern tip of Texas on the present-day Mexican border. It was hard to say, however, whether this strip of spongy ground, littered with oyster shells as sharp as glass, and looping around large salty lakes, was truly land. The men killed several cranes and a number of ducks. Shoals of crustaceans attracted thousands of birds, among them a large bird the men immediately named "big gullets" (La Salle informed them that the king's menagerie at Versailles had birds like these, called pelicans); others were named "spoonbills" because of their beaks; and the number and variety of eagles never ceased to amaze them. But there was still no fresh water, and the prospect of not finding any terrified them. The coast was definitely sloping southward. La Salle was forced to acknowledge that he had missed the mouth of the Great River — by 400 miles, although he didn't know it.

The three ships regrouped. It was clear that they had to turn back, but neither of the commanders had any idea how great a navigational error they had made. La Salle was convinced that the Mississippi, or at least an arm of it, flowed into Matagorda Bay,[11] which is a bay more than fifty miles wide, closed off by a long sand bar bristling with razor-sharp oysters. He asked Joutel, whom he trusted absolutely, to land first from the shallops with the greater part of the men. It would be his responsibility to choose a campsite. La Salle would join him afterward, as he could tell from the narrow channel that it would be difficult to bring the ships into the bay. Joutel succeeded in his task, despite the incompetence of most of the men accompanying him: "We were 120 or 130 men, when thirty good men would have been better by far and performed a great deal more, except when it came to eating, where the men were second to none."[12] A primitive camp was established at the head of the bay, by the mouth of a river, which La Salle, after inspecting it, was convinced "could be a branch of his river." He decided to have the two ships enter the bay. The *Aimable* was carrying all the provisions they needed to establish a permanent camp, as they expected to set up a bridgehead for a true exploration of the interior; the smaller *Belle* would be useful for going up the river. The *Belle* went first with La Salle on board and easily passed the bar. Aigron, who was captain of the *Aimable*, was acting bizarrely and in a way that boded ill for the operation. According to Minet, "The wine that Monsieur de La Salle had left for the captain and the pilot made them bolder than they should have been." Aigron refused the help of the pilot who had earlier passed the bar successfully and insisted that La Salle draw up a written order releasing him from any responsibility. He then had all his personal effects transferred to the *Joly*, even his private store of jam. La Salle stood on shore nervously watching Aigron's first maneuvers when suddenly he was startled by the sound of high-pitched yells. As if in a nightmare, he turned to see his workers on the run with Indians in hot pursuit. Showing the calm and authority for which he was legendary, he ordered the men around him to grab their weapons and charged toward the Indians.

By a miraculous bit of pantomime, he stopped the natives in their tracks and, grasping that several Frenchmen had already been brought to the Indian village, he asked to be taken there. At the moment he was entering the village, which consisted of about fifty huts, a cannon shot rang out. The Indians were terrified and fell to the ground. La Salle, who knew it meant that the *Aimable* was in trouble, allowed no trace of his anxiety to show. He was brought before a chief, who was surrounded by "several women who were completely naked except for a hide around the waist and who were not very pretty," and presented a gift of a dried tortoise, some jerked buffalo meat, and some pieces of fresh porpoise, which the chief accepted solemnly. He then asked leave to depart with his men and this was granted without objection, but on arriving at the beach in front of his own camp his worst fears were confirmed. The *Aimable* had struck bottom and their supplies for the year were pouring out a gash in its flank. The crew managed to save part of the flour and gunpowder, thanks to a shallop sent immediately by Beaujeu from the *Joly;* and the sea washed ashore a few barrels of wine and brandy, some cases of tools, and a hundred axes. But these disparate objects could not make up for losing the main bulk of the cargo, in particular the blacksmith's tools, his anvils, and the bricks intended for the forge. It would have been no dishonor, faced with a disaster of this magnitude, for La Salle to abandon the attempt, withdraw to Santo Domingo, and try to refit the expedition from there. He could not bring himself to do it. His greatness had always come from his courage and determination, and by some miracle of nature, he had always had the physical strength to accomplish his aims. Phenomenally capable on the Ohio, at Niagara Falls, and during his repeated crossings of Canada, he would have been so again in Texas had he been leading a handful of willing men, and if his health had not been shattered. But instead of enjoying the support of a few stout men, he was at the head of a community of more than a hundred. Here, his refusal to bow to necessity would work differently: his tenacity, always admirable before, now became a dangerous obstinacy. He was convinced that his river was nearby and he decided to stay. They would build a small fort, and he would resume exploring. Beaujeu then decided reasonably enough that he had accomplished his mission and prepared to leave in mid-March of 1685. With La Salle's consent, he would take back to France anyone who was afraid to remain in America.

Although they had quarreled so often, Beaujeu and La Salle parted on civil terms. The captain made a present of his nanny goat and billy goat, and a hen and a rooster, which, with Joutel's pigs, formed the start of a barnyard. La Salle was delighted to have his command all to himself — he would no longer have to justify his decisions to anyone. And he was glad to see part of the rabble he had been saddled with leaving. All too many of these craftsmen were staying behind, of the kind that would slack off at work, along with soldiers who were both impatient and undisciplined. Having families and marriageable girls along made matters worse, but La Salle's plan was to establish a base camp on the gulf and head into the backcountry with Nika to look for the Mississippi. He would also take a few officers, his brother, and his nephew, hoping they would form a close, efficient team.

The fort was built in a very few days, using materials salvaged from the wreck of the *Aimable,* on a site that proved to be quite horrible. The low dunes were unsheltered from the wind. The water that seeped in everywhere was brackish and green, and gave off an acrid smell. Eating mostly oysters and snakes and weakened by scurvy, the colonists were terrified of the Indians, who stalked the camp yipping and howling like wolves. Discouragement and bitterness became general. La Salle had no remedy to offer and was gone for weeks at a time exploring the bay aboard the *Belle* and pushing inland with a few men in a resolute effort to reach the great river. Exploring is one thing, being lost is another. Traveling along an unknown river can be strenuous and even dangerous, but the certainty that one is moving in a posted direction lays many anxieties to rest. That is why, on the American prairie, which has no landmarks, no variation, no signs of life in any direction, one feels intensely uneasy. La Salle had established colonies before in places where there were no whites — at Fort Frontenac on the deserted shores of Lake Ontario, at Fort Saint Joseph, and in the forest wilderness at Fort Crèvecœur — but he had never been deprived of a fallback position that was familiar (and we have seen that he did not think twice about retracing his steps, even at the cost of enormous hardship, when he felt it was necessary). He had always had the reassurance of knowing where he was; the terrible anguish that now gripped him and his companions was new. The coast along the gulf was hostile, and conditions were difficult, but La Salle's Canadian followers had survived hardships greater than this. The climate at this time of year was milder than farther north on the continent. And the men could provide for themselves by hunting buffalo, as the herds that had fled on their arrival had returned after several weeks. But the total isolation, the uncertainty as to where they were and what they would do, and the lack of any organization were unnerving. Nothing had prepared the men for being alone in this deserted tract of land. As difficult as it was to imagine the Canadian forest and the banks of the Saint Lawrence from a farm in Normandy or a Breton port, the men who crossed to the New World had possessed written descriptions on which to base their expectations. They also knew that ships sailed back to France on a regular schedule. In La Salle's entourage this boost to the general morale was lacking; and without regular rules or discipline the level of anxiety increased, causing irreparable damage. La Salle's coldness and reserve at first chilled, then irritated his companions. "When Monsieur de La Salle is among us," wrote Joutel, "joy is often banished."[13] His restraint was all the more disastrous in that he should, on the contrary, have been making every effort to inject some semblance of life and gaiety into the group. The colonists were traumatized by unexpected hardships and were dying at a terrifying rate. In spite of the injunctions of Joutel and La Salle, they poisoned themselves by eating unripe berries and drinking the standing water around camp. The women acted more reasonably, fetching water at a clear stream some distance away, and stayed healthier. In fact no woman or child died during those terrible early days. But even the most hardened found it demoralizing to start a settlement by laying out a cemetery and seeing its crosses grow more crowded every day.

La Salle decided to abandon the site as too unhealthy. Joutel stayed at the original encampment they called the "Big Camp" with the women, children and disabled men, while La Salle went into the interior with fifty workers. They followed a river which La Salle christened Cattle River (the present-day Lavaca) because he was so astonished at the number of buffalo that came down to the water to drink. Two leagues inland from the bay, or about five miles, he found flat ground on a slight elevation that he thought would do. Constructing the stockade and houses was more diffi- cult than they anticipated. Spring, though marked by an explo- sion of wildflowers that carpeted the plains in blue as far as the horizon, was surprisingly brief. It suddenly grew hot, and the heat was atrocious. The first settlers in Canada had been surprised by the cold; in Texas, it was the torrid summer that the Europeans found unbearable. The flowers gave way to dry, yellow grass, as stiff as barbed wire. "If I owned both Texas and hell," an officer at Fort Clark claimed in 1855, "I'd rent out Texas and live in hell."[14] Hauling logs was exhausting for men unaccustomed to such work. La Salle had to take over from carpenters unable to perform their tasks, and "he was so grieved not to accomplish things as he had hoped that he mistreated the men, often to ill effect." In August, finally, the colonists moved into the new fort, but the death of one of the most prominent members of the expedition cast a pall on the occasion. Sieur Le Gros was bitten by a rattlesnake at the Big Camp, when gangrene set in, the surgeon saw no alternative to amputating the leg, and Monsieur Le Gros "consented to it, though the surgeon had never performed the procedure be- fore."[15] Needless to say, the poor man died two days later.

The living quarters left much to be desired — the boards were so cracked and knot-holed that it was necessary to stretch buffalo hides over the roofs to keep out rain, but the hides wrinkled and split under the hot sun. And the plantings were practically all ruined by drought and insects. Still, once autumn returned, the country was not without charm. The blue spring flowers were re- placed by a thousand shades of yellow and gold, and there were grazing herds, although the vast plain where the eye finds nothing to arrest it filled even hardened men with mortal dread.

La Salle meanwhile could think only of finding "his river." In October he named Joutel commander of Fort Saint Louis — once again taking the king's name for the Texas fort. After drawing up an inventory and writing out Joutel's orders, particularly recommending that he guard the virtue of the young girls, La Salle set off inland with fifty men. They were heavily loaded with trade goods to appease any Indians they might meet and carried provisions in case game grew scarce. His immediate entourage consisted of his two nephews, a Huguenot secretary, his personal physician, Liotot, two servants, Dumesnil and Saget, and the faithful Nika.

He would have done better to go alone with Nika. The rest of the party had neither the strength nor the endurance to clear a trail through difficult terrain. Ten miles from the coast, the vegetation changes. The area, which Texans call the "Big Thicket," has such a profusion of vines and palms, such a tangle of aerial roots and high canes that it is virtually impenetrable. Slippery mosses, lichens, and algae develop in the humid shade underfoot. They dispersed in a lengthening column, and the officers lacked the moral authority to handle such a refractory group. La Salle's own nephew, Moranger, whose aggressiveness had already caused a number of incidents, was responsible for the first drama on the expedition. La Salle had asked him to bring up the rear and leave no one behind, knowing how difficult it was to catch up with others on an unmarked trail. ("No one would be so foolhardy," writes a contemporary traveler, "as to step off the trail alone even for a few yards."[16]) Moranger refused to wait for one of the Duhaut brothers, who had to stop to repair his bundle and his shoes. As they were traveling through reeds and rushes along what must have been the Colorado River, Duhaut lost his companions from sight. He hesitated among a number of "buffalo roads," and finally, "highly distraught, and not without reason,"[17] he decided to retrace his steps. He arrived at Fort Saint Louis after a nightmarish trek, traveling at night for fear of the Indians, and using the flint from his gun to cut open the deer and turkeys he managed to kill. He swore revenge.

In the meantime, La Salle pushed on. He crossed the Trinity and Sabine rivers, then stopped at a river so big and lazy that he at first mistook it for the Mississippi, though it was only the Red River, a tributary. He had traveled 300 miles as the crow flies, discovering a country that appeared fertile and was peopled by Indians who were hospitable though they hated the Spanish; they spoke a word in greeting that the Europeans transcribed as "Texas." During the trip, La Salle always kept a small notebook on hand where he wrote down all the words he learned in his exchanges with the Indians. After a few months he could make himself understood by using drawings together with the words he was sure of. He recovered his bearings after crossing several rivers that ran to the southwest, and he was certain that by continuing his progress in a northeasterly direction he would reach the main body of the Mississippi. Besides, the growing humidity and daily rain showers and storms reminded him of the climate his party had encountered going down the river. Feeling more confident, La Salle turned back toward Fort Saint Louis, leaving two men to camp on the banks of the Red River. He wanted to bring the *Belle* in along the coast carrying the supplies they would need to establish a second post at the mouth of this new river, which, if it was not the Mississippi, was at any rate near to it.[18] Determined to move quickly, La Salle hastened the pace, and on March 26, 1686, Joutel saw a dozen men "in quite poor shape, their clothes all ragged, [particularly the Abbé Cavelier], whose cassock was in tatters so that there was hardly a piece left large enough to wrap two sous' worth of salt."[19] When he recognized them, "there was much embracing" and Joutel was proud to show La Salle his rows of chicory, beets, and celery; the melons, asparagus, and pumpkins were growing well, and he had great hopes for the cotton plants whose seed he had brought from Petit Goave. Thinking that those at the fort might not have managed to hunt buffalo, La Salle arrived bringing a large load of meat; he was relieved to learn that the men had wanted neither for game nor for fish. They brought him up to date on all the details of their daily life. If it had been in his nature, La Salle would have smiled to see a miniature France flourishing on the plains of Texas.

This was thanks to Joutel, whose gaiety and natural balance led him to seek normal relations in the small community. He admired La Salle and had unquestioned loyalty for him; but La Salle's strictness and his sometimes unfair harshness seemed to him unsuited to a camp filled with disgruntled exiles. As soon as Joutel was in sole command of the fort, he lightened the atmosphere by organizing songs and dances, and putting the presence of young women to good account. For some reason, they adapted to the unaccustomed food and climate better than the men, perhaps because they did not drink excessive amounts of brandy. The results surpassed his expectations. One young woman, whom La Salle called the Princess because of her delicate manners, went out walking so often with Barbier, an old hand from Canada who had worked at the *Griffon* shipyard, that Barbier had gone to Joutel for permission to marry her, "fearful that Monsieur de La Salle on his return might be distressed and unhappy to find that he had ill-used one of his young charges." But Saint Louis, Texas, was truly an outpost of France, and Joutel had not forgotten the customs of his ancestors, according to which like married like. He answered Barbier gravely "that he counseled him against marriage, [as] he was an officer and his rank put him above a girl no one had known before she embarked." However, the Recollet friars observed that it was better for the young people to marry since "so many things had already been performed," and Joutel consented, troubled by the idea that the first child born in his colony might be a bastard. Another young woman, Mademoiselle Paris, was only waiting for La Salle to return to marry the Chevalier de La Sablonnière. But La Salle emerged from his journey through the swamps more keen on etiquette than ever. He refused to authorize the marriage because of the unequal social station of the young lovers, and turned to the problems raised by the expected child. The debate seems more appropriate to Versailles than to Texas, but the firstborn of a colony had right to a title of nobility. Barbier consequently claimed it for his child, while Madame Talon, whose son had been born on the high seas, wanted it for her own. La Salle was unwilling to accommodate his old companion, as he viewed "with distaste the prospect of starting the colony with a child born before its proper term." The dilemma was resolved by the infant's death. Problems of a different sort soon demanded his attention: the *Belle* had left with ten men on a scouting mission around the bay and had not returned. La Salle was gnawed by impatience. The ship was vital for establishing a fort on the Mississippi and for returning to Santo Domingo if necessary. After a month of searching all around the bay, they saw a boat appear on the horizon. Five men landed from it, bringing word of a disheartening accident. They had been in the shallop looking for water. The pilot of the *Belle* grew impatient waiting for them to return and came in toward shore. He was drunk, not an atypical state for him (water was in short supply, but there was plenty of brandy on board), and he sank the ship on a sand bank. The survivors managed to save only a few papers La Salle had stored on board along with his scarlet cape, which he believed would be safer there than in camp. Having now no ship, the party's only way to reestablish contact with France was to go north to the Illinois River and return by that route to Canada. La Salle confided this to Joutel, whom he decided to take with him. More secretive and closemouthed than ever, he chose twenty-eight men and set off once again, leaving Barbier in command of Fort Saint Louis. If he had had wings, he would have had a journey of 1,000 miles ahead of him. On foot, and counting the twisting of the Mississippi, he was starting on a trip of more than 3,500 miles.

❖ 14 ❖

Monsieur de La Salle's Death

1687

IN FORT SAINT LOUIS, TEXAS, ORDER STILL REIGNED, at least on the surface. The year 1686 ended with a solemn celebration of midnight Mass, performed with all possible pomp. The colony drank the king's health on Twelfth Night with nothing stronger than water, but with "a great deal of gaiety," and on January 12, 1687, the expedition set out. Every member packed carefully, for although La Salle was committed to returning to the fort to rescue its inhabitants once he reached Canada, most of his companions hoped if they made it to civilization never to set eyes on Texas again. Joutel reports that "each took a part of his best belongings."[1] The travelers cut up the sails from the *Belle* to make shirts and extra linen for themselves. Joutel's baggage consisted of "several shirts, scarves, handkerchiefs," as well as knives and other trade goods. On an earlier expedition, La Salle had bought a few horses at a village of Cenis Indians, and these allowed the party to travel with large loads. As always happened when La Salle went into action, he recovered "an evenness of temper [that] was reassuring to everyone; and by force of will he found solutions to everything, which lifted even the most dejected spirits," writes

Joutel.[2] Father Douay adds, "It would be difficult in history to find a more intrepid and invincible courage than was shown by Monsieur de La Salle in adverse circumstances; he was never defeated, and he always hoped to succeed in his enterprises with God's help, no matter what the obstacles."[3] On leaving the fort, where there remained seven women and their children, three clergymen, the young officer Sablonnière, a surgeon, and three workmen, under the command and keeping of Barbier, La Salle "delivered an eloquent address, with the winning air that was natural to him. All the small colony were present and were moved to tears by it, convinced that his voyage was necessary and his intentions of the purest."[4] But it is worth noting that, of the 180 people who had landed, less than forty were left — accident, sickness, and desertion had decimated the population of the small fort. If one imagines the emotions felt by those staying behind as well as by those leaving on the long upriver voyage, it is not surprising that Joutel writes that they separated "so sadly and tenderly, it seemed as if all carried a secret foreboding that they would never see each other again."[5] At the same moment, some five hundred miles away, Tonty was heading north again, after having gone down the Mississippi as far as the gulf to look for La Salle, whose fate worried him. In the best of worlds, the two expeditions would have met at the mouth of the Arkansas River, but the American continent, previously host to so many miraculous encounters, now frustrated the explorers with its inhuman scale.

La Salle gave the signal for departure and started out in the lead, as always, striding with long steps over the marshy prairie and never turning his head to see if his men were keeping pace. Behind him, the little group plodded onward, without gaiety or enthusiasm. Social distinctions, so clearly drawn in camp, grew blurred, and any solidarity or camaraderie between the men disappeared, never to return. Misadventures, grudges and fear had left their mark. Duhaut and Liotot, the surgeon, fanned their grievances in the course of long conversations. La Salle had ruined them, they had little confidence in the expedition's success and were irritated by the attitude of the La Salle clan — by

Robert's arrogance, his nephew's insolence, and Abbé Cavelier's incompetence. They took pleasure in egging each other on: Duhaut rehashed his bitter feelings at having been abandoned in the bush two years before, and the surgeon aired his resentment, of Moranger in particular, to whom he had given competent medical attention though he received only insults and harsh words in return. The servants took sides with their masters in these quarrels, spied on each other, argued, and made up only to complain of the hardships they were facing. The horses, though spared more than the men, were unequal to the task, and the men cursed under the weight of baggage they felt to be useless. Even the faithful Joutel grumbled at carrying "the old clothes and linen of these fine gentlemen, which we could easily have done without; but as they did not bear the burden of it, it cost them nothing."[6]

After two years in Texas, La Salle seemed to have mastered the art of traveling there. The march proceeded as planned, although the country was not easy to cross. The men tripped repeatedly, hindered by the tall, sharp grasses that wound around their legs; the sickening odor of stagnant water followed them, and they sank in it up to their knees, especially after a few days of rain. Lurking in the grasses were tarantulas as big as hen's eggs. The thickets, more impassable than large forests, were obstructed with debris, branches and cutting vines, and poisonous snakes hid in the undergrowth and struck invisibly. A path had to be cleared with an axe to open up a passage for the horses. At least the campsites were familiar, having been visited the year before. They crossed the rivers at known fords. It sometimes happened that they halted under a tree "where Monsieur de La Salle had caused the King's arms to be drawn, and others where various individuals had made crosses, carved into the bark."[7] One day, Nika recognized a Cenis Indian he had exchanged signs and broken words with on an earlier reconnaissance trip.[8] Encounters with the Indians were frequent and always friendly. "Monsieur de La Salle knew how to act with these peoples,"[9] says

Joutel, who was always divided between his admiration for La Salle and his exasperation with him for never "taking any counsel but his own."[10] The abundance of buffalo assured the men of food and their trails made traveling easier, for "when one walks in the wilds, one must follow their route. These animals have an instinct for avoiding pitfalls by taking the least difficult passage, where the ground is firmest, the woods and canes least thick, and where the best fords are located on the river." Every morning, the men made themselves footgear from fresh buffalo hide; it molded closely to their feet, drying and hardening during the day; at night they had to soak their feet in water to remove them. Crossing the many rivers was always a problem because of the quantity of baggage they carried, and because the horses could not swim fully laden. Whenever possible they felled a large tree across the river to use as a bridge, over which the men "passed their old rags from hand to hand."[11] This was so slow and awkward that La Salle decided to construct a boat. There was no birch bark in Texas, but the buffalo supplied every need. Several carcasses were stripped of their hide. The wool was scraped away and the hides stretched out to dry. They were then cut in squares to be sewn, using the animal's sinews. Meanwhile, the men lashed together what Joutel describes as a sort of framework onto which they attached the sewn hides by means of fasteners made of twigs. When the boat was finished, they turned it upside down to caulk the seams with suet and plug any small holes. These bull boats were still used on the Mississippi as late as the nineteenth century. Joutel admired the fact that buffalo, whose meat was far better than the meat from French cattle, at the same time provided nourishment, clothing, and a means of transportation. The Indians were impressed with the foreigners' skill, though they themselves had no use for boats of this kind, given how lightly they traveled. Throughout the course of the voyage, the Frenchmen never relaxed their guard and always posted sentinels around camp, although relations with the Indians were peaceful. Conditions were much less strenuous than La Salle and his old traveling companions had faced on their Canadian voyages. Food was plentiful, the winter climate mild, and the natives more curious than hostile.

Sometimes La Salle would decide to halt for several days to hunt and reprovision. The men would then build a palisade to protect the campsite; Father Anastase would hastily rig up an altar to say Mass; the officers would pull their prayerbooks from their bundles and, in the midst of the wilderness, settle down to their reading or amuse themselves by showing pictures to the Indians who wandered out of the woods to observe them in camp. According to Pierre Talon, a boy left by La Salle in a Cenis village for several months to learn the language, the Indians in the interior were gentle, polite, and extremely clean: they washed in the rivers every day at dawn, even when the water was icy cold, swam like fish, and, the young man added, they were "ironic and bantering, fun-loving and drunken."[12] After every encounter, La Salle took his notebook from his pocket and wrote down any new Indian words he had learned and the names of the different tribes, as he had discovered that talking about names was one of the best ways to open a conversation with the natives. He sometimes worked late, burning twisted rushes to supplement the candles they had to light the huts. Father Anastase, Abbé Cavelier, and Joutel recorded the main events of each day using a piece of charcoal as a pencil. Much later, they would all have the time to compose actual journals. The account kept by Abbé Cavelier is confused, irrational, and generally at variance with the other two. The texts by Father Anastase and Joutel always confirm each other, but Joutel's is much more lively and detailed. Meanwhile, the crew used their rest time to mend the packframes and saddles, while the Indians, who had not yet learned to protect horses in this way and were amazed at the loads the Frenchmen's horses could carry, watched them curiously. Others of the crew went hunting or visited the Indian villages. La Salle had instructed them that it was essential to smoke with the natives to ensure their goodwill, and no unpleasant incidents occurred during the voyage. From time to time the travelers met Spaniards or Frenchmen — the French were men who had stolen away from La Salle on earlier journeys and had adapted to their new existence to the point of being unrecognizable.

In mid-March, La Salle made camp two leagues from the Canoe River[13] on a site he knew from an earlier trip. Seeing that game was scarce, he sent seven men to fetch some corn that he had stored in a cache the previous year. He chose Duhaut, Liotot, Nika, Hiems, Tessier, and two servants, Saget and L'Archevêque. La Salle's sense of direction was as keen as ever. Like the Indians, he had "a much better idea than [others] of how to find trails and places he had visited previously."[14] His directions were accurate enough for the men to find the cache with no problem, but water had unfortunately seeped in and rotted the grain. Nika sighted a herd of buffalo in the distance and managed to kill two of them. A man went to give La Salle the news and ask for horses to carry back the sides of meat, and La Salle had the unfortunate idea of sending his nephew Moranger to supervise the operation. Moranger was as unfair, violent, and hot-tempered as ever, having learned nothing in two years. When he came across Duhaut smoking a portion of the meat, he rebuked him in an insulting tone for the way he was going about it. And when he noticed that Duhaut had set aside the marrow bones and offal for himself, according to the backcountry custom by which a hunter keeps the parts that are most likely to spoil, he gave vent to an access of rage. This tirade, reviving old grudges, was his downfall. Pushed to the brink and shaking with fury, Duhaut and Liotot decided on revenge. With Moranger separated as he was from the rest, they were conscious that he was in their power. Besides, they were no longer convinced that even La Salle was of any importance to them, as they were confident they could survive in the wilderness on their own and even find the Mississippi. In that solitary country, revenge could only mean death.

At nightfall, they conferred with their companions. If they killed Moranger, they would also have to kill Saget, his servant, and Nika. Nika, Monsieur de La Salle's Indian, was like his shadow. Not only were they inseparable and did they speak to each other in a language they alone understood, but Nika was the only person who never irritated their captain; he was the one who had taught him his woodcraft, the one who had never betrayed him, the one who, in silence, had made the whole adventure possible. To kill Moranger in front of Nika would be the same as killing him in front of La Salle, his uncle. Duhaut and Liotot were so enraged that they were determined to murder the Indian, although there were two men who objected. Hiems, a German sailor who had joined in Santo Domingo, thought Nika too valuable an asset to be harmed. As a hunter, Nika had a magical ability to find the trail, to move in the dark, to sense danger, to distinguish the poisonous from the edible, and he possessed a quiet strength that had often buoyed their downtrodden spirits. Tessier, the last surviving pilot, agreed with Hiems and pleaded for Nika's life. But the other two were on a rampage and wouldn't listen. They would do the deed alone, at night. Neither Hiems nor Tessier would interfere. That night, the first watch was given to the three marked men. When he was sure they were asleep, Liotot crept up to them, axe in hand. He fractured Saget's skull with a single blow; he turned and did the same to Nika. Moranger moved in his sleep as though he were waking up. The surgeon tried to hurry but had to hit him several times and call for help to finish him off. All was quiet again. The corpses were tossed out of camp, and the men spread dust over the large puddles of blood. But it was not over. The murderers were now afraid of La Salle and wanted to kill him too.

The tide of hatred and resentment had swept away the dikes of duty and order. When circumstances were at their worst, the men continued to observe the precepts of religion and the customs of society. But now, even though they faced no particular hardships, they had acted like savages — or rather, since the "savages" always obeyed a constraining code, like barbarians, flouting all laws and prohibitions. Two men had succumbed to their instinct for violence, and the compact that had allowed the group to survive in the empty plains of the New World was broken.

At camp, in the meantime, La Salle was concerned at not seeing his men return. He paced back and forth among the bark shelters, the glowing campfires, the stretched buffalo hides, and fire-blackened kettles; the others, lying on the ground, smoked or slumbered. Some neighboring Indians came and went through camp. Only Joutel kept La Salle company and tried to calm his fears. Did he think, La Salle asked, that the men could have "vile designs"? Joutel admitted that they did complain "of being often scolded," but they did not take him into their confidence, as they all knew him to be loyal to La Salle and "watchful of his interests." La Salle's worry shows that, in spite of his arrogance and apparent lofty detachment, he was in an anxious frame of mind. That he was alarmed when his companions were late and imagined that there might have been a plot (it had not, in fact, been planned beforehand) proves that he was attentive to the passions felt by his men. On the next day, March 19, he decided to go looking for them. He entrusted command of the camp to Joutel and asked Father Anastase to accompany him, as well as an Indian, who agreed to go for the price of an axe. Taking a further precaution he asked Joutel, who had the best gun, to lend it to the priest. All along the way, the priest reported, La Salle spoke of piety, grace, and predestination, citing his debt to the Lord for saving him from so many dangers during the twenty-odd years he had been traveling in America. Suddenly, he appeared overcome with a deep and unexplainable sorrow. He seemed so moved, the father said later, that he was hardly recognizable. La Salle soon recovered his equanimity, however, and examined his surroundings with the practiced eye of a woodsman. A group of eagles, circling over Duhaut and Liotot's camp like vultures, seemed a bad omen; worse, he saw Saget's stained scarf floating in the high grass. Fearing the worst, he fired a shot into the air, and by so doing gave the murderers warning of his arrival. Duhaut and Liotot hid like Indians flat on their stomachs in the tall, dry canes at the edge of the river, while L'Archevêque, who was wearing a hat, walked toward La Salle. "Where is my nephew?" La Salle shouted. "Gone to the dogs," answered L'Archevêque without taking his hat off. La Salle, shocked by his insolence, advanced on him furiously, prepared to knock the hat off. The servant backed away, as though defying him. La Salle approached in long strides. He was now within Duhaut's range. A shot rang out. La Salle dropped, hit in the head. He died without saying a word. Father Anastase, not knowing where the shot came from, stood petrified until Duhaut and Liotot came out of hiding and reassured him that he was safe. Meanwhile, they turned on the corpse with horrible brutality: "They stripped Monsieur de La Salle with the utmost cruelty, even removing his shirt. The surgeon in particular treated him with derision, calling him "Great Pasha" as he lay there dead and naked on the ground. Having stripped him, they dragged him into the brush where they left him to the mercy of the wolves and other wild animals."[15] His American adversaries, the Iroquois, would have spared La Salle such a mean death, as they knew how to honor a great man.

Thus perished, in a vile ambush set by his own people, a man who had sacrificed everything in service to an ambition that was vast, practical, and rooted in the passion for discovery rather than the mysteries of religion. A modern hero, he concentrated all his intelligence and energy on peaceful conquest. Victory for him resided less in capture than in knowledge.

But to return to the living. Duhaut and Liotot, sobered after their transport of rage, took hold of themselves and again assured Father Anastase that their anger had been nothing more than a momentary madness. They organized the return to camp, making it clear to their comrades that the murdering was over. They retraced the path they had taken several days before, followed by the horse carrying the sides of meat. With one look at

the downcast face of Father Anastase, Abbé Cavelier knew. He
fell to his knees, his grandnephew beside him, and begged
Duhaut in a piteous voice to spare him. Duhaut once more declared his peaceful intentions. It happened that Joutel was not in
camp but on a small hill where, according to La Salle's instructions, he was making a smoky grass fire to guide the men back to
camp. Surprised, he saw L'Archevêque walk toward him, seeming
"all disconcerted, as if he'd lost his way." L'Archevêque was a native of Bayonne who had been hired at Santo Domingo by
Duhaut; he had become friends with Joutel, and wanted to in-
form him of the calamity. Joutel was "entirely disconcerted" at
the news and remained confused for several moments as to what
to do. He believed the murderers might now attack him, but how
was he to take flight in the woods without a gun? L'Archevêque
reassured him somewhat, and Joutel agreed to return to camp.
He found Duhaut and Liotot at once furious, anxious, and uncertain. They had laid hands on all La Salle's belongings — and
Joutel's by the same token — and confiscated every firearm, an-
nouncing that they would take command of the expedition by
turns. Joutel hardly dared go near the abbé or Father Anastase,
who stood a short way off lest he should irritate his new masters.
He decided to be quiet and watch. The neighboring Indians noticed that four men were missing and tried to ask questions.
Nika's name kept returning to their lips. The ringleaders grew
more and more uneasy — perhaps the abbé had been right in
saying "that they had killed themselves when they killed
Monsieur de La Salle."[16] At nightfall, the watches had to be organized, and a truce was called. Duhaut announced that he had
acted "out of despair" but that he harbored no further grudge
against anyone, and he distributed the guns so that each could
stand watch as usual. More importantly, the party agreed on a
plan. They would stay among the Cenis villages for a time before
continuing their journey in order to exchange some of their
trade goods for corn and more horses. Buffalo were growing
scarce, a worrisome development, and gunpowder was running
low. While Duhaut, the two clergymen, the young nephew, and

L'Archevêque stayed in camp, Joutel, Hiems, Tessier, and Liotot went to visit the Indians. Once sure of their welcome, they fanned out into different encampments. Joutel was sorry he did not speak one of the Indian dialects, although it hardly hampered him. In the very first village, after the usual greetings — which in this region consisted of a chorus of yowls, followed by embraces and caresses — the natives brought him a Frenchman from Provence, an old acquaintance who had deserted the previous year: he was now completely naked, "pricked" with the designs of birds and animals in the style of the country,[17] and followed by a squaw. He gabbled in French, introducing what to Joutel's ear was a bizarre mixture of Indian words. Too content with his lot to dream of further voyages, he could not tell him where the Mississippi lay. However, one night when Joutel was resting, he noticed a naked man approach him carrying a bow and arrows, who sat down next to him without saying a word. Frightened by his peculiar visitor, Joutel grabbed his pistol and started to cock it when the man threw his arms around him. It was a Breton sailor named Ruter, who thinking that La Salle might have sent men to look for him had not dared approach Joutel during the day; a man from La Rochelle called Grollet had also settled with the Cenis Indians, "who took good care of them and gave them all they needed," including a fair number of wives. Joutel was amazed at how rapidly Ruter had changed: "He looked as though he had been a savage for ten years"[18] with his facial tattoos, bare feet, and his crude blanket of turkey feathers, held in place with string. Only his leisurely gait might have betrayed him for a European. Ruter and Grollet were able to tell Joutel that he was heading in the right direction to reach the Big River. For Joutel, who had been a soldier, Indian life held no temptations. Perhaps he felt too old for the pleasures of a libertine existence, or perhaps he was afraid of dying outside his religion — or he may just have had his fill in the course of long years of campaigning and wanted to go home. At any rate, neither Ruter nor Grollet could persuade him to stay, nor could the head of the village, although he offered Joutel his daughter, a shapely girl. Back at the main camp, he confided to the clerics his determination to continue toward the northeast and return to Canada. Duhaut, on the other hand, wanted to go back to the fort, build a boat, and sail to the Antilles. The plan was crazy, as Joutel saw it, since they had no skilled carpenters, but it had the advantage of ridding him of Duhaut, who was treating his quasi-prisoners quite roughly. Time was passing, and the month of April was nearly over, but no one could move because, on Duhaut's orders, Hiems and his servants had gone to different villages to look for horses — this was always a tricky proposition because the Indians set great store by their horses, which were few and enormously useful. Hiems and the others were adapting well to the soft and indolent life of an Indian village, and were in no hurry to return. Spirits in camp took a downturn when Duhaut announced that he too had decided to go north. Joutel had such hatred for him that he confessed to Abbé Cavelier his desire to kill Duhaut; but the abbé, being cowardly, preferred to put his trust in God and deterred Joutel from his plans of vengeance and freedom.

On May 1, divine intervention took the form of the extravagant person of Hiems. He appeared, followed by Ruter, Grollet, and about twenty Indians, greeted those in camp rather coldly, and went off to confer with Duhaut. He wanted to part with the expedition and insisted on receiving his share of the spoils, consisting of La Salle's personal effects and weapons. Duhaut refused. Hiems became angry: "Pay me my wages then, since you have killed my master," he shouted, and, without waiting for an answer, he fired. Duhaut fell stone dead four yards away. At the same moment Ruter shot Liotot, sending three bullets through his body. The surgeon was alive long enough to say confession; then, over Abbé Cavelier's objections and his own pleas (he still hoped the Indians could nurse him back to health), he was dispatched with a pistol.[19] The astonishment of the Indians at the French style of reunion was so plain that the survivors, afraid it might have a bad influence, tried to explain to them the logic of the slaughter. The presence of the Indians actually helped cool tempers. Hiems, who had decided to stay with the Indians, or at least with the beautiful Indian women, divided up the party's wealth. In return, Abbé Cavelier gave him a note, written in Latin, saying that Hiems was innocent in the slaying of his brother. Joutel, with the two clergymen, young Cavelier, De Marle (one of the few surviving officers), and a young man from Paris called Barthélemy, carrying hatchets, knives, and food for fifteen days and leading six horses, set off at the end of the month of May.

They advanced slowly, rarely going farther than six leagues in a day, or a little over a dozen miles. They still had more than 300 miles to go before reaching the Mississippi where it is joined by the Arkansas. They halted frequently, often stopping at Indian villages, where Joutel prudently replenished their supply of grain by exchanging knives and needles. The Indians always welcomed their arrival. In one village, Joutel was clearly distraught at having lost a horse when its leather halter was chewed by dogs; the Indians showed him a species of nut tree whose bark made excellent straps. Only one drama cast a shadow over the expedition. In June, young De Marle, taking a dip in the river although the current was strong and he couldn't swim, was swept away and drowned, despite his comrades' efforts. The party continued its eastward progress, angling slightly north. In July, the rivers they crossed were teeming with alligators, and La Salle had said these only appeared south of the Arkansas. And on July 14, after traveling for two months, they were approaching a very large river when they caught sight of a big cross set in the ground on the opposite shore. A few yards beyond it was a small house, not an Indian hut but a real house, with a roof, a chimney, and an actual door. Two men in trousers, wearing hats and carrying guns, were watching them, and having gotten a good look at the travelers, they fired off a salvo in welcome and immediately directed the Indians to take several canoes across to bring the travelers back.

The two Frenchmen, Couture and de Launay, both from Rouen, had come down the Mississippi with Tonty looking for La Salle, and they had volunteered to stay for some time at the fort on the Arkansas in case La Salle should arrive in the area. When they learned of his death, the two men wept, but advised that the news should be kept secret, particularly from the Indians. The Indians' great respect for La Salle was a virtual guarantee of their good conduct, but it was uncertain how they would react to the news of his death. The travelers should present themselves as his emissaries. Joutel and Cavelier agreed. The abbé had other reasons as well for wanting to keep the assassination of his brother hidden. They were given a dugout canoe, well-suited for travel on the Mississippi, and taking several Indians who had offered to guide them they set off again. They still had more than 600 miles to cover before reaching the Illinois River. Going up the Mississippi in the month of August was an arduous task, and would have been far more difficult if the Indians along the way had not all welcomed them with great generosity. La Salle's name was a passport that opened hearts and stores of food to them.

Finally, on September 16, they were at the foot of the rock at Saint Louis, Illinois, back in New France under Tonty's protection. Joutel wanted to hurry on to Quebec in order to cross to France before the last boat sailed, but bad weather made travel on the Great Lakes impossible, and he resigned himself to wintering at Fort Saint Louis. This worked to the abbé's advantage. Tonty had some furs belonging to La Salle. Cavelier asked to have them, showing him a note from his brother. Tonty, who was the soul of honesty, handed them over immediately, which he need not have done if the fact of La Salle's death had been known. Joutel said nothing. Cavelier was reassured by his silence, and promised to reimburse him part of what he had lost and pay his wages. Joutel smiled, and again said nothing. In the spring, when the time came to organize their trip to the Saint Lawrence, Joutel offered to work as a paddler, just so he could buy himself a shirt when he got to Montreal; he knew Cavelier well enough not to count on his promises. They left on May 21, 1688, reached Montreal on July 14, and boarded one of the first boats for La Rochelle on September 4. On November 7, they slept in Rouen, in their own beds.

Only then, when he had converted his furs into ringing silver and was happily restored to his own home rich and intact, did Cavelier write Seignelay the news of La Salle's death. He also described what had happened to the colonists who had stayed on the gulf, but neither the king nor his minister were inclined to rescue these unfortunates. When Tonty finally learned the truth from Couture, who arrived in Illinois in September, he decided to take action. He went down the Mississippi by canoe with five Frenchmen, a Shawnee warrior, and two Indian captives. He found signs of Hiems near the Red River, and went with several Indians to the village where Hiems had been adopted, but a quick inspection convinced Tonty that the natives had murdered him. An unpleasant scene in the chief's hut, added to their inability to get local guides and the loss of all their ammunition, forced Tonty's party to turn back.

It was the Spaniards, guided by one of La Salle's deserters, who eventually revisited the fort on the gulf. Having discovered the wrecked hulls of the *Aimable* and the *Belle*, Spanish colonists had been concerned for several years that Frenchmen were living in the heart of what they considered their empire. A small troop left the province of Nuevo Leon to cross the rugged country of south Texas, and entered Saint Louis Bay. They advanced unopposed; nothing broke the silence and dryness of the desert. On April 22, 1689, in the distance, they saw a palisade and the remains of cabins. They approached. Although their men were ready for battle, they were terrified by the silence, which could only be the silence of death. They urged their horses on and entered the encampment to find nothing but ruin and desolation. The doors had been ripped from their hinges, the barrels staved in, the books torn; and on the prairie there were half-gnawed corpses, one still gripping what must have been a skirt. A group of Indians stood nearby, wrapped in their buffalo robes, silent and impassive. They belonged to nomadic tribes along the gulf that were much crueler and more barbarous than the Cenis. The Spanish commander somehow managed to learn that two foreigners were living with a tribe in Texas, and he arranged for them to be brought to him. He waited until, at dawn on May 1, two men appeared, their faces covered with geometric designs, and wearing ragged leather clothes. They were L'Archevêque and Grollet, who had decided to try Spanish jails rather than end their lives among the Indians. All that is known of the fate of Barbier, Father Zénobe, the Princess, Madame Talon, and young La Sablonnière and their comrades comes from the accounts of these two men. In January 1688, an Indian party made a surprise attack on the fort, where the colonists were in a weakened state from smallpox. Everyone was killed except an Italian, a young Parisian named Breman, and the Talon children. The Indians led them away, and they were "saved by the native women, who, feeling compassion for their youth, carried them on their backs into their huts while their husbands massacred the rest. They were raised and loved by these same native women, as though they had been their children."[20] Two or three years later, the Indians turned their captives over to the Spanish. What happened to the Italian and Breman is not known, but the six Talon children resurfaced: the young girl and her two small brothers went to Spain; the two older boys were impressed into the Spanish navy, and returned to France and freedom when they were captured by the French in 1696 during a naval battle. They reappeared in Brest in 1698. Twelve people are known for certain to have returned from La Salle's final expedition.

Epilogue

Frontenac dies in Canada in 1698, called back there eight years before to deal with the deteriorating situation. Threatened by the English and the Iroquois simultaneously, Canada had seemed on the point of disintegration. The governorship was not an attractive posting, but the former governor accepted it, perhaps secretly pleased at the failure of his successors in office, moved by the admiration of the Indians — they carried him on a litter during his last campaign to spare him the fatigue of the warpath — and comforted by the Canadians' vote of confidence. At his death, the power of the Iroquois had waned and they would never be a threat to the colonists again. The English who besieged Quebec had been driven back; the route to the Great Lakes was still open to the French; and the forts along the Mississippi were secure. Peace was reestablished in November 1698, and the news traveled to the king by the last boat that year. Exhausted by his efforts, Frontenac took to his bed, where a mortal chill spread through him. He had only the strength to write a new will in favor of his wife, asking that his heart be sent to her in a lead or silver urn. Madame de Frontenac is reported to have refused this last gift, saying that his heart had not belonged to her while he lived, and she did not want it now that he was dead. She did accept the small fortune he had amassed. If he had lived another year, he would have learned that Iberville and Bienville, sons of his old interpreter Le Moyne, had successfully laid the foundations of a new colony in New France at the mouth of the Mississippi in 1699.

The long conversations with La Salle from the winter of 1673 had borne fruit, though neither was on hand for it.

FIFTY YEARS LATER

The French, true to the bold concept of occupying points of settlement, were masters of a great corridor formed by the Mississippi and its fifty-four affluents, joining the two capitals Quebec and New Orleans (this city was founded officially in 1723 and named in honor of Louis XV's regent). America seemed destined to be French, until the Seven Years' War in Europe resulted in a reordering of the New World. France was defeated and forced to abandon all its overseas possessions. Canada became English, and only the extraordinary tenacity of its first settlers kept alive the language and religion of their ancestral land. Rather than cede Louisiana to the British, Louis XV gave it to his cousin the king of Spain, Charles III.

A CENTURY LATER

The inhabitants of Louisiana became French again, practically without knowing it, thanks to a secret article to the Treaty of Ildefonso, signed by Napoleon Bonaparte and Charles IV. But this was not the last of their tribulations. In 1803, Bonaparte was still in possession of his common sense and his flair for business; convinced that France could not keep this distant possession, he sold Louisiana to the young republic of the United States for 15 million dollars, a sum almost equivalent to the fortune of the richest man in America, John Jacob Astor, and therefore a respectable price for a territory that was largely wilderness. The name was kept; and the word, first pronounced by La Salle in 1682, still sounds sweetly to French ears, a memory of the Sun King fluttering over a heterogeneous America, among the ancient tribes of Arkansas and Texas. In 1810, with the arrival of steamboats, the Mississippi at last became the great navigational route imagined by La Salle. Until then, only flatboats had trafficked on the river, riding the current to New Orleans with the goods on which that city's trade depended. The captain would dismantle his boat on arrival, selling its pine planks and beams, sawn in the northern forests, to the local building trade. Subsequently, the Mississippi carried traffic in both directions. The North and the South were joined, and La Salle's ambition was fulfilled.

La Salle shares with most explorers the sorrowful honor of being assassinated and then forgotten by his countrymen. These unappeased ghosts remain in our memory if a beautiful river or a spectacular bridge is named after them. Hudson and Verrazano have had this good fortune. We remember La Pérouse mainly because of a small Parisian street immortalized by Marcel Proust. La Salle, the man who gave Louisiana and much more to France, did not fare as well. He has no epitaph in Paris. America, the country he explored, gave his name to a car — the big comfortable La Salle of the fifties — a final irony for this tireless walker.

Bibliographical Note

The footnotes provide full bibliographical information, but I wish to acknowledge separately my debt to Francis Parkman, the great nineteenth-century historian (1823–1893), so like Michelet in his scope, power, and enthusiasm. He has been for me a source of constant inspiration. I wish also to draw attention to the three main studies of La Salle published in French and to two English-language studies:

Pierre Leprohon, *Cavelier de La Salle, fondateur de la Louisiane* (1933, reprinted in 1984, André Bonne).

Roger Viau, *Cavelier de La Salle* (Mame, 1960).

Yves Cazaux, *Le Rêve américain, de Champlain à Cavelier de La Salle* (Albin Michel, 1988).

Edmund Boyd Osler, *La Salle* (Longman, 1967).

John Upton Terrell, *La Salle: The Life and Times of an Explorer* (Waybright and Talley, 1968).

None of these works could have been written without the enormous labor performed by Pierre Margry (1818–1894), Director of the Archives of the Admiralty and the Colonies. Mining this vast resource, as well as other public archives and a number of private collections, he made possible the publication of the most important documents relating to the French explorers in North America. These texts (published as *Découvertes et établissements des Français dans l'Amérique Septentrionale 1614–1754*) were of such interest to American historians that Francis Parkman arranged for the United States Congress to subscribe for 500 copies in order to help finance their publication.

Notes

CHAPTER 1 FROM ROUEN TO QUEBEC

1. François Bluche, *La Vie quotidienne au temps de Louis XIV* (Paris: Hachette, 1984), chapter 6.
2. From *Archivum historicum Societatis Jesu*, IV, cited in Gilbert J. Garraghan, "La Salle's Jesuit Days," *Mid-America, XIX* (Chicago: Illinois Catholic Society, 1937), 93–103.
3. Jean de Viguerie, "L'instruction des enfants," in *L'Education en France, XVIème–XVIIIème siècle* (Paris, 1978).
4. A minimal amount: one needed ten times as much, or 4,000 livres, in order to live comfortably. See for example the discussion of Angélique's marriage in Molière's *Le Malade imaginaire* for a contemporary bourgeois perspective. Mme de Maintenon, the royal mistress, received 4,000 livres per month for her personal expenses, a sum thought modest by Saint-Simon.
5. Jean-Pierre Bardet, *Rouen au XVIIème et XVIIIème siècles* (Paris: Sedes, 1983). This is an exceptional proportion for France at this period.
6. Arundel de Condé, *Dictionnaire des anoblis normands (1600–1790)* (Rouen, 1976), cited in Bluche, *Vie quotidienne.*
7. Bluche, *Vie quotidienne,* 272.
8. Quebec is the oldest town in North America. New York, originally named New Amsterdam, dates from 1625 and Boston from 1630.
9. Bluche, *Vie quotidienne,* chapter 5.
10. All details of life on shipboard are drawn form Jean Merrien, *La Vie quotidienne dans la marine au temps du Roi-Soleil* (Paris: Hachette, 1964).
11. *The Jesuit Relations: Jean Enjalran, October 13, 1676.* Trilingual edition — French, Italian, and Latin — with an English translation by Reuben Gold Thwaites (Cleveland: Burroughs, 1896–1901), LX, 108.
12. *Kebec* means "narrowing" in Huron.
13. Jean Enjalran in *Jesuit Relations,* LX, 110.
14. Chrestien Le Clercq, *Nouvelle Relation de la Gaspésie* (Paris: Auroy, 1691), 344.
15. François-Marc Gagnon and Denise Patel, *Hommes effarables et bestes sauvages: Images du Nouveau Monde depuis les voyages de Jacques Cartier* (Quebec: Boréal, 1986), 51.
16. Ibid., 80.
17. Ibid., 84.

CHAPTER 2 CLEARING THE LAND

1. *Canada* is an Indian word that, according to Jacques Cartier, was used to denote encampments along the Saint Lawrence in the vicinity of Quebec. When he asked the Hochelaga Indians where he was during his second voyage in 1541, they answered, "Canada." The name stuck.
2. Louis-Armand de la Hontan, *Voyages* . . . (La Haye, 1703), 65.
3. Francis Parkman, "La Salle and the Discovery of the Great West," *France and England in America* (New York: Library of America, 1983), I, 1315.
4. These equivalents are drawn from *Atlas Historique du Canada* (Canada: Presses de l'Université de Montréal, 1987), plate 53. An English-language edition of this work is available from University of Toronto Press.
5. W. J. Eccles, *France in America* (East Lansing: Michigan University Press, 1990).
6. Pierre Margry, "Récit à un ami de l'abbé de Gallinée," in *Découvertes et établissements des Français dans l'Amérique Septentrionale, 1614–1754* (Paris: Maisonneuve, 1876–1886), I, 353.
7. The lumberjacks of Northern Michigan ate carpenter ants to ward off scurvy, and at the beginning of this century one could still buy vials of these insects in the United States as a "winter's end tonic." Edwin Way Teale, *Wandering through Winter* (New York: Saint Martin's Press, 1981), 276.
8. Duc de Saint-Simon, *Mémoires* (Paris: Gallimard, Bibliothèque de la Pléiade, 1953), III, 83.
9. Details taken from Jean Provencher, *C'était l'hiver* (Quebec: Boréal Express, 1986).
10. Remember that the *annual* allowance allotted La Salle by his brothers came to 400 livres.
11. Brébeuf, *Relations des Hurons*, 1636, 117, cited in Parkman, "The Jesuits in North America," *France and England in North America*, I, 447.
12. Marcel Trudel, *Histoire de la Nouvelle-France* (Quebec: Fides, 1966), II, 386.
13. Père LeClerc, *Premiers établissements de la foi* (Paris: 1961), cited in Séraphin Marion, *Relations de voyageurs* (Paris: Presses Universitaires de France, 1923), 47.
14. Gabriel Sagard-Théodat, *Histoire du Canada* (Paris: Librairie Tross, 1886), I, 165.
15. Ibid., II, 33.

16. Le Jeune, *Relation* of 1633, cited in Trudel, *Histoire de la Nouvelle-France*, II, 391.
17. Biard, *Relation*, 1636, cited in Trudel, *Histoire de la Nouvelle-France*, II, 391.
18. Cf. Parkman, *France and England in North America, passim.*
19. Marion, *Relations de voyageurs*, 149.

CHAPTER 3   MONSIEUR DE LA SALLE'S INDIAN

1. Jean Delanglez, "A Calendar of La Salle's travels, 1643–1683," in *Mid-America*, XXII, 278–305.
2. Margry, *Découvertes et établissements*, "Relation de l'abbé de Gallinée," I, 118.
3. Margry, *Découvertes et établissements*, "Relation du sieur de La Mothe Cadillac," V, 82.
4. Margry, *Découvertes et établissements*, "Relation de l'abbé de Gallinée," I, 127.
5. Ibid., I, 129.
6. See Marguerite Yourcenar's superb essay "Agrippa d'Aubigné and *Les Tragiques*" in *The Dark Brain of Piranesi and Other Essays* (New York: Farrar, Straus and Giroux, 1984).
7. Madame de Sévigné, Letter to Monsieur and Madame de Grignan, February 23, 1680, in *Letters of Madame de Sévigné* (New York: Dutton, 1937), I, 61.
8. Archer Butler Hulbert, *The Ohio River: A Course of Empire* (New York: Putnam's Sons, Knickerbocker Press, 1906).
9. La Salle, cited by Parkman, *France and England in North America*, I, 743.
10. Jean-Claude Lasserre, *Le Saint-Laurent, grande porte de l'Amérique* (Lyon: Presses Universitaires de Lyon, 1980).

CHAPTER 4   THE GOVERNOR'S EAR

1. W. J. Eccles, *Frontenac, The Courtier Governor* (Toronto: McClelland and Stewart, 1959), 20.
2. Tallemant des Réaux, *Historiettes* (Paris, 1840), IX.
3. The Frondeurs were members of Parliament and royal princes who tried to curb royal absolutism during the regency of Queen Anne. The troubles started in 1648 when Louis XIV was only ten years old, and soon turned into a real civil war. Peace was restored in 1653.

4. Mademoiselle de Montpensier, *Mémoires* (Paris: Charpentier), II, 226.

5. Ibid., II, 263.

6. Saint-Simon, *Mémoires*, I, 623.

7. Madame de Sévigné in a letter to her daughter dated April 6, 1672, in *Lettres* (Paris: Gallimard, Bibliothèque de la Pléiade, 1972), I, 471.

8. From Frontenac's correspondence, published in *Rapport de l'archiviste de Québec* (Quebec, 1920), Letter to Minister Colbert, November 2, 1672.

9. *Onontio,* which means "Big Mountain" in Iroquois, is a literal translation of the name of Canada's first governor, Montmagny. The name went on to be applied to all subsequent governors.

10. *Dictionary of Canadian Biography* (Toronto: University of Toronto, 1966).

11. Letter from Frontenac to the minister, November 1673, in *Rapport de l'archiviste de Québec*, 37.

12. Ibid., 36.

13. Paul du Poisson, "Letter to Father ***," in *Jesuit Relations*, LXVII, 292, cited in Raymond Douville and Jacques-Donat Casanova, *La Vie quotidienne en Nouvelle-France* (Paris: Hachette, 1964), 179.

14. Pierre Boucher, *Histoire véritable et naturelle des moeurs et productions du pays de la Nouvelle-France* (Paris: Lambert, 1664), chapter IV. This book was commissioned by the king in 1662.

15. Letter from Frontenac to the minister, November 1673, in *Rapport de l'archiviste de Québec*, 41.

16. Examples of the pipes may be found in the Musée de l'Homme in Paris. See No. 239 in the catalogue "Naissance de la Louisiane, tricentenaire des découvertes de Cavelier de La Salle," 1982.

17. See "Journal du voyage du comte de Frontenac," in *New York Colonial Documents* (Albany: ASM press, 1866), IX, 95–103.

18. *Dictionary of Canadian Biography.*

19. See the "Journal du voyage," in *New York Colonial Documents.*

20. Parkman, *France and England in North America*, I, 785.

CHAPTER 5   A DIVIDED COLONY

1. Frontenac, Letter to the minister, November 1673, in *Rapport de l'archiviste de Québec*, 40.

2. Ibid.

3. Ibid., 39. In his previous letter, Frontenac had perhaps shown more accuracy in warning Colbert of "how changeable and untrustworthy

are the Iroquois, who are perfectly capable of breaking their treaty with us should they see us as weak, for they have a natural inclination toward war, and it may be touched off by nothing more than a dream of one of their old women." Ibid., 15.

4. Parkman, "Count Frontenac and New France," *France and England in North America*, II, 31.

5. Frank G. Roe, *The Indian and the Horse* (Norman: University of Oklahoma Press, 1955).

6. Pierre Deffontaines, *L'Homme et l'hiver au Canada* (Paris: Gallimard, 1957), 95.

7. Letter from Minister Colbert to the governor, May 17, 1674, in *Rapport de l'archiviste de Québec*, 53.

8. Marcel Trudel, *La Population du Canada en 1663* (Montreal: Fides, 1973), 31.

9. Letter from Frontenac to the minister, November 14, 1674, in *Rapport de l'archiviste de Québec*, 78.

10. Letters of nobility granted to La Salle by Louis XIV, Bibliothèque Nationale. They appear as No. 12 in the catalogue "Naissance de la Louisiane," 16.

11. Margry, *Découvertes et établissements*, "Account of the expenses incurred by Monsieur de La Salle," I, 329.

12. Françoise Deroy-Pineau, *Marie de l'Incarnation, Marie Guyart, femme d'affaires, mystique, mère de la Nouvelle-France, 1599–1672* (Paris: Robert Laffont, 1989), 197.

13. Parkman, *France and England in North America*, I, 793.

14. Jean-Claude Dubé, *Les Intendants de la Nouvelle-France* (Montreal: Fides, 1984).

15. Louis Hennepin, *Nouvelle Découverte d'un très grand pays* (Pays-Bas: Utrecht, 1697), 5.

16. Parkman, *France and England in North America*, I, 309.

17. Letter from Talon to Colbert, November 10, 1670, in Parkman, idem., I, 1260.

CHAPTER 6   A CANADIAN SEIGNEUR

1. Margry, *Découvertes et établissements*, "Récit à un ami de l'abbé de Gallinée," I, 380.

2. Ibid.

3. Ibid., I, 370.

4. The route passes north of Baffin Island and, depending on conditions, continues around Victoria Island either to the north or to the

south, then follows the coast of Alaska to the Bering Strait. This route is almost completely ice bound. The cost of constructing ice breakers to open the route to large ships would be absolutely prohibitive. See *National Geographic*, August 1990, 2.

5. Parkman, *France and England in North America*, I, 750.

6. Margry, *Découvertes et établissements*, "Rapport de La Mothe Cadillac," V, 107. The expression comes from the fact that the young men rolled bark in the shape of torches and lit them at night to go from cabin to cabin. The young women would sleep near the door and stop the man they liked, putting out his torch.

7. Frontenac, Letter to the minister, November 2, 1672 in *Rapport de l'archiviste de Québec*, 20.

8. Ibid.

9. Margry, *Découvertes et établissements,* "Accusations du comte de Frontenac à Colbert," I, 334.

10. Hennepin, *Nouvelle Découverte*, 32.

11. Margry, *Découvertes et établissements*, "Mémoire sur le projet du sieur de La Salle," I, 334.

12. *Relation of 1637*, cited in Douville and Casanova, *La Vie quotidienne des Indiens au temps de la colonisation française* (Paris: Hachette, 1967).

13. Margry, *Découvertes et établissements*, I, 334.

14. Ibid., I, 333.

15. Father Le Jeune's *Relation*, cited in Douville and Casanova, *La Vie quotidienne des Indiens.*

16. Edwin Way Teale, *Journey into Summer* (New York: Saint Martin's Press, 1981), 221.

17. Fanny Kelly, *Narrative of My Captivity among the Sioux Indians* (Chicago: Lakeside Press, 1990), 144.

18. Margry, *Découvertes et établissements*, "Mémoire sur le projet du sieur de La Salle," I, 331.

19. Margry, *Découvertes et établissements*, "Récit à un ami de l'abbé de Gallinée," I, 389–390.

20. Margry, *Découvertes et établissements*, Letter to the prince de Conti, I, 393.

21. Frontenac, Letter to Colbert, November 11, 1674, in Margry, *Découvertes et établissements*, "Louis Joliet et le père Marquette," I, 262.

22. Ibid. The portage the governor refers to is the one around Niagara Falls.

23. Colbert, Letter to Duchesneau, April 28, 1677, in Margry, *Découvertes et établissements*, I, 329.

24. Margry, *Découvertes et établissements*, "Récit à un ami de l'abbé de Gallinée," I, 346.

25. Margry, *Découvertes et établissements*, "Mémoire au roi, présenté sous la Régence," I, 423–432.
26. Parkman, *France and England in North America*, I, 806.

CHAPTER 7   THE SOUND OF THE GREAT WATERS

1. Frontenac, Letter to Colbert, November 11, 1674, in Margry, *Découvertes et établissements*, I, 258.
2. Louis Hennepin, *Description de la Louisiane* (Paris: Auroy, 1685), 55.
3. In this case, the French name has survived. The name Huron was given to Indians along the lake's shores because of their hairstyle — shaved on the sides and raised in a ridge across the top — ressembling a boar's head, *hure* in French.
4. Approximately a thousand miles.
5. Margry, *Découvertes et établissements*, "Relation des découvertes et voyages du sieur de La Salle," I, 441.
6. Ibid.
7. Ibid.
8. Augustus Porter, *The Beginning of the Commerce on the Great Lakes* (New York, 1914), 25.
9. Chateaubriand, *Mémoires d'outre-tombe* (Paris: Gallimard, Bibliothèque de la Pléiade, 1957), I, 245.
10. La Salle, Letter to one of his partners, September 29, 1680, in Margry, *Découvertes et établissements*, II, 62.
11. Hennepin, *Description de la Louisiane*, 95.
12. Ibid., 68.
13. Margry, *Découvertes et établissements*, "Relation des découvertes du sieur de La Salle," I, 444.
14. This corresponds approximately to the current metric ton, but measures varied widely in the seventeenth century. See Merrien, *La Vie quotidienne*, 30.
15. Hennepin, *Description de la Louisiane*, 69.
16. Ibid., 76.
17. Chateaubriand, *Mémoires d'outre-tombe*, I, 243.
18. Margry, *Découvertes et établissements*, "Relation des découvertes du sieur de La Salle," I, 444–445.
19. Ibid., II, 20–21.
20. Hennepin, *Description de la Louisiane*, 124.
21. Margry, *Découvertes et établissements*, "Relation des découvertes du sieur de La Salle," I, 446.
22. The Bay of Stinking Waters, so called because it gave off a strong

sea smell. Fathers Allouez and Dablon, who explored the region to found a mission there, called their settlement Green Bay. Delighted with their lush surroundings, they believed they had arrived, they said, at paradise on earth but added that the path leading to it was as difficult as the path to Heaven. Cf. the *Relations* for 1670–1671.

23. Frontenac's correspondence is larded throughout with references to information transmitted by the Jesuits. The governor used the Jesuits but was so distrustful of them that any allusion to their doings was always in code.

24. Margry, *Découvertes et établissements*, Letter to Thouret from La Salle, II, 71.

25. Margry, *Découvertes et établissements*, I, 452.

26. Ibid., I, 402.

27. Ibid., I, 460.

CHAPTER 8   THE ILLINOIS PRAIRIES

1. Margry, *Découvertes et établissements*, "Cavelier de La Salle de 1679 à 1681," I, 463.

2. William Cronon, *Changes in the Land: Indians, Colonists, and the Ecology of New England* (New York: Hill and Wang, 1983), 28.

3. The Indian name was *Theakiki*. Its present name, Kankakee, may be a corruption of it. Along different segments, La Salle called it the "Seignelay" and the "Divine," in honor of Madame de Frontenac and her friend. A map drawn by Frontenac's engineer, Raudin, makes the reference even more precise, calling it the "Rivière de la Divine ou de l'Outrelaise."

4. Margry, *Découvertes et établissements*, "Cavelier de La Salle de 1679 à 1681," I, 463.

5. Hennepin, *Description de la Louisiane*, 192.

6. Ibid., 189.

7. This is a small town in Illinois having the same name as the river and the city in Canada.

8. Margry, *Découvertes et établissements*, "Cavelier de La Salle de 1679 à 1681," I, 466.

9. Ten bushels at a very rough estimate.

10. Margry, *Découvertes et établissements*, I, 467

11. Margry, *Découvertes et établissements*, "Relation de Henri de Tonty," I, 583.

12. Margry, *Découvertes et établissements*, Letter from La Salle, II, 41.
13. Ibid.
14. Margry, *Découvertes et établissements*, Letter from La Salle, II, 44.
15. Ibid.
16. Tonty's Relation, cited in Régine Hubert-Robert, *Histoire de la Louisiane Française* (New York: Editions de la Maison Française, 1943), 25.
17. Margry, *Découvertes et établissements*, Letter from La Salle to a friend, II, 227.
18. Margry, *Découvertes et établissements*, "Voyage de La Salle," II, 138.
19. Margry, *Découvertes et établissements*, Letter from La Salle to a friend, II, 227.
20. Ibid., II, 172.
21. Ibid., II, 233.
22. Ibid., II, 87.
23. Ibid., II, 69.
24. Ibid., II, 225.
25. Ibid., II, 53.
26. Ibid., II, 251.
27. Ibid., II, 50.
28. Ibid., II, 259.
29. Ibid., II, 55.
30. Ibid., II, 60.
31. Ibid., II, 61.
32. Ibid., II, 84.
33. Ibid., II, 88.
34. Mademoiselle d'Allonne also had an extraordinary story. She was captured by the Iroquois in 1687. She turned up again in Albany, having been freed several years later thanks to the governor of New York, whom she helped negotiate a peace treaty with the Indians. She returned to Montreal to settle and sued for the right to engage in trade on her lands at Fort Frontenac. She even went to France to plead her case. She was granted permission on condition that she farm her land. Feeling too weak to leave Montreal, however, she died there in 1718 at the age of 72.

CHAPTER 9 INDIAN TERRITORY

1. Margry, *Découvertes et établissements*, "Cavelier de La Salle de 1679 à 1681," I, 503.

2. Ibid., I 505.
3. Ibid., II, 128.
4. Ibid., I, 522.
5. Ibid., II, 325.
6. Ibid., I, 529.
7. Margry, *Découvertes et établissements*, "Tonty's Narrative," I, 529.
8. Ibid., I, 585.
9. Ibid., I, 583.
10. Ibid., II, 148.
11. Ibid., II, 152.
12. This incident is one of the rare cases where La Salle's letter and the Abbé Bernou's text (which is always considered the official account of the explorer's discoveries) do not coincide. The accounts of the council and the offering of gifts are identical, but the Abbé leaves out the whole episode of Ouabicolcata's resurrection. Either the clergyman refused to give credit to such an absurd act or he thought it so unlikely that it would discredit his whole account. I decided to follow La Salle because I am convinced that the incredible influence he had over the Indians — no Indian ever betrayed him — is explained precisely by his talent for entering into their way of thinking. All other Europeans and particularly the clergy (whose mission, after all, it was) tried to impose an alien concept of existence on the native peoples.
13. Margry, *Découvertes et établissements*, II, 235.

CHAPTER 10   THE MISSISSIPPI RIVER

1. Roger Viau, *Cavelier de La Salle* (Paris: Mame, 1960).
2. Margry, *Découvertes et établissements*, Letter from La Salle to Thouret, II, 159.
3. Ibid., II, 173.
4. Deroy-Pineau, *Marie de l'Incarnation*, 241.
5. Abbé Bernou, "Mémoire pour Monseigneur le marquis de Seignelay, 1682," in Margry, *Découvertes et établissements*, II, 277.
6. Margry, *Découvertes et établissements*, II, 159.
7. By way of comparison, a carriage pulled by good horses on the road between Paris and Dieppe in the eighteenth century traveled seventeen leagues (sixty miles) in nine hours. Cf. Benedetta Craveri, *Madame du Deffand et son monde* (Paris: Le Seuil, 1987), 24.
8. Jonathan Raban, *Old Glory, an American Voyage* (New York: Simon and Schuster, 1981).

9. George W. Kendall, *Across the Great Southwestern Prairies* (New York: Readex Microprint, 1966), 83.
10. Chateaubriand, in *Voyage en Amérique, Oeuvres romanesques et voyages* (Paris: Gallimard, Bibliothèque de la Pléiade, 1969), 743.
11. Chateaubriand, *Oeuvres complètes* (Paris: Pourrat, 1837), XII, 109.
12. Margry, *Découvertes et établissements*, II, 173.
13. Chateaubriand, *Voyage en Amérique*, 720.
14. Margry, *Découvertes et établissements*, II, 159.
15. Margry, *Découvertes et établissements*, Letter from Father Zénobe Membré, II, 208.
16. Ibid.
17. Margry, *Découvertes et établissements*, "Prise de possession," II, 183.
18. Margry, *Découvertes et établissements*, II, 211.
19. Chateaubriand, *Atala*, prologue, in *Oeuvres romanesques et voyages*, 33–34.
20. Ibid.
21. Margry, *Découvertes et établissements*, "Relation de Joutel," II, 215.
22. Ibid., IV, 53.
23. Ibid., II, 191–192.
24. Margry, *Découvertes et établissements*, Letter from the King to Monsieur de La Barre, August 5, 1683, II, 310.

CHAPTER 11   QUARRELING IN QUEBEC

1. Cronon, *Changes in the Land*, passim.
2. W. J. Eccles, *The Canadian Frontier, 1534–1760* (New York: Holt, Rinehart and Winston, 1969).
3. Margry, *Découvertes et établissements*, Letter from Monsieur Tronson, I, 277.
4. Vicenzo Coronelli was summoned to Paris by Louis XIV to make two giant globes, one terrestrial and the other celestial. These amazing objects, which measured five yards in diameter, were set on a base which was itself a masterpiece of fine furniture making. Coronelli worked very quickly. He finished his globes in 1683 after two years, and had the sections of smaller globes printed and sold. He then undertook the *Specchio del Mare*, a superb collection of ocean charts, and reproduced many maps of cities in another work, *Il Teatro della Città*. Several years later, he made a very beautiful map of New France. The cartouche containing the title shows Indians shooting their bows and Europeans hunting bear and beaver. He was fond of local color, and another cartouche shows a man roasting on a spit

and a group of natives with one of them about to bite into a human leg that he is holding in his hand. Engraving dated 1688, coll. David Stewart, Montreal.

5. Longitude sightings remained very approximate until the eighteenth century. Only with the invention of the modern chronometer in 1765 could time be told accurately enough to determine longitude precisely.

6. Raban, *Old Glory*.

7. Margry, *Découvertes et établissements*, "Tonty's Narrative," I, 611.

8. Margry, *Découvertes et établissements*, II, 289.

9. Today it is called "Starved Rock," because in the Indian wars that followed Pontiac's assassination (he was a chieftain allied to the French and who led an Indian coalition against the English to drive them from the area) a party of Indians took refuge there and chose to die of starvation rather than give themselves up.

10. Letter from Frontenac to the minister, November 2, 1672, in *Rapport de l'archiviste de Québec*.

11. W. J. Eccles, *Essays on New France* (Toronto: Oxford University Press, 1987), 137.

12. Letter from the minister to Frontenac, June 13, 1673, in *Rapport de l'archiviste de Québec*.

13. Ibid.

14. Letter from Frontenac to the minister, November 2, 1672, in *Rapport de l'archiviste de Québec*.

15. Ibid.

16. Ibid., 11.

17. John Hare, Marc Lafrance, David-Thierry Ruddel, *Histoire de la ville de Québec, 1608–1871* (Quebec: Boréal, 1987), 81.

18. *Canadian Dictionary of Biography*.

19. Letter from Frontenac to the minister, November 1673, in *Rapport de l'archiviste de Québec*.

20. Letter from Colbert to Frontenac, May 1, 1677, cited by Henri Lorin, *Le Comte de Frontenac* (Paris: Colin, 1895), 122.

21. Margry, *Découvertes et établissements*, "Tonty's Narrative," I, 613.

22. Margry, *Découvertes et établissements*, II, 314.

23. Margry, *Découvertes et établissements*, Letter from La Salle, April 2, 1683, II, 216–217.

24. Margry, *Découvertes et établissements*, Letter from La Salle, May, 1683, II, 321.

CHAPTER 12   A NEW DEPARTURE

1. Saint-Simon, *Mémoires*, II, 156.
2. *La Gazette* was published from 1631 until the Revolution. It folded in 1792 and was published again under the name *Gazette de France* until the end of the century.
3. *Larousse du XIXème siècle.*
4. Margry, *Découvertes et établissements,* "Mémoire du sieur de La Salle pour rendre compte à Monsieur de Seignelay," III, 18.
5. La Salle uses both the Indian name *"Mississippi"* and the name "Colbert" with which he had christened the river earlier ("Mémoire sur le projet du sieur de La Salle" in Margry, I, 361).
6. Ibid., 359. He emphasizes the fact in answer to slanderous charges that had been leveled at him and recalls that "the official deed, notarized and signed by all his men, was placed in Monsieur Colbert's hands last year by the Comte de Frontenac" (Margry, III, 19).
7. Ibid., II, 360.
8. Margry, *Découvertes et établissements,* "Motifs des entreprises," III, 23.
9. La Salle is making a blunder. The river he refers to, the present Red River, flows from the north and not from the west. It therefore did not run through the area under discussion.
10. Margry, *Découvertes et établissements,* II, 362.
11. Ibid., II, 360 and III, 23.
12. Ibid., II, 361.
13. Saint-Simon, *Mémoires,* IV, 956.
14. Ibid.
15. Margry, *Découvertes et établissements,* II, 377 and 382.
16. All the details come from Margry, *Découvertes et établissements,* "Joutel's Narrative," III.
17. Margry, *Découvertes et établissements,* Letter from the minister to sieur Arnoul, II, 391.
18. One of these families came from Canada and was called Talon, though they were unrelated to the former provincial administrator.
19. For more details, see Marc Villiers du Terrage, *La Dernière Expédition de La Salle au Mexique* (Paris: Maisonneuve, 1931). It appears that all the witnesses disagree on the exact composition of the party.
20. Margry, *Découvertes et établissements,* "Mémoire pour servir d'instruction au sieur de Beaujeu," II, 384. La Salle received a copy of his orders in a letter from the king (Margry, II, 382).
21. Margry, *Découvertes et établissements,* Letter from Beaujeu to the minister II, 399.

22. Ibid., Letter from Beaujeu to Villermont, II, 439.
23. Ibid., Letter from Beaujeu to the minister, June 21, 1684, II, 400.
24. Ibid., Beaujeu to Villermont, II, 428.
25. Ibid., II, 425.
26. Ibid., II, 445.
27. Ibid., II, 438.
28. Ibid., Letter from La Salle to the minister, II, 405–406.
29. Ibid., Letter from La Salle to his mother, II, 470.

CHAPTER 13 TRISTES TROPIQUES

1. Claude Lévi-Strauss, *Tristes Tropiques* (New York: Atheneum, 1975), 17.
2. Margry, *Découvertes et établissements*, "Relation de Joutel," III, 93.
3. Ibid.
4. Ibid., 95.
5. Ibid., 105.
6. The men received eight sous a day for food.
7. Margry, *Découvertes et établissements*, "Relation de Joutel," III, 99.
8. Ibid., II, 496.
9. Ibid., III, 102.
10. Ibid., III, 125.
11. Three large rivers flow into the bay, one of which is the Colorado.
12. Margry, *Découvertes et établissements*, "Relation de Joutel," III, 125.
13. Ibid., 234.
14. David G. McComb, *Texas: A Modern History* (Austin: University of Texas, 1989).
15. Margry, *Découvertes et établissements*, "Relation de Joutel," III, 182.
16. Mary Laswell, *I'll Take Texas* (New York: Houghton Mifflin, 1958), 237.
17. Margry, *Découvertes et établissements*, "Relation de Joutel," III, 207.
18. Abbé Cavelier affirmed that the river was in fact the Mississippi, but it is uncertain on what he based his conclusion. La Salle admitted his doubts to Joutel, saying "that he had not found his river." "Relation de Joutel" in Margry, III, 220.
19. Ibid., III, 219.

CHAPTER 14 MONSIEUR DE LA SALLE'S DEATH

1. Margry, *Découvertes et établissements*, "Relation de Joutel," III, 259.
2. Ibid.
3. Douay in Margry, *Découvertes et établissements*, II, 327.
4. Ibid., II, 330.
5. Margry, *Découvertes et établissements*, "Relation de Joutel," III, 259.
6. Ibid., 279.
7. Ibid., 335.
8. Ibid., 310.
9. Ibid., 266.
10. Ibid., 278.
11. Ibid., 303.
12. "Examination of Pierre and Jean Talon, by order of the Comte de Pontchartrain on their arrival from Vera Cruz," September 14, 1698, in Margry, III, 615.
13. This river is called the Trinity today. The expedition had covered about a third of the distance to the Mississippi.
14. Margry, *Découvertes et établissements*, "Relation de Joutel," III, 320.
15. Ibid., III, 330.
16. Ibid., III, 224.
17. These tattoos, darkened by finely ground charcoal and different for men and women, astonished Joutel, who had never seen the like before.
18. Margry, *Découvertes et établissements*, "Relation de Joutel," III, 353.
19. Ibid., III, 371.
20. Examination of the Talon children, in Margry, III, 617.

Index